THE SELLING OF SUPREME COURT NOMINEES

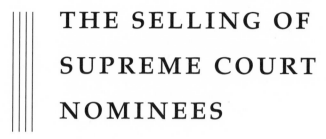

THE SELLING OF SUPREME COURT NOMINEES

JOHN ANTHONY MALTESE

THE JOHNS HOPKINS UNIVERSITY PRESS

BALTIMORE AND LONDON

To Benjamin, Samuel, Susan, and Scott

© 1995, 1998 The Johns Hopkins University Press
All rights reserved. Published 1995
Printed in the United States of America on acid-free paper

Johns Hopkins Paperbacks edition, 1998
9 8 7 6 5 4 3 2 1

The Johns Hopkins University Press
2715 North Charles Street
Baltimore, Maryland 21218-4363
The Johns Hopkins Press Ltd., London

Library of Congress Cataloging-in-Publication Data will be found
at the end of this book.

A catalog record for this book is available from the British Library.

ISBN 0-8018-5883-6 (pbk.)

CONTENTS

In 1987, a new term entered the vocabulary of American politics: *to Bork*, a verb that John Anthony Maltese defines as "to unleash a lobbying and public relations campaign of the kind employed successfully against Robert Bork." Bork, a distinguished, aggressively conservative legal scholar and a federal appeals court judge, had been nominated to the Supreme Court by President Ronald Reagan. More than 300 liberal interest groups publicly opposed his nomination, as did the Democrats who controlled the Senate. Bork's active political support was similarly impressive: more than 100 conservative interest groups backed him. Reagan spoke publicly in his favor more than thirty times, and Bork himself spent several days testifying on his own behalf in nationally televised hearings before the Senate judiciary committee. In the end, Bork's nomination was defeated in the Senate by a vote of 58 to 42, the largest margin of rejection for a Supreme Court nominee in history.

In the wake of the failed Bork nomination, a chorus of critics, led by the Twentieth Century Fund Task Force on Judicial Section, urged a return to a golden age when the qualifications of Supreme Court nominees were considered without the taint of politics. Prominent legal scholars, such as Stephen Carter, and influential senators, such as Paul Simon, weighed in with likeminded proposals. Yet, as if to mock their efforts, President George Bush's Supreme Court nomination of Clarence Thomas in 1991 provoked one of the most politically passionate struggles in history. (Thomas was narrowly confirmed.)

Efforts to depoliticize the nominating process are misguided, according to Maltese. "The problem," he writes, "is that the apolitical nature of that golden age is largely fictitious." As early as 1795, President George Washington's nomination of John Rutledge to be chief justice was "Borked" by

Federalists who objected not to Rutledge's legal qualifications (which, like Bork's, were exemplary) but rather to his political views. During the century that began five years later, more than one in four Supreme Court nominations failed, seldom because a nominee was professionally unqualified.

To be sure, the politics of Supreme Court nominations is different now from what it was during the eighteenth and nineteenth centuries. Although partisanship has always been involved, what has changed is the range of political participants and the public character of their efforts. Presidents and senators, animated by party politics, used to be the main contestants in the largely private political struggles over nominations. Until 1913, when the seventeenth amendment gave the people the right to elect senators, and 1929, when the Senate began debating Supreme Court nominations in open session, interest groups had little access to the process. Once those barriers fell, however, interest groups marched forward boldly. Is it any surprise that the first nominee to be kept off the Supreme Court because of interest group pressure (John J. Parker) was rejected in 1930? Similarly, the combination of an open process and political conflict acted as a magnet to draw the attention of the news media. And once the media spotlight was focused on the process, presidents and, increasingly, the nominees themselves stepped into it to make their voices heard.

Maltese's book is illuminating on all these points. It is also—dare I say it?—a good read. He has joined sound, original historical and political analysis to lively storytelling in a way that few modern scholars attempt and fewer achieve. *The Selling of Supreme Court Nominees* is a book that sells itself.

MICHAEL NELSON

PREFACE AND ACKNOWLEDGMENTS

Unlike other studies of Supreme Court appointments, this one is not a polemic, nor does it concentrate on a single appointment or provide a general historical overview of each appointment. Instead, through the use of unpublished archival documents, interviews with participants in the process, a canvass of contemporaneous newspaper accounts, and a review of secondary sources, it treats the selection of Supreme Court justices as a political process and analyzes the evolution of that process over time. Each chapter deals with a particular aspect of the process and uses case studies to illustrate the argument.

Chapter 1 begins by reviewing the constitutional underpinnings of the Supreme Court appointment process. Using the 1970 nomination of G. Harrold Carswell as a case study, it demonstrates ongoing tensions between the two most significant players in the appointment process: the president (who has the constitutional power to nominate justices) and the Senate (which has the constitutional power to offer its "advice and consent"). These tensions are exacerbated by the inherent ambiguity in the constitutional language relating to Supreme Court appointments. The chapter argues that constitutional language is only a starting point for understanding the Supreme Court appointment process. At the root of the matter, the process is a political one and can be understood only by looking at our political system and how it has evolved over time.

Chapter 2 serves as a brief overview of the early appointment process (from George Washington through Abraham Lincoln and the Civil War). Using the 1795 nomination of John Rutledge as a case study, it demonstrates that politics has always played a role in the process. Indeed, Rutledge was the first nominee to be "Borked." However, the appointment process was relatively closed in those early years. For the most part, participation was limited to the president and the Senate. Clashes between the participants were based primarily on partisan cleavages. To the extent that the press entered the picture, it was as a partisan organ perpetuating a particular party line. The closed nature of the process began to change after the Civil War, when the concerns of organized interest groups became an additional factor in determining the outcome of Senate votes on Supreme Court nominees.

Chapter 3 looks at the social and technological changes that led to the rise of organized interest groups in the latter half of the nineteenth century. These groups quickly recognized the power of the Supreme Court to influence public policy and therefore sought to influence the appointment process. The chapter focuses on the emergence of these groups as a significant new player in the process. The 1881 nomination of Stanley Matthews serves as a case study of early interest-group involvement in the Supreme Court confirmation process, involvement that appears to have been quite successful (and that did not mirror existing partisan cleavages).

Despite the ongoing desire of groups to influence Senate votes on Supreme Court nominees, two structural factors helped to thwart the institutionalization of routine group involvement in the nineteenth century. First, senators were not popularly elected but were chosen by state legislatures.[1] This undermined the potent threat of electoral retaliation against senators now enjoyed by interest groups. Second, Senate consideration of Supreme Court nominees took place in almost absolute secrecy. Public hearings were nonexistent, and what hearings did take place were among the most secretive in the Senate. Even floor debate took place in executive session. Moreover, the Senate usually acted very quickly on Supreme Court nominations. Both committee action and floor debate often took place with little discussion and no roll-call votes. Thus, even if interest groups could retaliate against senators, they often did not know whom to retaliate against. Besides, given the haste and secrecy of Senate deliberations, interest groups seldom had either the time or the opportunity to influence the outcome in the Senate.

Both of these structural impediments were removed in the twentieth century. The 1913 passage of the Seventeenth Amendment to the Constitution provided for the direct election of senators, and Senate rule changes in 1929 lifted the veil of secrecy by opening floor debate on nominations. Chapter 4 argues that these changes directly affected the confirmation process by making senators more accountable to a broader constituency. All of a sudden, public opinion mattered in a very direct way. Thus, public hearings became a way for senators to test the waters and assess public sentiment on nominees. This new openness, coupled with the new threat of electoral retaliation, paved the way for interest groups to become major players in the Senate confirmation process. Chapters 4 and 5 contain two cases—the ill-fated nominations of John J. Parker in 1930 and Clement Haynsworth in 1969—that serve as examples of the new power that interest groups began to exert over the confirmation process.

Interest groups played a major role in defeating both Parker and Haynsworth, but much changed between 1930 and 1969. Those changes are examined in chapters 6 and 7. Chapter 6 looks at how three players in the confirmation process—organized interests, the nominees themselves, and presidents—responded to the opening of Senate deliberation on Supreme Court nominations. Chapters 4 and 5 showed how senators became more responsive to public opinion; chapter 6 shows how that change prompted players in the process to wage their own campaigns to mobilize public opinion as a way of influencing the Senate voting outcome. Soon, carefully calculated public appeals became commonplace. At the same time, the presidency itself underwent major changes. The president became a policy leader, and a large White House staff emerged with specialized units performing highly specific functions to assist the president in policy formulation and implementation. Chapter 7 looks at those changes in the presidency and how they have affected the president's role in the Supreme Court appointment process. Particular emphasis is placed on attempts by presidents to increase their policy leadership by influencing judicial decision-making through court appointments. Staff units now serve as resources for screening potential nominees and generating support for them.

Finally, chapter 8 looks at President Bill Clinton's appointments of Stephen Breyer and Ruth Bader Ginsburg and examines various proposals to reform the process. As we shall see, "to Bork or not to Bork" remains a question of paramount importance, but it is one that has been asked in one form or another since the days of Washington and Jefferson.

I am grateful to many people for their help in the preparation of this book. Its topic is one that I stumbled onto in 1987 at the National Archives' Nixon Presidential Materials Project, then housed in Alexandria, Virginia. While conducting research for my book *Spin Control*, I found several folders of documents concerning White House attempts to "sell" its nomination of Clement Haynsworth in 1969. Although the Nixon White House publicly claimed to be staying above the fray of politics during Haynsworth's Senate confirmation proceedings, the documents clearly showed the White House engaging in a bare-knuckled political fight. I wrote a paper based on the documents, which I presented at the 1988 annual meeting of the American Political Science Association and published in *Judicature* in 1989.

I have Michael Nelson to thank for urging me to expand that original research. He read all of the various drafts of this book with great care and did much to improve it. I would never have finished it without his gentle prodding and enthusiastic support. (I took much longer to complete this study than I had promised, but neither Mike nor Henry Tom, executive editor at the Johns Hopkins University Press, lost faith. I am grateful to both of them.)

I presented portions of this book as conference papers at various meetings of the American Political Science Association and the Southern Political Science Association. I am grateful to the discussants, fellow panelists, and audience members who offered suggestions for improvement. Many others read all or part of the manuscript and offered helpful comments. I am particularly grateful to Woody Howard, for encouraging my early involvement in this project; to James J. Holmberg, of the Filson Club Historical Society in Louisville, Kentucky, for giving me permission to quote from a letter written by John Marshall Harlan; to Phil Shipman, of the Senate Judiciary Committee, for his cheerful help; to Charlie Euchner, for his close reading of an early draft; to Karen Maschke, for collaborating on a related paper concerning interest group involvement in Senate Judiciary Committee hearings; and to Frank Langr, for his clipping service.

In addition, I am grateful for the valuable comments of an anonymous reviewer and for a generous Herbert Hoover Presidential Research Grant that facilitated a visit to the Herbert Hoover Library in West Branch, Iowa. The staffs at the Hoover Library, the Nixon Presidential Materials Project, the Library of Congress, the National Archives, and the Department of Agriculture Library were a joy to work with.

My colleagues at the University of Georgia have provided an ideal climate for writing this book. I am particularly grateful to my department chair, Tom Lauth, and to Larry Beth, Lief Carter, John Clark, Del Dunn, Vally Koubi, Brad Lockerbie, and Susette Talarico for their friendship, support, and advice. I am especially indebted to Scott Ainsworth. He read my drafts, gave advice, and co-authored a paper on Stanley Matthews and the National Grange that was based on a portion of chapter 3 of this manuscript, which in turn strengthened this work. He and his wife, Susan Nees, are valued friends who have always been there when I needed them. Many other friends offered support throughout this book's long gestation, especially Pete and Beth Digeser, Janine Holc, and Tim Smith.

Finally, I would like to thank my parents. My mother, Eva May Beekman Campbell Maltese, died during the writing of this book. She was a woman of extraordinary grace and gentle good humor. I am very grateful for her example. I am also grateful for my father, John. He is a remarkable man with an exuberant spirit and a generous heart, and I love him very much.

THE SELLING OF SUPREME COURT NOMINEES

INTRODUCTION

On April 6, 1994, eighty-five-year-old Justice Harry A. Blackmun announced his intention to resign from the United States Supreme Court. Appointed by President Richard Nixon in 1970 as a conservative "law and order" judge, Blackmun was, by 1994, the most reliable liberal voter on the Court. He wrote the controversial 1973 abortion rights decision, *Roe v. Wade*, the case that extended the constitutional right of privacy to protect a woman's right to obtain an abortion. He also wrote a scathing dissent in *Bowers v. Hardwick*, a 1986 case in which the court refused to strike down a Georgia sodomy law on privacy grounds.[1] Even on law enforcement issues, where his conservative views were the slowest to change, Blackmun moved to the left. He often supported civil liberties claims, took an expansive view of federal courts' use of habeas corpus to redress the claims of state defendants, and in his last year on the bench became the only sitting justice to disavow the death penalty, saying he would "no longer tinker with the machinery of death."[2]

By 1992, the 7-to-2 majority of *Roe v. Wade* had dwindled to a bare 5-to-4 majority (with only two members treating abortion rights as expansively as the *Roe* majority had). Concurring in *Planned Parenthood of Southeastern Pennsylvania v. Casey*, Blackmun lamented the dilution of *Roe* and the tenuousness of the majority. "In one sense, the Court's [majority] approach is worlds apart [from the dissenters' view that *Roe* should be overturned]," he wrote. "And yet, in another sense, the distance between the two approaches is short—this distance is but a single vote." Blackmun added: "I am 83 years old. I cannot remain on this Court forever, and when I do step down, the confirmation process for my successor well may focus on the issue before us today."[3]

President Bill Clinton's 1993 appointment of Ruth Bader Ginsburg increased the Court's margin of support for *Roe* by one justice. Still, advocates on both sides of the abortion issue poised themselves to take a stand on President Clinton's nominee to replace Blackmun. It would be only the second opportunity for a Democratic president to nominate a Supreme Court justice since 1968. A president's Supreme Court appointments are among his most important (and most contentious). As a tool for influencing judicial policymaking, they are an important part of presidential power. Symbolically, they are a test of presidential strength.

From 1789 through 1994, U.S. presidents made 149 nominations to the Supreme Court.[4] Of these, 120 were confirmed by the Senate, but only 112 of the 120 were seated on the Supreme Court.[5] Edwin M. Stanton died three days after he was confirmed in 1869, and seven other nominees declined their seat after Senate confirmation.[6] The remaining twenty-nine nominations were unsuccessful, of which twenty-seven may be classified as "failed" nominations because Senate opposition blocked them (see table 1).[7] The Senate formally voted to reject twelve of these twenty-seven failed nominations. It passively rejected ten others, either by voting to "postpone" consideration of the nomination or by taking no action at all. In those cases, the nomination died at the end of the Senate session. Presidents withdrew the remaining five nominations in the face of certain Senate defeat. (The nomination of Walworth was first postponed and then withdrawn.)

Although presidents have succeeded in securing Senate confirmation of their Supreme Court nominees 80.5 percent of the time, the rate of unsuccessful nominations (19.5%) is the highest for any appointive post requiring Senate confirmation.[8] Moreover, the failure rate shot up to 29 percent during the twenty-five-year span from 1968 through 1993. This failure rate is indicative of the profound effect that Supreme Court appointments can have on public policy. By defining privacy rights, interpreting the First Amendment, setting guidelines for the treatment of criminal defendants, and exercising its power of judicial review in a host of other areas, the Supreme Court establishes public policy.

In theory, impartial judges objectively applying the law according to set standards of interpretation should all reach the same "correct" outcome in cases that come before them. But, in practice, there are very different views among judges about how to interpret legal texts. Moreover, judges are human beings who are influenced, at least in part, by their backgrounds, personal predilections, and judicial philosophies. Quite simply, different judges will reach different conclusions when confronted with the same case. Thus, participants in the Supreme Court appointment process often use it as a way to influence policy outcomes.

In a 1969 memo to President Richard Nixon, White House aide Tom Charles Huston noted that judicial nominations were "perhaps the least

TABLE 1. Failed Supreme Court Nominees, 1795–1987

Nominee and Year of Nomination	President and Party	Composition of Senate	Action
John Rutledge, 1795	Washington (F)	19 F, 13 DR	Rejected 14–10
Alexander Wolcott, 1811	Madison (DR)	28 DR, 6 F	Rejected 24–9
John J. Crittenden, 1828	J. Q. Adams (NR)	28 J, 20 NR	Postponed 23–17
Roger B. Taney, 1835	Jackson (D)	20 D, 20 W	Postponed 24–21
John C. Spencer, 1844	Tyler (W)	28 W, 25 D	Rejected 26–21
Reuben H. Walworth, 1844[a]	Tyler (W)	28 W, 25 D	Postponed 27–20
Edward King, 1844[a]	Tyler (W)	28 W, 25 D	Postponed 29–18
Edward King, 1844	Tyler (W)	28 W, 25 D	Withdrawn
John M. Read, 1845	Tyler (W)	28 W, 25 D	No action
George W. Woodward, 1845	Polk (D)	31 D, 25 W	Rejected 20–19
Edward A. Bradford, 1852	Fillmore (W)	35 D, 24 W	No action
George E. Badger, 1853	Fillmore (W)	35 D, 24 W	Postponed 26–25
William C. Micou, 1853	Fillmore (W)	35 D, 24 W	No action
Jeremiah S. Black, 1861	Buchanan (D)	36 D, 26 R	Rejected 26–25
Henry Stanbery, 1866	A. Johnson (R)	42 U, 10 D	No action
Ebenezer R. Hoar, 1869	Grant (R)	56 R, 11 D	Rejected 33–24
George H. Williams, 1873	Grant (R)	49 R, 19 D	Withdrawn
Caleb Cushing, 1874	Grant (R)	49 R, 19 D	Withdrawn
Stanley Matthews, 1881	Hayes (R)	42 D, 33 R	No action
William Hornblower, 1893	Cleveland (D)	44 D, 38 R	Rejected 30–24
Wheeler H. Peckham, 1894	Cleveland (D)	44 D, 38 R	Rejected 41–32
John J. Parker, 1930	Hoover (R)	56 R, 39 D	Rejected 41–39
Abe Fortas, 1968	Johnson (D)	64 D, 36 R	Withdrawn
Clement Haynsworth, 1969	Nixon (R)	58 D, 42 R	Rejected 55–45
G. Harrold Carswell, 1970	Nixon (R)	58 D, 42 R	Rejected 51–45
Robert H. Bork, 1987	Reagan (R)	55 D, 45 R	Rejected 58–42
Douglas Ginsburg, 1987	Reagan (R)	55 D, 45 R	Withdrawn

Note: F is Federalist, DR is Democratic Republican, NR is National-Republican, D is Democrat, W is Whig, R is Republican, J is Jacksonian, and U is Unionist. Tyler, Fillmore, and Andrew Johnson were not elected.

a. Reuben Walworth's nomination was later withdrawn. Edward King was nominated twice.

considered aspect of Presidential power. . . . *In approaching the bench, it is necessary to remember that the decision as to who will make the decisions affects what decisions will be made.* That is, the role the judiciary will play in different historical eras depends as much on the type of men who become judges as it does on the constitutional rules which appear to [guide them]."[9] Thus, Huston urged Nixon to set specific criteria for the types of judges to be nominated in an effort to influence judicial policymaking. If the president "establishes *his* criteria and establishes *his* machinery for insuring that the criteria are met, the appointments will be *his*, in fact, as in theory."[10] In

TABLE 2. Supreme Court Nominations by Unelected Presidents

President and Nominee	Confirmation Successful	Confirmation Unsuccessful[a]
John Tyler		
John C. Spencer		X
Reuben Walworth		X
Edward King		X
Edward King (2d nomination)		X
Samuel Nelson	X	
John M. Read		X
Millard Fillmore		
Benjamin R. Curtis	X	
Edward A. Bradford		X
George E. Badger		X
William C. Micou		X
Andrew Johnson		
Henry Stanbery		X
Chester Arthur		
Horace Gray	X	
Roscoe Conkling[b]	X	
Samuel Blatchford	X	
Theodore Roosevelt		
Oliver W. Holmes	X	
William R. Day	X	
Calvin Coolidge		
Harlan F. Stone	X	
Harry Truman		
Harold H. Burton	X	
Fred M. Vinson	X	
Gerald Ford		
John Paul Stevens	X	
Total	11	9

a. Rejection, withdrawal, postponement, or no action.
b. The Senate confirmed Conkling, but he declined the seat.

response, Nixon wrote: "RN *agrees.* Have this analysis in mind when making judicial nominations."[11] Nonetheless, the failure rate of Supreme Court nominees demonstrates that a president's Supreme Court nominations are not simply "his." Article II, section 2, of the Constitution requires that the Senate offer its "advice and consent" on nominees. This gives the Senate the power to screen presidents' Supreme Court nominations by confirming or rejecting them. Moreover, an increasingly wide array of actors participate in the Senate confirmation process, all with hopes of influencing the outcome.

For many years, the Senate's confirmation process was all but closed to public scrutiny. The Senate Judiciary Committee, which is responsible for initial hearings on Supreme Court nominees, held its proceedings behind closed doors until the twentieth century and rarely even kept records of its proceedings. In 1881, the *New York Times* reported that the "Judiciary Committee of the Senate is the most mysterious committee in that body, and succeeds better than any other in maintaining secrecy as to its proceedings."[12] Even floor debate on nominations was generally held in executive session. With rare exceptions, presidents and Supreme Court nominees maintained absolute public silence during the confirmation process. No nominee testified during confirmation hearings until 1925 (with nominees routinely testifying only since 1955); nor did presidents routinely engage in public campaigns on behalf of their nominees until the 1980s. Although interest groups attempted to influence the Supreme Court confirmation process as early as 1881 and were responsible for blocking the nomination of John J. Parker in 1930, they have been powerful repeat players in the process only since the late 1960s.

In addition to being an opportunity to influence public policy, Supreme Court appointments are a test of presidential strength. "Weak" presidents—those who are unelected, those who face a Senate controlled by the opposition, and those in their terminal year in office—are statistically less likely to secure confirmation of their Supreme Court nominees:

—*Unelected presidents.*[13] Unelected presidents have made twenty Supreme Court nominations, of which only eleven were successful (see table 2). Thus, the 84.4 percent presidential success rate for elected presidents is high compared to only 55 percent for unelected presidents. However, the "weakness" of unelected presidents may be time bound or related to other factors. Beginning with Chester Arthur in 1882, all nine nominations by unelected presidents have been successful.

—*Divided government.* Presidents have made thirty-three Supreme Court nominations when the opposition party controlled the Senate (see table 3). During these periods, presidents had a success rate of 54.5 percent (compared to 87.9 percent when the same party controlled both the presidency and the Senate).[14]

—*Presidents in their terminal year in office.*[15] The Senate has considered twenty-five Supreme Court nominations during the terminal year of presidential terms but has confirmed only thirteen of them (see table 4). Thus, the presidential success rate dropped from 86.2 percent during their early years in office to only 52 percent during their terminal year.

TABLE 3. Supreme Court Nominations Made When the Opposition Party Controlled the Senate

President and Nominee	Confirmation Successful	Confirmation Unsuccessful[a]
John Quincy Adams		
John J. Crittenden		X
John Tyler		
John C. Spencer		X
Reuben Walworth		X
Edward King		X
Edward King (2d nomination)		X
Samuel Nelson	X	
John M. Read		X
Millard Fillmore		
Benjamin R. Curtis	X	
Edward A. Bradford		X
George E. Badger		X
William C. Micou		X
Andrew Johnson		
Henry Stanbery		X
Rutherford Hayes		
William B. Woods	X	
Stanley Matthews		X
Grover Cleveland		
Lucius Q. C. Lamar	X	
Melville W. Fuller	X	
Rufus W. Peckham	X	
Dwight Eisenhower		
John M. Harlan	X	
William J. Brennan	X	
Charles E. Whittaker	X	
Potter Stewart	X	
Richard Nixon		
Warren E. Burger	X	
Clement Haynsworth		X
G. Harrold Carswell		X
Harry A. Blackmun	X	
Lewis F. Powell Jr.	X	
William H. Rehnquist	X	
Gerald Ford		
John Paul Stevens	X	
Ronald Reagan		
Robert H. Bork		X
Douglas Ginsburg		X
Anthony Kennedy	X	

TABLE 3. *Continued*

President and Nominee	Confirmation Successful	Confirmation Unsuccessful[a]
George Bush		
David H. Souter	X	
Clarence Thomas	X	
Totals	18	15

a. Rejection, withdrawal, postponement, or no action.

Any combination of these weak situations further undermines a president's ability to secure confirmation of Supreme Court nominees. Unelected presidents facing divided government have made twelve nominations, with a success rate of only 25 percent. Terminal-year presidents facing divided government also made twelve nominations, again with a success rate of 25 percent. Unelected presidents in their terminal year have made eleven nominations, only one of which was successful. Presidents have made seven nominations when all three weak situations occurred, and again only one was successful.[16]

The long periods of divided government that have marked the years since 1969 have contributed to the increasingly contentious nature of recent confirmations. So, too, has the "transformative" nature of many recent Supreme Court vacancies, in which single appointments had the potential to alter key voting blocs on the Court, thereby determining the direction of future policy decisions by the Court on such controversial issues as abortion.[17] In such an atmosphere, interest groups eagerly entered the fray, waging massive lobbying and public relations campaigns for and against judicial nominees.

The nomination of Robert Bork in 1987 was unprecedented in the history of Supreme Court confirmation politics in terms of the breadth of involvement by organized interests (more than 300 groups publicly opposed Bork and more than 100 supported him),[18] the degree of grassroots support that these groups generated, the extensive use of marketing techniques in the nomination struggle, the length and detail of Bork's public testimony before the Senate Judiciary Committee, and the number of witnesses appearing at the televised hearings. The process even generated a new verb: *to Bork,* which means to unleash a lobbying and public relations campaign of the kind employed against Robert Bork. It also entails the *defeat* of the nominee—as was the case with Bork. When President George Bush nominated Clarence Thomas to replace retiring Justice Thurgood Marshall in 1991, the National Organization for Women (NOW) convened a press

TABLE 4. Supreme Court Nominations Made by Presidents in Their Terminal Year in Office

President and Nominee	Confirmation Successful	Confirmation Unsuccessful[a]
John Adams		
John Jay[b]	X	
John Marshall	X	
John Quincy Adams		
John J. Crittenden		X
Andrew Jackson		
Roger B. Taney	X	
Philip P. Barbour	X	
William Smith[b]	X	
John Catron	X	
Martin Van Buren		
Peter V. Daniel	X	
John Tyler		
Reuben Walworth		X
Edward King		X
Edward King (2d nomination)		X
Samuel Nelson	X	
John M. Read		X
Millard Fillmore		
Edward A. Bradford		X
George E. Badger		X
William C. Micou		X
James Buchanan		
Jeremiah S. Black		X
Rutherford Hayes		
William B. Woods	X	
Stanley Matthews		X
Grover Cleveland		
Melville W. Fuller	X	
William Harrison		
George Shiras Jr.	X	
Howell E. Jackson	X	
William Taft		
Mahlon Pitney	X	
Lyndon Johnson		
Abe Fortas		X
Homer Thornberry		X
Total	13	12

a. Rejection, withdrawal, postponement, or no action.
b. The Senate confirmed, but the nominee declined the seat.

conference in New York to announce its opposition to Thomas. Leaders Patricia Ireland, Gloria Steinem, and Flo Kennedy all stated their opposition to Thomas at the press conference, but Kennedy unleashed the strongest rhetoric. "We're going to Bork him," she exclaimed. "We need to kill him politically."[19]

As a result of this new atmosphere, critics have complained that the confirmation process has been perverted. In 1988, a Twentieth Century Fund task force of distinguished scholars, lawyers, and public officials studied the Supreme Court confirmation process and made suggestions for reform. The task force concluded that the modern confirmation process was "dangerously close to looking like the electoral process." It further noted that the selection process had become "very much a national referendum on the appointment, with media campaigns, polling techniques, and political rhetoric that distract attention from, and sometimes completely distort, the legal qualifications of the nominee."[20] To improve the situation, the task force suggested that Supreme Court nominees no longer be required to testify before the Senate Judiciary Committee and that the committee and the Senate "base confirmation decisions on a nominee's written record and the testimony of legal experts as to his competence."

The point was to limit the public visibility of the process, thereby limiting the opportunity for political grandstanding. The task force concluded that "the hearings, the witnesses called to testify, and the questions asked of them should be confined to the ability and capacity of the nominee to carry out the high tasks of serving on the Supreme Court." The task force made it clear that the "ability and capacity" of nominees referred only to their legal competence, not to how they would vote on specific issues before the Court.[21]

The controversial recommendations of the Twentieth Century Fund Task Force on Judicial Selection have been largely ignored, as was evidenced by the highly visible and contentious Thomas hearings in 1991. In its final days, the Thomas nomination became a media spectacle as the Senate Judiciary Committee held public hearings to investigate charges that Thomas had sexually harassed a former employee. The way the Senate handled the charges prompted renewed criticism of the confirmation process. Many argued that the charges should have been investigated behind closed doors, and in a timelier fashion. The impression that emerged of the all-male Judiciary Committee was of a group generally insensitive to the issue of sexual harassment. During the 1993 confirmation hearings for Ruth Bader Ginsburg, the Judiciary Committee (no longer an all-male body) conducted some of its questioning of the nominee behind closed doors to set a precedent for future cases, where sensitive issues, such as harassment charges, could be broached outside of public view.

Controversy over the Bork and Thomas battles and the recommendations of the Twentieth Century Fund Task Force serve as a potent reminder of the long-standing, vigorous debate over how the Supreme Court appointment process should operate. Article II, section 2, of the United States Constitution says that the president "shall nominate, and by and with the Advice and Consent of the Senate, shall appoint . . . Judges of the supreme Court." But what exactly does "advice and consent" mean? What is the proper role of the Senate vis-à-vis the president? What criteria should the Senate use to judge a nominee? What role should public opinion and organized interests play in the process?

The Twentieth Century Fund Task Force on Judicial Selection suggested a return to a golden age, when Supreme Court nominees were not required to testify, when the factious whims of public opinion were ignored by senators, when the legal qualifications of nominees were considered without the taint of political motivation, and when senators deliberated behind closed doors rather than posturing in the glare of television lights. The problem is that the apolitical nature of that golden age is largely fictitious.

Notwithstanding the unique characteristics of the Bork battle, politics has been a part of the Supreme Court selection and confirmation process since the earliest days of the Republic. As early as 1795, the Senate rejected President George Washington's nomination of John Rutledge to be chief justice because of the overtly partisan motivations of the emerging Federalist and Democratic-Republican parties. As we shall see in chapter 2, Rutledge could hardly be faulted for his judicial qualifications. He had already won confirmation from the Senate as an associate justice of the Supreme Court in 1791, had served as the chief justice of South Carolina, and had chaired the Committee of Detail (responsible for writing the first draft of the United States Constitution) at the Constitutional Convention of 1787. Instead, Rutledge drew fire from Federalists for his public opposition to the Jay Treaty, a cornerstone of Federalist policy. The active involvement of partisan Federalist newspapers fanned the opposition.

The Rutledge experience cannot be discounted as a mere anomaly. Henry Paul Monaghan points out that, in the century following the Rutledge defeat, "the Senate rejected or tabled Supreme Court nominations for virtually every conceivable reason, including the nominee's political views, political opposition to the incumbent president, senatorial courtesy, interest group pressure, and on occasion even the nominee's failure to meet minimum professional standards."[22] Likewise, Joel B. Grossman and Stephen L. Wasby note that "nominations to the Supreme Court in the 18th and 19th centuries were expected to be subject to politically motivated attacks."[23] Indeed, slightly more than one out of every four nominations (26.7%) failed in the nineteenth century, and those failures were seldom based on a lack of qualifications.[24] Even a contemporaneous account by Lord Bryce, in his treatise *The American Commonwealth*, suggests that the Senate could reject a nominee "on any ground which it pleased, as for instance, if it disapproved his political affiliations, or wished to spite the President."[25]

What, then, has changed? The pages that follow address that question and trace the emergence of the modern Supreme Court appointment process, the study of which is essential to understand efforts to influence the judicial process and to understand presidential power.

As we shall see, modern presidents have reacted to changes in the selection process by developing their own strategic resources to help secure confirmation of their judicial nominees, resources used to "sell" their Supreme Court nominees. Presidents now have an unprecedented ability to communicate directly with the American people, to mobilize interest groups, and to lobby the Senate. For each of these areas, specialized White House staff units have evolved to advise presidents and to implement strategic initiatives. The modern institutional presidency is a system of government centered in the White House, a system in which presidents and their staff oversee the formulation and implementation of policy. Increasingly contentious confirmation battles with active interest group involvement have made presidents even more reliant on centralized resources to mobilize public opinion, generate group support, and lobby senators to combat opponents of their judicial nominees.

CHAPTER ONE

⦀ THE PRESIDENT VERSUS
⦀ THE SENATE

In the spring of 1970, President Richard Nixon and the Senate had been squabbling for nearly eight months over the Supreme Court vacancy left by the resignation of Associate Justice Abe Fortas. The Senate rejected the president's first choice, Clement F. Haynsworth, after a protracted battle. Now it was on the verge of handing the same fate to Nixon's second choice, G. Harrold Carswell.

On April 1, 1970, only nine days before the final Senate vote on Carswell, Senator William B. Saxbe (R-Ohio) released to the press a letter he had just received from the president defending his nominee. Nixon offered this interpretation of the president's appointment power: the central issue surrounding the battle over Carswell, he wrote, was "the constitutional responsibility of the President to appoint members of the Court—and whether this responsibility can be frustrated by those who wish to substitute their own philosophy or their own subjective judgment for that of *the one person entrusted by the Constitution with the power of appointment.*"[1]

The language of the letter angered many senators because Article II, section 2, of the Constitution clearly states that the president's power is to *nominate.* Appointment comes only with "the Advice and Consent of the Senate." The clause clearly dictates that the two branches share power. Although the precise scope of advice and consent is open to debate, Nixon's interpretation of the clause left the Senate virtually powerless. "If the Senate attempts to substitute its judgment as to who should be appointed," Nixon continued, "the traditional constitutional balance is in jeopardy and the duty of the President under the Constitution is impaired. . . . What is at stake is the preservation of the traditional constitutional relationships of the President and the Congress."

Release of the letter provoked an immediate storm of controversy. On the floor of the Senate, Birch Bayh (D-Ind.), the leader of the Senate opposition to both Haynsworth and Carswell, passionately intoned that the president's interpretation was "wrong as a matter of constitutional law, wrong as a matter of history, and wrong as a matter of public policy."[2] Many Republicans agreed. Senator Robert Griffin of Michigan, the Republican whip in the Senate who had led the successful fight against Lyndon Johnson's nomination of Associate Justice Fortas to be chief justice in 1968, published a law review article on the advice and consent clause shortly after the withdrawal of the Fortas nomination. In it, he wrote that Senate approval of Fortas "would have been a disservice to the nation and would have constituted an abdication of the 'advice and consent' power of the Senate." He concluded that it was "important to recognize that this power of the Senate with respect to the judiciary is not only real, but it is at least as important as the power of the President to nominate."[3] Democrats gleefully read from Griffin's article and placed the full text of it in the *Congressional Record*. Griffin himself admitted in floor debate that he would not retreat from his writings "one inch." "I feel just as strongly now about the importance of the Senate's responsibility in the appointing process as I did during the debate on Mr. Justice Fortas," he said.[4]

Griffin then tried to move the issue to Carswell's qualifications. He argued that Carswell was "one of the best trained and most experienced nominees who has been nominated for the Supreme Court." The Senate should focus on the nominee's qualifications, he argued. Instead, much of the opposition to Carswell was motivated by "political" considerations that were really "directed against the President [rather] than the person of Judge Carswell."[5]

In fact, it can be argued that qualifications were not Judge Carswell's long suit. Angered by the defeat of Haynsworth, which Nixon felt was motivated by politics and largely attributable to the fact that Haynsworth was a southerner, the president had responded with what some observers felt was the "spite nomination" of Carswell.[6] As one leading Republican senator who eventually voted against Carswell later put it: "I learned that the Justice Department had rated Carswell way down below Haynsworth and a couple of other candidates. That made it clear that the choice of Carswell was vengeance—to make us sorry that we hadn't accepted Haynsworth."[7] Nixon's close White House adviser Charles Colson admits that Carswell was chosen "in a pique over what had happened to Haynsworth."[8]

Clearly, the Carswell nomination resulted from great haste. Nixon was determined to nominate a southerner as part of his strategy for winning the South in the 1972 presidential election, and he ordered the Justice Department to come up with another southern nominee when the Senate defeated Haynsworth.[9] With little in the way of a background check, the

Justice Department chose Carswell, a Floridian who had recently been appointed to the U.S. Court of Appeals for the Fifth Circuit. Perhaps the administration reasoned that no controversy would arise over the nomination since Carswell had so recently won confirmation. If so, the reasoning was faulty, since Senate scrutiny of nominees for lower federal courts is often pro forma. Some commentators have suggested that this haste and a determination to choose a southerner, more than spite, motivated the choice of Carswell.[10]

Whatever the rationale, Colson claims that the White House announced the Carswell nomination before it even had a chance to review any of the judge's decisions. Colson recalls that he and another White House aide, Egil ("Bud") Krogh, frantically went through the *Federal Reporter* in an effort to find cases that Carswell had written. In an interview, Colson exclaimed: "This was *after* he was named—*after* Nixon did an announcement!" Colson paused and laughed. "That was kind of a bad show."[11]

Within days of the nomination, Ed Roeder, a reporter in Jacksonville, Florida, unearthed a bombshell that the White House and Justice Department had overlooked in their cursory investigation of Carswell. The bombshell was a speech that the nominee had made at an American Legion meeting in 1948, when the twenty-eight-year-old Carswell was running for a seat on the Georgia state legislature. The speech was damning in its rancor and its explicit racism:

> Foremost among the raging controversies in America today is the great crisis over the so-called Civil Rights Program. Better [it] be called, "Civil Wrongs Program." . . . By this "Civil Wrongs Program" the Federal Government is asked to go beyond its constitutional powers and usurp the powers of the individual states.
>
> I am a southerner by ancestry, birth, training, inclination, belief and practice. I believe the segregation of the races is proper and the only practical and correct way of life in our states. I have always so believed, and I shall always so act. I shall be the last to submit to any attempt on the part of anyone to break down and to weaken this firmly established policy of our people.
>
> If my brother were to advocate such a program, I would be compelled to take issue with and to oppose him to the limits of my ability.
>
> I yield to no man as a fellow candidate, or as a fellow citizen, in the firm, vigorous belief in the principles of white supremacy, and I shall always be so governed.[12]

Soon more evidence of Carswell's alleged racism surfaced.[13] This evidence stunned the White House. When a White House Daily News Summary reported an allegation by the *New York Times* that Carswell had chartered an "all-white athletic booster club while serving as U.S. Attorney in

1953," Nixon penned one helpless phrase in the margin: "*My god!*"[14] Shortly thereafter, when his news summary reported that Carswell's leading opponent, Senator Birch Bayh, "belonged to and was honored by a college fraternity which barred Negroes from membership in its charter," Nixon wrote "*good*" in the margin.[15] At one point, Nixon even suggested that the White House leak the fact that other liberal senators who opposed Carswell, such as George McGovern and Hubert Humphrey, had lived in homes subject to restrictive racial covenants, but an aide quickly reminded the president that he had also owned property with restrictive racial covenants.[16]

Carswell's record as a judge only reinforced his racist image. During the Haynsworth battle, the staff of Republican Senator Charles Mathias prepared a confidential memorandum that they distributed to moderate and liberal Republicans. The memo pointed out that, as moderate federal judges in the South retired, the Nixon administration intentionally replaced them with "segregationist Democrats or Dixiecrats." The memo particularly emphasized Nixon's appointments to the Fifth Circuit. It noted, for instance, that Nixon's most recent appointment, Charles Clark, was "a leading strategist in Mississippi's resistance to desegregation" and a "close associate of William Harold Cox, [a] segregationist District Court Judge." But the memo was especially notable for what it said about the recent appointment of Carswell to the Fifth Circuit. His appointment "is described by Southern lawyers as an even more unfortunate choice than Clark, since Carswell is older, less intelligent, and more set in his ways. As a district court judge, he has been repeatedly reversed and reproached by the Fifth Circuit for his rulings involving desegregation of everything from reform schools to theaters. But his chief technique, say civil-rights lawyers, is prolonged temporization."[17] Mathias later said that the White House saw the memo when it circulated in November 1969. Thus, when Nixon nominated Carswell to the Supreme Court in January 1970, he must have realized that the nomination would anger moderates and liberals in the Senate.[18]

After his nomination, Carswell tried vehemently to disassociate himself from his earlier actions, but he could not shake the charges of racism— nor the charges of his mediocrity. Jeb Stuart Magruder, the deputy director of the White House Office of Communications, was part of a task force set up by the White House to plan Carswell's confirmation strategy. White House Congressional Relations Director Bryce Harlow and Deputy Attorney General Richard Kleindienst co-chaired the group. Other White House aides in the group included Charles Colson, Communications Director Herbert G. Klein, and Lyn Nofziger, a member of the congressional relations staff who was responsible for writing speeches for friendly representatives and senators. The group also included Republican senators Robert Dole of Kansas and Howard Baker of Tennessee and William Rehnquist and John

Dean of the Justice Department. Nixon later appointed Rehnquist to the Supreme Court and Ronald Reagan elevated him to chief justice in 1986.

Magruder remembers that the daily 8:00 A.M. meetings of the task force "were increasingly punctuated by groans of frustration and hoots of disbelief as our nominee's ineptitude became more and more apparent. . . . Few if any of us thought he was well qualified for the Supreme Court, but the issue was that we could not endure a second straight defeat on a Supreme Court nomination."[19] According to Nixon aide John Ehrlichman, Bryce Harlow told the president that the Senate thought Carswell was "a boob, a dummy." "And what counter is there to that?" Harlow asked—"he is."[20] Nixon's White House press secretary, Ronald Ziegler, says simply: "Carswell did not deserve to be [a] Supreme Court Justice."[21] Even Nixon reportedly concluded that Carswell was "a bad egg."[22]

The Carswell nomination became the object of public ridicule when his leading supporter, Senator Roman Hruska (R-Neb.), called Carswell's mediocrity a virtue. Responding during a television interview to a question about Carswell's qualifications, Hruska said: "Even if he is mediocre, there are a lot of mediocre judges and people and lawyers. They are entitled to a little representation, aren't they? We can't have all Brandeises, Cardozos and Frankfurters, and stuff like that there."[23] Hruska's response shocked the White House. "We couldn't believe it," Magruder later recalled. "That one remark made our nominee a national joke."[24]

Again, Nixon tried to turn the tables. He noted an editorial in the *Indianapolis News* that advised Senator Bayh to cease attacking Carswell's mediocrity because Bayh had failed his bar exam in 1960. Bayh was reportedly "one of less than a dozen to flunk the test while 112 were passing it."[25] The president then instructed his aides to order pro-Carswell spokespeople to repeat the charges for the benefit of a wider newspaper and television audience.[26] Magruder responded cautiously to Nixon in a memo. "Senators will usually not attack one another on such a personal basis," he reminded the president, "and lawyers—who have taken Bar exams and know how rough they are—seldom attack on this basis. Thus, this subject was not aired directly to any great extent by our spokesmen." However, Magruder noted that the story had "played prominently in the news since being mentioned in the *Indianapolis News*."[27]

This atmosphere of desperation politics served as a prelude to the Saxbe letter. Charles Colson, a former assistant to Senator Leverett Saltonstall (R-Mass.), suggested the letter. Colson had left a successful law practice to join Nixon's presidential campaign in 1968 as part of the Key Issues Group that developed policy papers and worked with special interest groups in Washington.[28] Another member of the Key Issues Group was Bryce Harlow, who recommended that Colson join the White House in late

1969 as a liaison with organized groups throughout the country. Colson soon attracted Nixon's attention. The president admired Colson's willingness to play "hardball" with administration opponents.[29] Colson quickly enjoyed virtually unrestricted access to the president—one of only two or three aides who had such cachet. He and the president met often to talk about "gut politics" and to exchange views on what Colson called "hand-to-hand political combat."[30]

As Magruder recalls, Colson developed the idea at the height of the Carswell battle "that the Senate could not reject a Supreme Court nominee because he was conservative and/or mediocre, but only on the grounds of impropriety." Colson presented this idea at a meeting of the Carswell task force and suggested that they find a senator to "write the President for guidance, and for the President to respond with this theory of the Senate's proper role in the confirmation process." The task force rejected the proposal as "both bad law and bad politics," Magruder recalls. Undaunted, "Colson took his plan directly to Nixon, who liked it."[31] The White House arranged for Senator Saxbe to write the letter to the president. As directed by the White House, Saxbe expressed concern about the charges against Carswell and requested a reply from the president.[32] Saxbe had not publicly stated how he would vote on Carswell, but he privately agreed to announce his support after getting a letter from the president that reiterated Nixon's commitment to Carswell.[33]

Nixon's response, actually written by Colson, was not thoroughly researched. Many argue that it contained historical inaccuracies. Colson later described the circumstances that produced the letter:

> I wrote that letter as a draft and took it to Bryce Harlow who was in charge of the maneuvering of the Carswell nomination. And I said, "Here's what I think the president ought to write, but we better check it out carefully. This is *my* recollection from 'Federalist Paper' [76]," which I had happened to have done a paper on in law school—which was the only reason I knew about it.
>
> [Harlow] walked in to Nixon [and showed him the letter], and Nixon said, "That's a *great* letter," and gave it to [his secretary] Rose Woods and said, "Type it up." [Nixon then] signed it, handed it back to Bryce, and Bryce took it up to the Hill. Nobody in the Justice Department looked at it. Nobody in the White House looked at it. . . . It was done by me as a rough draft. It was a *first* draft. That came out, signed by the president, word for word the way I dictated it. Things slipped through the cracks on that one.[34]

In fact, the Constitution provides no clear guidelines concerning the Senate's advice and consent function. For that matter, the Constitution does not even spell out the basic qualifications of potential Supreme Court nominees. The framers were careful to point out precise qualifications for congressmen, senators, and presidents but said nothing about Supreme Court justices.[35] Since federal statutes have not clarified the issue, it "is legally possible, though scarcely conceivable, that a non-citizen, a minor or a non-lawyer could be appointed to the Court."[36] The silence of the Constitution has contributed to controversies over the proper role of the president and the Senate in the Supreme Court appointment process.

The advice and consent clause says simply that the president "shall nominate, and by and with the Advice and Consent of the Senate, shall appoint . . . Judges of the supreme Court." The clause's language places no explicit limit on the Senate's consent function. In fact, the Senate may actually relinquish some of its power by not aggressively exercising its advice function. Although the Senate has almost never offered formal advice to presidents about whom to nominate (one exception was in 1874 when President Ulysses S. Grant sought the advice of Senate leaders before nominating Morrison Waite to be chief justice), an increased advice function may limit interbranch conflict during the later confirmation stage of the process. Arguably, the Senate would find it difficult to oppose a nominee that it played a role in selecting. In the wake of the Clarence Thomas hearings in 1991, Senator Paul Simon (D-Ill.) submitted a resolution to the Senate calling for it to exercise the advice portion of the advice and consent clause.[37] Media analysts like David Broder and David Gergen also encourage the Senate to exercise its constitutional authority to advise the president.[38] Senator Joseph Biden (D-Del.), chairman of the Senate Judiciary Committee, promised hearings on how to improve the process.

Years after the controversies of the Nixon administration had faded, Charles Colson argues that the basic thrust of the Saxbe letter was "quite accurate as a matter of historical interpretation." Colson feels that the framers of the Constitution did intend that the appointment power rest primarily with the president, and that the advice and consent clause was "sort of an afterthought to protect against nepotism. That was the principal reason [for the clause]."[39] Colson based his conclusion on "Federalist 76," in which Alexander Hamilton explains that the Senate's consent function would serve as "a check upon a spirit of favoritism in the President" by preventing the appointment of "unfit characters from State prejudice, from family connection, from personal attachment, or from a view to popularity."[40] Some legal scholars agree with Colson's argument that Alexander Hamilton—an ardent supporter of a strong executive—gave short shrift to the Senate's affirmative role in offering advice and consent. For instance, Henry Paul Monaghan writes: "The *Federalist* assumed that the power to appoint was an inherently executive function and insisted that the president's power to nominate was virtually equivalent to the power to appoint."[41]

But if this interpretation of Hamilton is correct, Hamilton quickly abandoned his own position. As we shall see in the next chapter, Hamilton, for purely political motives, spearheaded the drive to convince the Senate to reject President Washington's nomination of John Rutledge in 1795. Such a case demonstrates the potential weakness of reading too much into the original intentions of the framers. Besides, Hamilton's views in the *Federalist Papers* represent only one interpretation of vague constitutional language. Even the doctrinaire *Federalist Papers* can themselves be interpreted so as to contradict President Nixon's sweeping claim in the Saxbe letter.[42]

The language of the advice and consent clause, like so much Constitutional language, resulted from compromise. The framers' debate over appointment power reflected a more general split at the Constitutional Convention between "presidentialists" and "congressionalists."[43] Both camps agreed that national power had to be increased. The Articles of Confederation, adopted in 1781, had established an all but powerless federal government consisting of a weak legislature, no single executive, and no independent judiciary. But the fifty-five men who assembled in Philadelphia in 1787 to revise the structure of government were divided over where the strength of the new national government should reside. Presidentialists wanted a strong executive to promote "energy and efficiency in government."[44] Congressionalists, who feared the threat of monarchy and thus feared executive authority, preferred increasing the power of the national legislature. The competing interests between large and small states further complicated the debate over the appointment power.[45]

The original Virginia Plan called for legislative appointment by both chambers. The convention first debated that proposal on June 5. Presidentialists, led by James Wilson, quickly opposed the plan and called for executive appointment of judges. As introduced on June 15, the New Jersey Plan also embraced executive appointment (although the New Jersey Plan called for the executive to be elected by the legislature). A variety of other plans also surfaced. James Madison, who later changed his mind, suggested that judicial appointments be made by the Senate alone; the Committee of the Whole suggested that judges of the Supreme Court be appointed by the Senate and that inferior federal judges be appointed by the lower chamber; and Alexander Hamilton suggested executive appointment subject to Senate approval.

The convention rejected both executive appointment and executive appointment subject to the advice and consent of the Senate on July 18. On July 21, James Madison suggested executive appointment that could be vetoed by a two-thirds vote of the Senate. That proposal also failed, and the Convention finally settled, by a 6-to-3 vote, on appointment by the Senate alone. The Committee of Detail subsequently incorporated the provision for Senate appointment in its draft of the Constitution, but the provision faced renewed opposition from presidentialists at the end of August. As a result, the convention submitted the appointments clause, together with other disputed provisions, to the Committee on Postponed Matters. The committee substituted the advice and consent language that finally made its way into the Constitution. Staunch presidentialists, such as James Wilson, opposed the compromise, arguing that it still gave too much power to the Senate, but the compromise prevailed.[46]

Given the rancorous debate over the appointments clause, it is reasonable to assume that ambiguities in the compromise provision were intentional. After all, the framers designed the language to accommodate competing positions and to placate various interests. Ambiguity allowed for a degree of consensus that otherwise would have been impossible to achieve, since it allowed various framers to cling to differing interpretations of the same Constitutional language. Obviously, consensus that language is acceptable does not necessarily translate into consensus on what that language means. Thus, presidentialists could argue that the advice and consent clause allowed the Senate only a minimal role, one limited, as Hamilton writes in "Federalist 76," to checking "a spirit of favoritism in the President" and deterring the appointment of "unfit characters." Congressionalists, on the other hand, could interpret the advice and consent clause as allowing a vigorous role for the Senate in the confirmation process.

James E. Gauch points out that the congressionalists went into the compromise with the clear upper hand. After all, the plan for Senate appointment of judges had won the approval of the convention. Gauch argues that "there is not even a hint that the compromise entailed a drastically curtailed role for the Senate, except with the power to nominate." Moreover, he concludes that vigorous opposition to the compromise by presidentialists "strongly suggests that the Senate still had a meaningful role."[47]

But what exactly does a "meaningful role" entail? Does it, for example, allow the Senate to reject a nominee solely on the basis of ideology? The framers did not directly confront that issue, but at least some early observers predicted, and sanctioned, ideologically motivated rejections;[48] in fact, the Senate rejected nominees on ideological grounds from the very beginning. Even George Washington seemed to admit that the Senate could reject nominees for whatever reason it wanted. In a 1789 message to a Senate committee on treaties and nominations, Washington wrote that just "as the President has a right to nominate without assigning reasons, so has the Senate a right to dissent without giving theirs."[49]

In practice, the amount of power exercised by the Senate has ebbed and flowed with changing political circumstances. Likewise, support for an aggressive senatorial role has come variously from both ends of the political spectrum depending upon whose toes are being pinched. When economic conservatives controlled the Court through the first thirty-seven or so years of the twentieth century, progressives and economic liberals demanded strict scrutiny of Supreme Court nominees. Such was the case in 1930 when President Herbert Hoover nominated former Associate Justice Charles Evans Hughes to replace William Howard Taft as chief justice. Senate opponents disagreed with Hughes's economic views and feared that he would further "judicial activism" by reading economic rights into the Constitution through ambiguous language, such as the due process clauses of the Fifth and Fourteenth Amendments. They waged an unsuccessful fight against Hughes that prompted the *New York Herald Tribune* to editorialize that the emphasis on Hughes's political and economic views was "a ridiculous approach to an examination of a man's fitness for judicial office. The primary requisites for such an office are integrity, wide experience, capacity and intellectual independence. Mr. Hughes has all these. His enemies attacked him because his political and economic opinions differed from theirs." As a result, the *Tribune* charged Senate opponents of perpetrating a "disgraceful spectacle."[50]

But liberals insisted that they opposed Hughes to prevent the Court from imposing policy choices that the Constitution did not dictate. During floor debate, Senator Clarence Dill (D-Wash.) said: "Democrats and Republicans should realize when they vote to confirm Mr. Hughes as chief justice that they will vote to put a man in that position who will read into the decisions of the court doctrines that will overturn and destroy practically everything that liberals like Jefferson and Jackson stood for" because Hughes would vote to protect "property rights" above "human rights."[51]

During the liberal Warren Court era of the 1950s and 1960s, the situation reversed. Conservatives became the ones who decried "judicial activism," this time perpetrated by liberals on the Court who read personal liberties, such as a right to privacy, into the Constitution. Like their opponents during the Hughes battle, these conservatives called for strict scrutiny of Supreme Court nominees. For instance, as a private attorney in 1959, William Rehnquist wrote that "the Supreme Court has assumed such a powerful role as a policy-maker in the government that the Senate must necessarily be concerned with the views of the prospective justices . . . as they relate to broad issues confronting the American people, and the role of the Court in dealing with those issues. . . . The Senate is entitled to consider those views, much as the voters do with regard to candidates for the presidency . . . or U.S. Senate."[52] But when they controlled both the Supreme Court and the presidency in the 1970s and 1980s, conservatives such as Bruce Fein and William Bradford Reynolds argued for a very limited Senate role in the confirmation process.[53] Liberals now were the ones likely to call for strict scrutiny of judicial nominees, just as they did in the 1920s and 1930s when they charged the conservative Supreme Court with unprincipled activist rulings. In the early 1990s, with both the Senate and the presidency controlled by moderate-to-liberal Democrats, conservatives once again urged strict scrutiny of nominees.

Understanding the confirmation process requires a look beyond formal constitutional language. At root, getting jurists on the bench is a political process, shaped by changing political dynamics and reflecting contemporaneous concerns and balance of power.

CHAPTER TWO

IN THE BEGINNING

During the early years of our Republic—from the presidency of George Washington through the Civil War—participation in the Supreme Court appointment process was relatively closed, limited primarily to the president and the Senate. Although the partisan press played some role, it mostly perpetuated a particular party line. This closed nature of the process did not change until after the Civil War, when organized interests began to be an important additional player.

As this chapter suggests, politics has been an important part of the selection of Supreme Court justices ever since the administration of George Washington. Even the first nine Supreme Court nominations, which encountered no opposition during the confirmation process and which were routinely approved by the Senate by voice vote, were not completely devoid of political considerations. In those early appointments, however, political considerations were more evident in the initial selection of the nominee by the president than in the Senate confirmation process. That continued to be the case in many of the nominations since then.

Originally, the Supreme Court consisted of six members: five associate justices plus the chief justice.[1] During the spring and summer of 1789, Washington gathered suggestions for potential nominees to the Court. Although he became president on April 30, 1789, Washington did not submit his Supreme Court nominations to the Senate until September 24 of that year. They were the last of his nominations for posts in the new government. The delay, he explained, was because he considered the Supreme Court appointments to be his most important.[2] Speculation about potential High Court nominees was widespread well before Washington was sworn in. As early as July 1788, some newspapers predicted that Washington would be president of the new government and that John Adams would be the chief justice.[3] Adams, who did not aspire to be chief justice, became vice president instead.[4]

By April 1789, suggestions for High Court nominees came to Washington from all sides. Many simply volunteered their services in letters to the new president.[5] Shortly after his inauguration in New York City, Washington marked a file drawer in his office "sup'r ct." There he placed such letters along with the names of other potential nominees that had been suggested to him. According to Richard Barry, Washington was in the habit of opening the drawer and "spreading the items in front of callers and bringing up the subject for comment, while he would listen to the arguments about the various candidates."[6]

In choosing justices, President Washington insisted that they be men who had strongly supported the new Constitution.[7] Washington's nominee for chief justice, John Jay, had supported ratification of the Constitution as one of the authors of the *Federalist Papers*. Of Washington's first choices for the remaining five associate justice seats, three (John Blair, John Rutledge, and James Wilson) had been delegates to the Constitutional Convention in the summer of 1787, and two of those three (Rutledge and Wilson) had served on the Committee of Detail, which wrote the first draft of the Constitution. Although the remaining two nominees had not been members of the Constitutional Convention, Washington had no doubts about their loyalties. William Cushing had vigorously supported ratification of the Constitution as vice president of the Massachusetts ratifying convention, and Robert H. Harrison was a close friend of Washington's who had served as his private military secretary during the Revolutionary War.[8]

As with all his appointments, President Washington also sought geographical balance so as not to antagonize any of the states. In fact, the choice of Jay as chief justice was as much a recognition of the role that his state of New York had played in securing ratification of the Constitution as it was a choice for Jay himself.[9] On September 25, 1789, Washington sent Alexander Hamilton a list of his various appointments together with the state from which they came (*DH*, 9n).[10] His first six Supreme Court nominees came from New York, South Carolina, Pennsylvania, Massachusetts, Maryland, and Virginia.

Throughout the preceding months, states had been promoting favorite son nominees to the Court. Some newspapers participated in that promotion. For instance, on February 21, 1789, Philadelphia's *Federal Gazette* called upon Washington to choose a chief justice from Pennsylvania, pointing out that the "southern states give a President and the eastern states a Vice-President: upon these generous and just principles Pennsylvania humbly puts in her claim to furnish a CHIEF-JUSTICE for the United States" (*DH*, 606). On March 9, the same paper reported its pleasure at hearing that "many thousand federalists" had voiced their support for Pennsylvania's James Wilson to be chief justice (*DH*, 609). The *New-York Journal* responded on April 16 that their correspondent, upon reading the *Federal Gazette* account, was confident that many thousands of Federalists throughout the country felt that Wilson was *not* the proper choice for chief justice, "b[e]ing convinced that there are characters in the other states of the union, as well as in that of P[e]nnsylvania, who are more deserving of it" (*DH*, 611–12). Since political conditions dictated that no state could offer more than one member of the Supreme Court, individuals from the same state often jockeyed for a nomination. Such competition took place between William Cushing and John Lowell, both of Massachusetts (*DH*, 601).

The president submitted his Supreme Court nominations to the Senate on September 24, 1789. The Senate unanimously confirmed all six two days later (*DH*, 9–10). Washington seemed particularly eager to inform his old friend, Robert Harrison, of the Senate action. The president mailed the six men their commissions along with personally written cover letters between September 29 and October 5, but he singled out Harrison and wrote him a separate, warm letter first, on September 28. Washington wrote that

> it has been the invariable object of my anxious solicitude to select the fittest characters to expound the Laws and dispense Justice. To tell you that this sentiment has ruled me in your nomination to a seat on the Supreme Court of the United States, would be but to repeat opinions with which you are already well acquainted. . . . Your friends, and your fellow-citizens, anxious for the respect of the Court to which you are appointed, will be happy to learn your acceptance—and no one among them will be more so than myself. . . . This letter is . . . an early communication of my sentiments on this occasion and as a testimony of the sincere esteem and regard with which I am, Dear Sir, Your Most Obed't and Affectionate H'ble Serv't. (*DH*, 35)

Nonetheless, Harrison alone declined a seat on the Court. He did so in a letter to the president on October 27, 1789, in which he returned his commission (*DH*, 37–38). Although less than forty-five years old, Harrison was in failing health. Washington sent Harrison his commission yet again on November 25, together with a letter urging him to reconsider his decision (*DH*, 40). Secretary of the Treasury Alexander Hamilton, who had worked with Harrison and Washington during the Revolutionary War, also urged Harrison to reconsider. "We want men like you," Hamilton concluded in a letter written on November 27. "They are rare in all times" (*DH*, 41). Harrison appears to have briefly accepted the encouragement to reconsider, but after an effort (aborted by poor health) to travel from Annapolis, Maryland, to the seat of government in New York, Harrison declined the appointment again (*DH*, 33, 42). He died less than three months later. Washington nominated James Iredell of North Carolina on February 8, 1790, to fill the seat left vacant by Harrison, and the Senate unanimously confirmed Iredell two days later (*DH*, 64–65, 692–93). Likewise, when Washington nominated Thomas Johnson in 1791 and William Patterson in 1793 to fill vacancies on the Court, the Senate responded with unanimous approval. Not so in 1795, however, when the Senate rejected Washington's nomination of John Rutledge for chief justice. As we shall see, brute politics motivated the rejection of Rutledge.

The Shelling of John Rutledge

Washington's choice of Rutledge for chief justice initially appeared to be a safe one. The Senate had unanimously confirmed Rutledge as an associate justice of the Supreme Court in 1789. In fact, Washington had seriously considered naming him chief justice then. Rutledge's credentials were impeccable. He had chaired the South Carolina delegation to the First Continental Congress in 1774, served as governor of South Carolina in 1779 (after serving as president of the South Carolina Republic from 1776 to 1778), was chosen by the legislature to serve as chief judge of the South Carolina Court of Chancery in 1784, and attended the Constitutional Convention of 1787 where, as chairman of the Committee of Detail, he oversaw the writing of the first draft of the United States Constitution. President Washington appointed him to the United States Supreme Court in 1789, but Rutledge resigned in 1791 to become chief justice of the South Carolina Court of Common Pleas (*DH*, 15–18). He nonetheless aspired to be chief justice of the United States Supreme Court, and when in 1795 he learned that Chief Justice Jay would resign to become governor of New York, he immediately wrote Washington (on June 12) to inform him of his availability (*DH*, 94–95).

Although observers had long expected Jay's resignation, he did not formally tender it to the president until June 29, 1795, after the Senate had already adjourned for the summer (*DH*, 13). Justice Iredell, in a letter to his wife, Hannah, on July 2, bitterly complained about the timing of the resignation (*DH*, 760). He was "astonished" that Jay sent his resignation after the Senate adjourned. "Whatever were his reasons," he wrote, "I am persuaded it was utterly unjustifiable." Iredell feared that an unfilled vacancy would make his participation in circuit duties that fall "unavoidable"—an irksome task that would keep him away from his family.[11]

The Senate recess, however, did not keep Washington from making an appointment. Under Article II, section 2, of the Constitution, the president has the power "to fill up all Vacancies that may happen during the Recess of the Senate, by granting Commissions which shall expire at the End of their next Session." Under such recess appointments, individuals may serve temporarily without the advice and consent of the Senate. President Washington had already made a recess appointment to the Supreme Court in 1791, giving Thomas Johnson a temporary commission to fill the associate justice seat left by Rutledge. Thus, when Washington received Jay's resignation on July 1, 1795, he signed a temporary commission making Rutledge chief justice that same day.[12] The next day, the administration made public the terms of the Jay Treaty with Great Britain.[13] This seemingly unrelated event became an important factor in Rutledge's eventual defeat.

The treaty, negotiated by Rutledge's predecessor, attempted to resolve lingering disputes between the United States and Great Britain. British troops still remained in the United States in western forts, Americans owed debts to British merchants incurred before the Revolutionary War, and disputes remained unresolved about American property that had been confiscated from British loyalists.[14] Washington was especially concerned that the United States not be drawn into the war between France and Great Britain. Thus, he used the Jay Treaty as a way of reassuring the British of America's neutrality. By maintaining neutrality, however, the United States reneged on the terms of its Treaty of 1778 with France. Moreover, American sympathies tended to lie with France. Thus, many Americans opposed the Jay Treaty, especially since Britain had granted few concessions in negotiating the treaty.

The battle lines over the treaty reflected the emergence of political parties in this country. Thomas Jefferson, the leader of the emerging Democratic-Republican party, led the opposition to the Jay Treaty. Federalists, led by Alexander Hamilton, called for ratification of the treaty. In the midst of this, Rutledge publicly criticized the treaty at a meeting held at Saint Michael's Church in Charleston, South Carolina, on July 16. The meeting took place after he had been named chief justice but before newspapers in Charleston had announced his appointment, probably before Rutledge himself knew of the appointment, and certainly before Rutledge had formally received his commission.[15] He spoke extemporaneously, but at length, about what he considered the specific flaws in the treaty. Having done so, he concluded his remarks by praising France and suggesting the impropriety of negotiation with Great Britain.

Rutledge's criticism of Jay and the treaty was uninhibited. He was, after all, among like-minded friends. Nor did he hold a friendly view of John Jay that might have served to temper his remarks. In fact, he apparently harbored a grudge against Jay because Washington had named him the first chief justice of the Supreme Court, an honor that Rutledge had wanted. In a June 12 letter to the president, Rutledge reminded Washington that several of his friends were "displeased" by his acceptance of an associate justice seat on the Supreme Court, suggesting that his "Pretensions to the Office of Chief-Justice were, at least, equal to Mr. Jay's, in point of Law-Knowledge, with the Additional Weight, of much longer Experience, & much greater Practice" (*DH*, 94).

Rutledge apparently did not consider the possible impropriety of speaking out against the treaty and criticizing John Jay, although he had less reason to think about the impropriety of such criticism if he did not yet know of his interim appointment as chief justice. Besides, he likely had no idea that his remarks would be widely publicized. However, a correspondent for the *South-Carolina State-Gazette* attended the meeting and on July 17 the newspaper carried a lengthy description of Rutledge's remarks (*DH*, 765–70). Newspapers around the country subsequently reprinted the story (*DH*, 767n). Soon, opponents of the treaty everywhere were quoting Rutledge's line-by-line criticisms of the treaty.[16] In short, Rutledge found himself labeled as a leader of the opposition, which Federalists did not take kindly to. Thus, partisan newspapers throughout the country focused attacks on Rutledge.

The association of newspapers with a particular political party was a relatively recent phenomenon. Even during the debate over the ratification of the Constitution, most newspapers were not attached to political parties or specific political leaders.[17] That changed with the establishment of the new federal government in New York, where Alexander Hamilton started the *Gazette of the United States* as a newspaper designed to serve as the official mouthpiece of Federalist views.[18] The paper, edited by John Fenno, first appeared on April 15, 1789.[19] In return for touting the incumbent Federalist position (and for sharply criticizing opponents of the Federalists), the government awarded the publisher patronage in the form of printing orders from the Treasury Department and, for a time, the printing of the laws.[20]

When the seat of government moved to Philadelphia in 1791, the *Gazette of the United States* followed. There it faced a rival newspaper, the *National Gazette*, that represented the opposition views of the Democratic-Republicans, led by Jefferson. Philip Freneau edited the *National Gazette*. The rival newspapers mirrored the breach between Hamilton and Jefferson and may have widened it. The newspapers also helped to consolidate the Democratic-Republican party.[21] The newspapers' polarized positions and editorial attacks on each other drew attention from around the country. As a result, other newspapers followed their lead, aligning themselves with one side or the other.[22]

Attacks in such papers went to extremes in personal vilification. The Philadelphia paper, the *General Advertiser* (better known as the *Aurora*), replaced the *National Gazette* as the primary mouthpiece of the Democratic-Republicans in 1793. It deemed most of President Washington's actions unconstitutional, accused him of overdrawing his salary, and labeled him "a frail mortal, whose passions and weaknesses are like those of other men, a spoiled child, a despot, an anemic imitation of the English kings."[23] On December 3, 1796, the *Aurora* declared: "If ever a nation was debauched by a man, the American nation has been debauched by Washington. If ever a nation has suffered from the improper influence of a man, the American nation has suffered from the influence of Washington. If ever a nation was deceived by a man, the American nation has been deceived by Washington."[24] Vituperation became rampant as newspapers split over the French question and the Jay Treaty.

In that context, a rabidly partisan press covered the Rutledge speech criticizing the Jay Treaty. As a result, the United States experienced its first public "shelling" of a Supreme Court nominee. Philadelphia newspapers published detailed reports of Rutledge's speech on July 28, 1795. Federalists promptly registered their shock. Oliver Wolcott Jr., who succeeded Alexander Hamilton as secretary of the treasury later that year, wrote Hamilton on July 28: "To my astonishment, I am recently told that Mr. Rutledge has had a tender of the office of Chief Justice. By the favour of heaven the Com[missio]n is not issued, and now I presume it will not be" (*DH*, 772). On July 29, Secretary of State Edmund Randolph (who had conveyed the news to Rutledge on July 1 that Washington had chosen him as chief justice) wrote the president that the "conduct of the intended Chief Justice is so extraordinary, that Mr. Wolcott and Col. [Timothy] Pickering [the secretary of war] conceive it to be proof of the imputation of insanity" (*DH*, 773).[25] Pickering himself wrote the president two days later that "private information as well as publications of [Rutledge's] recent conduct relative to the treaty, have fixed my opinion that the commission intended for him ought to be withheld" (*DH*, 774).

Nonetheless, Rutledge arrived in Philadelphia on August 10. Two days later, he received his temporary commission (dated July 1) and was sworn in as chief justice (*DH*, 96–97). The Senate had already ratified the Jay Treaty, and President Washington signed it on August 14. In light of Rutledge's opposition to the treaty, Federalists began suggesting that Senate confirmation of him would be an extreme embarrassment to their party.[26] Thus, Federalists began to denounce Rutledge publicly. Writing under the pseudonym "Camillus," Alexander Hamilton said that Rutledge had spoken "in a delirium of rage."[27] In August and September, northeastern papers carried an open letter to Rutledge from "A Real Republican," saying that the office of chief justice was "too important and dignified" for Rutledge, who was "a character not very far above mediocrity."[28] It also called for a thorough inquiry into Rutledge's personal affairs before Senate action on his nomination.

The letter implied that Rutledge had not repaid debts and suggested that suits for recovery be brought against him. To be confirmed as chief justice, a person "should be conspicuous for his love of justice in his private dealings, and in his official conduct." But "if anything can be discovered in either, that suggests even a doubt on this point, he must lose the confidence and the respect of the people, [and] his usefulness and his reputation are gone for ever." "To save yourself from disgrace," the letter concluded, "it is the earnest wish of your friends that you may decline the appointment; since with these charges, exhibited by common fame, and believed by the people, it will be impossible . . . for the Senate at their next session, to approve your [nomination]."

Jeffersonian newspapers defended Rutledge and carried responses to "A Real Republican," to which the anonymous writer, in turn, responded.[29] Amid the charges and countercharges in the newspapers, President Washington formally submitted his nomination of Rutledge to the Senate on December 10, 1795. Alexander Hamilton immediately began lobbying senators to defeat Rutledge, claiming that the chief justice was insane.[30] According to Rutledge's biographer, "no senator talked with Rutledge personally while the question of his confirmation was before the Senate."[31] Five days later, the Senate rejected the nomination by a vote of 14 to 10.[32]

Not only was the Rutledge nomination the first to be widely debated in the public press, it was the first in which Senate debate on the nominee was open to the public. No authentic reporting of the debates of Congress took place for nearly a century after Congress first convened. In other words, debates were not published with legislative sanction and supervision (as they are now in the *Congressional Record*).[33] Thus, newspapers served as the only tool for publishing the proceedings of Congress, but their accounts were often sketchy and inaccurate. Although the House of Representatives allowed access to reporters from the very beginning, the Senate deliberated in secret until 1795. The Senate sanctioned the building of public galleries that year during its recess. When the body reconvened on December 9, it opened its doors to the public for the first time. Thereafter, the Senate denied access to the public only during executive sessions.[34]

In the wake of the Rutledge rejection, the December 16, 1795, Philadelphia *Columbian Centinel* wrote that the "opening of the doors of the *Senate*, though very inconvenient on account of the building, will *open* the eyes of many people; who will therein see many of the first rate talents, patriotism and firmness. The negative they have put on the nomination of [Rutledge] is an instance of the latter" (*DH*, 813). Already, evidence existed of the inaccuracy of newspaper coverage of Senate proceedings. Newspapers reported that the Senate rejected the Rutledge nomination by, variously, a vote of 14 to 8, 12 to 10, and 14 to 9 (*DH*, 99 n.3).

Vice President John Adams wrote to his wife soon after the defeat, on December 17, that the Senate vote "gave me pain for an old Friend, though I could not but think he deserved it. C[hief] Justices must not go to illegal Meetings and become popular orators in favour of Sedition, nor inflame the popular discontents which are ill founded, nor propogate Disunion, Division, Contention and delusion among the People" (*DH*, 813). Adams's sentiments foreshadowed the Sedition Act passed by Congress during his presidency in 1798, an act designed to suppress opposition newspapers and public criticism of Federalist policies.[35] Under the act, any criticism of the government or its leaders constituted seditious libel; violators were subject to arrest.

Others were less harsh than Adams. The Boston *Independent Chronicle*, on December 31, wrote an eloquent defense of Rutledge after his defeat: "The Treaty, at the time Judge Rutledge expressed his mind, was a subject of public investigation; and every freeman was in duty bound to declare his sentiments with respect to it. The Judge exercised this right, and for doing it he is abused in the public papers, and even marked by an official act, as an enemy to the Government" (*DH*, 823). The essay concluded that "the honorable Judge" must feel a satisfaction from having acted in a manner "becoming a free citizen."

Rutledge resigned his temporary commission on December 28, 1795; it is not clear whether he knew by then of the Senate action on his nomination (*DH*, 100). He returned to private practice in Charleston, but the Federalist press (the *American Minerva*, for example) continued to profess that he was mentally deranged (817). The Philadelphia *Columbian Centinel* on December 26 bluntly stated that he was "insane" (*DH*, 820) to which the Boston *Independent Chronicle* of January 7 sharply retorted that "*insanity* by the political quacks of the present day is, an independent mind (*DH*, 824–25). But reports of an abortive suicide attempt by the humiliated Rutledge fueled the stories of his mental incompetence.

So ended the first controversial nomination to the United States Supreme Court, and so began a long-standing tradition in controversial nominations: name-calling, public appeals, charges of personal impropriety, and political retribution. To use modern parlance, John Rutledge had been "Borked."

The Trend Continues

Politically motivated appointments and rejections continued throughout the nineteenth century. George Washington and John Adams appointed only Federalists to the Supreme Court. When the Federalists lost both the presidency and the Senate to the Democratic-Republicans in the elections of

1800, the lame duck Federalists passed legislation increasing the size of the lower federal judiciary as part of an effort to "pack" the courts with loyal Federalists (many of whom had been unsuccessful political candidates in 1800). Their goal was to maintain a foothold of power in the federal judiciary, where they would enjoy tenure for life. The Federalist's court-packing efforts infuriated the Democratic-Republicans.

During the Federalist lame duck period (November 1800–March 1801), President John Adams also had the opportunity to fill the chief justice post on the Supreme Court. He chose John Marshall, whose appointment had a tremendous impact on the Court. By modern standards, the Supreme Court had very limited jurisdiction, but many of its early decisions directly affected the development of governmental power. The most fundamental debate throughout the early years of the United States revolved around the issue of states' rights versus national supremacy. That is, how much power did the states cede to the national government through the Constitution?

That debate permeated the Constitutional Convention and continued well after the Constitution's ratification. The debate helped to form early partisan cleavages: Federalists favored a strong national government while the Democratic-Republicans favored states' rights. Opponents in this debate interpreted the Constitution very differently. States' rights advocates favored a narrow interpretation of the Constitution (now often referred to as strict construction). They felt that the Constitution was a compact among the states, and that the states had delegated to the new national government only those powers specifically enumerated in the Constitution. All other powers, they felt, were reserved to the states. Because of this, they felt that judges should apply the Constitution narrowly and not use ambiguous constitutional language as a vehicle to read into the document additional powers of the national government.

Federalists took a quite different view. They felt that the Constitution was a compact among the people, rather than the states, and that the national government had broad powers beyond specifically enumerated provisions of the Constitution. In fact, many of them argued that the national government had all powers not specifically prohibited to it by the Constitution. Moreover, they treated the Constitution as an organic, living document that could be interpreted broadly.

Thus, who controlled the Supreme Court was very significant. The early domination of the Court by Federalists set important precedents that increased the power of the national government over the states. The Federalist Court, led by Chief Justice John Marshall, also read the Constitution broadly to create the Supreme Court's power of judicial review in *Marbury v. Madison*.[36] This unenumerated power gave the Supreme Court the authority to review actions of other branches of government (including laws passed by Congress) and to strike down those actions if they violated the Constitution.

The policy implications of the power of judicial review are far-reaching, since it allows the Court to strike down policies that may have the support of a majority of the American people when those policies are based on questionable constitutional principles. The problem then becomes one of constitutional interpretation: How does the Court decide exactly what violates the Constitution? For example, do laws that prohibit abortions violate the Constitution? Laws that criminalize consensual sexual acts among adults? Minimum wage laws? Child labor laws? Laws prohibiting flag burning? Does prayer in public schools violate the Constitution? What about nativity scenes at Christmastime on government property? The answers are not easy ones, and the danger is that the Court will read constitutional language so broadly that a simple majority of the Court can substitute its policy preferences for those representing the people.

Although these questions did not come before the Court in the early 1800s, important questions involving such things as federalism, commerce, and taxation did. Thus, it is not surprising that, when Democratic-Republicans took control of the government in 1801, they wanted to repopulate the Supreme Court and the rest of the federal judiciary with members of their own party. The issue transcended mere partisanship. At stake were important policy considerations involving the scope of governmental power. After an unsuccessful attempt to remove Federalist Supreme Court justices through impeachment, the Democratic-Republicans slowly replaced justices through natural attrition. But their first opportunity did not come until 1804. Thomas Jefferson appointed three justices during his eight years in office, but appointing the justice who would give the Democratic-Republicans a majority on the Court fell to Jefferson's successor, James Madison. "The death of [Justice William] Cushing is opportune," Jefferson wrote in a letter to Attorney General Caesar Rodney, "as it gives an opening for at length getting a republican majority on the supreme bench. . . . I trust the occasion will not be lost."[37] Jefferson repeated that sentiment in a letter to President Madison:

> The nation ten years ago declared its will for a change in the principles of the administration of their affairs. They then changed the two branches depending on their will, and have steadily maintained the reformation in those branches. The third, not dependent on them, has so long bid defiance to their will, erecting themselves into a political body, to correct what they deem the errors of the nation. The death of Cushing gives an opportunity of closing the reformation by a successor of unquestionable republican principles.[38]

But filling the vacancy proved troublesome for Madison, who was an unexpectedly weak president with little control of Congress. His first choice, Levi Lincoln (President Jefferson's attorney general), declined due to ill health. Madison attempted to coerce Lincoln into accepting by nominating him anyway. The Senate confirmed him the next day, but Lincoln remained steadfast in his refusal to accept the post. A month later, on February 4, 1811, Madison nominated Alexander Wolcott, a prominent Democratic-Republican politician from Connecticut. Federalists denounced the nomination. Wolcott, as a U.S. collector of customs, had already earned their wrath through his vigorous enforcement of the Embargo and Non-Intercourse Acts.[39] Moreover, Wolcott had little legal experience. The Federalist press fanned the opposition, and given Wolcott's lack of legal qualifications, even Democratic-Republican senators found it difficult to support him. The Senate rejected him on February 13. Madison then nominated, and the Senate confirmed, John Quincy Adams (the son of President John Adams), who served as Madison's minister to Russia and later as president. Adams also refused the seat. Nearly eight months passed before Madison submitted another nomination: Joseph Story of Massachusetts.

Almost nothing is known about why Madison chose Story. Jefferson staunchly opposed him, saying that Story was "unquestionably a tory" and, at thirty-two, "too young."[40] As a member of Congress, Story had opposed Jefferson on the Embargo Act, and he was a personal friend of Chief Justice John Marshall. Although a nominal Republican, he gave every indication of Federalist leanings. But Madison knew Story's uncle. Aware of Jefferson's opposition, wary of Story's Federalist sympathies, and concerned about Story's lack of judicial experience, Democratic-Republican senators did not cheer the nomination. Under other circumstances, they might have voted against Story. But the Supreme Court seat had been vacant for over a year, and the Senate on November 18, 1811, wearily confirmed Story without a roll-call vote. As Jefferson feared, Story quickly aligned himself with Marshall, although he earned a reputation as one of the great Supreme Court justices.[41]

Partisan politics led to the defeat of eleven more Supreme Court nominees over the next fifty years. A Senate controlled by the opposition stymied John Quincy Adams's lame duck nomination of John J. Crittenden in 1828, John Tyler's nominations of John C. Spencer, Reuben H. Walworth, Edward King, and John M. Read in 1844–45,[42] and Millard Fillmore's nominations of Edward A. Bradford, George E. Badger, and William C. Micou in 1852–53. Andrew Jackson faced a Senate evenly divided between Democrats and Whigs when he nominated his old crony, Roger B. Taney, in 1835. Taney had served as Jackson's attorney general and, under a temporary recess appointment, as Jackson's secretary of the treasury. While treasury secretary, Taney defied the Senate by following the president's order to remove government deposits from the Bank of the United States. Furious, the Senate rejected Taney's treasury nomination in 1833. Unwilling to give Taney lifetime tenure on the Supreme Court when it had already rejected him as treasury secretary, the Senate rejected his 1835 associate justice nomination. Late that year, Jackson renominated Taney for chief justice. The Senate, now controlled by Democrats, confirmed him in March 1836.

Presidents who enjoyed a majority in the Senate made the remaining two defeated nominations, but James Buchanan's lame duck nomination of Jeremiah S. Black came less than a month before the 1861 inauguration of Abraham Lincoln. Moreover, sectional differences divided the Senate. Armed with the opposition of fellow Democrat Stephen Douglas, who lost the presidency to Lincoln, the Senate rejected Black by one vote.[43] James K. Polk, on the other hand, was in his first year of office when he nominated George W. Woodward in 1845. Polk also enjoyed a Senate controlled by fellow Democrats, but Woodward's nativist leanings angered Senate Democrats, who had repudiated nativism during the preceding election. The opposition of Democratic Senator Simon Cameron from Woodward's home state of Pennsylvania sealed the defeat of the nomination. (Cameron later became a Republican.) Not only was Pennsylvania home to a large ethnic population, but Woodward had run against Cameron for the Senate seat that Cameron now held.[44] Six Democrats (led by Cameron) joined all twenty-five Whigs in voting against Woodward.

The ten years following the Civil War saw four more failed Supreme Court nominations. Sectional and partisan rivalries, coupled with the legitimate fear that the Court might use judicial review to strike down Reconstruction policies, led to a particularly politicized appointment process. Congress even used its power to reduce the size of the Supreme Court from ten to seven justices to prevent President Andrew Johnson from appointing justices who might oppose Reconstruction.[45] Barring impeachment, Congress could not remove sitting justices, but the reduction prevented Johnson from filling vacancies until the number of justices fell below seven. (Congress has changed the size of the Supreme Court a number of times, often for blatantly political purposes. The Court has had nine members since 1869.)

Some scholars argue that Congress's concern that Reconstruction not be undermined led to unusually aggressive Senate scrutiny of nominees in the period immediately after the Civil War, resulting in a disproportionate number of rejections.[46] But the post–Civil War years also saw dramatic changes in technology. These changes led to the rise of organized interests in this country, a development that had a significant impact on the American political order and the Supreme Court selection process.[47]

CHAPTER THREE

‖ THE RISE OF ORGANIZED
‖ INTERESTS

The Supreme Court appointment process, which was relatively closed in the early part of our history, began to change in the wake of the Civil War, largely because of the emergence of powerful interest groups designed to further the relatively narrow concerns of a particular group (such as farmers). This chapter looks at that development and the role that interest groups began to play, as early as 1881, in the Supreme Court appointment process.

Political motivations have always played a role in the Supreme Court appointment process, but the players in that process have changed over time. Today, it would be hard to imagine the process without the active involvement of organized interests. When Ronald Reagan nominated Robert Bork in 1987, over 400 groups lobbied for or against his confirmation. Testimony by representatives from interest groups is now a standard part of Senate Judiciary Committee hearings on nominees. But such involvement by a broad range of groups on a regular basis is a recent phenomenon that dates back only to the late 1960s or so.[1]

Nonetheless, interest groups have played an active, although irregular, role in the Supreme Court confirmation process since 1881, when a variety of organized interests including the National Grange and the Anti-Monopoly League lobbied against the two nominations of Stanley Matthews to be an associate justice.[2] The Matthews nominations are a milestone because of that. Prior to Matthews, Senate opposition blocked seventeen Supreme Court nominations, but each was a result of partisan politics, sectional rivalries, senatorial courtesy, or lack of qualifications. Organized interests played no role because they were largely nonexistent.

That changed in the years following the Civil War. As John P. Frank writes, the "simultaneous development of railroad empires, manufacturing monopolies and farm poverty" led to "a growth of widespread political movements based on class interests."[3] Farmers and laborers mobilized, as did those who sought to protect big business against governmental intrusion. Increasingly, the Supreme Court had to decide the constitutionality of laws affecting business. Were government regulations that set maximum rates for railroads or minimum wages for workers constitutional? Were government limits on the number of hours that employees could work constitutional? Were income taxes constitutional? Antitrust legislation? Child labor laws? The outcome of such decisions profoundly affected a wide array of economic interests. As a result, outside groups began to take an interest in the Supreme Court selection process.

At least two structural factors stalled the institutionalization of routine group involvement in Senate consideration of Supreme Court nominees in the 1800s. First, senators were not popularly elected but chosen by state legislatures. This undermined the potent threat of electoral retaliation against senators that interest groups now enjoy. Second, Senate consideration of Supreme Court nominees took place in almost absolute secrecy. Senate Judiciary Committee hearings of the type we are now accustomed to were nonexistent. Hearings, which were usually pro forma, were not open to the public, witnesses did not testify, and the nominee did not appear. Even floor debate took place in executive session. Under Senate rules, floor debate on all nominations was closed unless two-thirds of the Senate voted to open it—a very rare occurrence. Moreover, the Senate usually acted on Supreme Court nominations very quickly. Both committee action and floor debate often took place with little discussion and no roll-call votes. Thus, interest groups seldom had either the time or the opportunity to influence the Senate confirmation process.

Both of these impediments to interest group involvement were removed in the twentieth century. The ratification of the Seventeenth Amendment to the Constitution in 1913 led to the direct election of senators, and Senate rules changes in 1929 opened floor debate on nominations.[4] In turn, the Senate Judiciary Committee began to open its hearings to the public on a regular basis. Not surprisingly, these developments led to a steady increase in interest group involvement in the Senate confirmation process.

Even though interest groups did not routinely participate in the Senate confirmation process prior to the twentieth century, their earlier efforts should not be ignored. In fact, interest groups played an important role in blocking President Rutherford B. Hayes's nomination of Stanley Matthews in 1881. Interest groups also influenced Senate opposition to President James A. Garfield's renomination of Matthews later that year. The Senate finally confirmed Matthews, but by only one vote—and not along party lines.

The Matthews Defeat

President Hayes's nomination of Matthews may be viewed as a reward to an old friend, one who had done as much as any single individual to secure Hayes the presidency. Their lifelong friendship began in college and continued through their stints as officers in the same Union regiment during the Civil War. Later, both practiced law in Cincinnati before turning to political careers.[5] When Hayes ran for president in 1876, Matthews not only supported his old friend but played an active role in securing one of the most controversial outcomes of any U.S. presidential election.

In the election, Hayes lost the popular vote to his Democratic opponent, Samuel J. Tilden. In part due to the help of Matthews, Hayes eventually secured a majority of electoral votes, but that victory hinged on questionable popular returns in Florida, Louisiana, and South Carolina. When initial counts failed to determine a clear winner, Congress established a bipartisan electoral commission to determine the outcome of the election. President Ulysses S. Grant named Matthews, as the Republican counsel, to argue Hayes's case before the commission. Matthews convinced the commission not to investigate the conduct of the balloting itself, thus ensuring that the validity of the certified results presented by the states would not be questioned. Since Republican-backed, militarily controlled Reconstruction governments still dominated the states with the questionable returns, it was not surprising that their results favored Hayes.[6]

Still, the commission's results did not guarantee Hayes's election, because a filibuster led by southern Democrats in the House of Representatives stalled the electoral count. Again, Matthews came to the rescue by playing a major role in the negotiations between Hayes and the recalcitrant southern Democrats. A conference in Matthews' room at the Wormley Hotel a week before the inauguration of the still unelected president was due to take place played an important role in securing the Compromise of 1877, which gave Hayes the presidency. In short, considerable credit can be given to Matthews for Hayes's ultimate victory.[7]

When Justice Noah H. Swayne resigned from the Court on January 21, 1881, Hayes immediately nominated Matthews to replace him. That Hayes nominated anybody came as a surprise, since he had only a little more than a month left in office. Most people assumed that Hayes would leave the choice of the nominee to his successor and fellow Republican, James A. Garfield. To Hayes's surprise, the nomination provoked a storm of controversy—not because of charges of cronyism but because of Matthews' ties to railroad interests. As a lawyer, Matthews had long represented the railroads; in 1875, he served as president of the National Railway Convention,[8] and he apparently received a retainer from railroad financier Jay Gould during the three years that Matthews served in the U.S. Senate (1877–79).[9] During that time, Matthews ardently defended railroad interests in proposed legislation. When Hayes nominated him, Matthews was under the full employ of Gould.

The National Grange, an organization of farmers that had long opposed the extortionate rates that railroad monopolies charged to ship their products, quickly mobilized against the Matthews nomination. In the early 1870s, the Grange had successfully lobbied state legislatures to pass regulatory legislation that, among other things, set caps on railroad rates. Those so-called Granger Laws faced judicial review and the Supreme Court sustained their validity, but the Grange learned in the process that it had to lobby both for the passage of legislation *and* the appointment of judges who would sustain that legislation.[10] In that spirit, the leader of the National Grange condemned politicians and political parties who "continue to nominate and urge men for legislative and judicial positions who are known to be in the employ or under the control of the 'Great Railroad Monopolies.' "[11]

To the Grange, no one was more under the control of the Great Railroad Monopolies than Stanley Matthews. As the *Cincinnati Grange Bulletin* put it: "How many more railroad lawyer senators made into judges of the Supreme Court will it take to rouse the so-called Granger decisions, and take the strong arm of the law from the side of the people?"[12] In particular, the Grange feared that Matthews would prove to be the decisive vote necessary for the Court to strike down the Thurman Act of 1878, which Matthews had violently opposed as senator. Congress passed the Thurman Act to force the Pacific railroads to pay interest on more than $64 million worth of thirty-year bonds that the United States government had issued to finance the completion of the transcontinental railroad. When issuing the bonds, Congress expected the railroads to pay the interest as it came due semiannually. But the railroads used the ambiguous language of the legislation to argue that both principal and interest could be paid in one lump sum at the end of the thirty years.

The Grange viewed the railroads' effort to stall payment of the loan as just one more example of corporate abuse. The railroads had already sold inflated stock and engaged in a variety of other corrupt business practices to increase their earnings and, with a virtual monopoly on transportation to the West Coast, charged extortionate rates. The Grange actively supported the legislation. The railroads, of course, bitterly opposed the act, with Stanley Matthews as their chief spokesperson in the Senate. Despite the railroads' opposition, the act passed in April 1878.[13] The *New York Times* hailed the legislation as an "utter defeat for the Jay Gould lobby."[14]

The railroads promptly challenged the Thurman Act in court, arguing that it altered the terms of a contract between the government and the railroads and was unconstitutional because it violated the railroads' vested rights. In a 5-to-3 opinion issued in May 1879, the Supreme Court upheld the constitutionality of the act. Chief Justice Waite, joined by Justices Miller, Swayne, Clifford, and Harlan, formed the majority; Justices Bradley, Strong, and Field dissented.[15] Corporate interests fumed at the opinion, while grassroots organizations such as the Grange rejoiced.

By the time Hayes nominated Matthews in 1881, voting blocs on the Court were shifting. Matthews would replace Justice Swayne (who had voted in the majority in the railroad case). Moreover, two other justices who supported government regulation of the railroads were so incapacitated by age and illness that they no longer participated in Court decisions. One of them, Justice Ward Hunt, did not participate in Court rulings for the last five of his nine years on the bench (having abstained from the Thurman Act case because of illness). Congress finally induced Hunt to resign in 1882 by passing a special act that waived the requirement that public officials serve ten years before being allowed to retire with full pay.[16] It had no such luck with the other incapacitated justice, Nathan Clifford, who had voted to uphold the Thurman Act but, subsequently, had lost control of his mental faculties. Clifford's family finally convinced the justice to leave Washington for his home in Maine, issuing a statement that he would resign upon his arrival there. Clifford, however, defied them. He may have agreed to leave Washington, but he flatly refused to resign from the Court. His death soon ended the impasse.[17]

The upshot of these illnesses and changes was that Matthews, if confirmed, might prove to be the decisive vote in overturning the sinking fund case and nullifying the Thurman Act. That was no small issue. Not only was there strong public support for the act, but the legislation had originated in the very same Senate Judiciary Committee that was to vote on Matthews' confirmation. The chairman of the committee was none other than Senator Allen Thurman (D-Ohio), the author of the act; and a solid majority of the Democratically controlled committee stood strongly behind it.[18] Even George Edmunds, the ranking Republican member of the committee, had strongly advocated the Thurman Act.[19] These men viewed Matthews as an agent for the railroads and thus as an enemy of their interests.

Populists and a variety of interests joined the opposition, with the Grange at the forefront. The Grange, which was well versed in lobbying state legislatures, had already set its sights on Congress. As the leader of the Grange said in his annual address of 1881: "There are favors which we need and reforms which we seek, which must be obtained, if at all, through the legislative department of government. This can only be reached through the influence of public opinion, by petition, or the ballot box."[20] Grange newspapers around the country beseeched their readers to oppose Matthews, and much of the popular press joined the crusade. The *Louisville Post* asked: "Shall Stanley Matthews, who sat in the Senate as the attorney for the Pacific railroads, wear the silk gown as their attorney on the bench of the Supreme Court?"[21]

Even the *New York Times*, noting his close ties to the railroad industry, questioned Matthews' impartiality and suggested that he lacked "judicial character." "He may have been honest and conscientious in what he has done," the editorial said, "but he has neither been judicial nor judicious. He is by nature an advocate, one-sided as to the cause which he espouses, superficial in his study and his thought, and carried to his conclusions by the intensity of his zeal rather than by the depth and accuracy of his reasoning."[22] Matthews' clear stand on the railroad issue would erode "public confidence in the impartiality of the highest judicial tribunal in the land," the *Times* added in a subsequent editorial.[23] "The fact that he has acted in the Senate as the attorney of great railroad corporations whose relations with the Government have been in the past, and are almost certain to be in the future, matter for judicial review, is, of itself, enough to disqualify him from sitting on the Bench of the Supreme Court."[24]

Alarmed, Matthews wrote to the president and asked him to "help me out of the complications in the Senate which now seem to threaten my humiliating defeat."[25] President Hayes seemed surprised by the opposition, confiding in a letter dated February 5 that there had been "more active opposition than I looked for."[26] He refused to withdraw the nomination and instead directed a lobbying campaign on Matthews' behalf. The *New York Times* noted on February 9 that "remarkable efforts" were "being made on [Matthews'] behalf by his friends both in and out of the White House."[27] Well aware that the Judiciary Committee would not approve Matthews, his friends tried to convince the Senate to discharge the Judiciary Committee from considering the nomination and simply bring the matter to the consideration of the full Senate. There they felt that Matthews would be confirmed by a small margin. But to discharge the committee of its responsibility to review the nomination would be virtually unprecedented, and the stratagem failed.[28] Thus, the nomination remained in the Judiciary Committee, where it died at the end of the session. Matthews' opponents had succeeded in blocking his appointment.

Matthews' Renomination

Privately, President-elect Garfield refused to lend his support to President Hayes's nomination of Matthews, even when a delegation from Cleveland, Ohio (the largest city in Garfield's home state) asked him to do so.[29] Publicly, Garfield begged off from any expression of opinion on the nomination.[30] Thus, most observers assumed that, when Garfield took office on March 4, he would submit his own nominee. To the shock of almost everyone, Garfield instead resubmitted the Matthews nomination on March 14.[31] It is not clear why he did so, although some argue that it was because of strong corporate pressure led by Jay Gould.[32] During the 1880 presidential campaign Garfield had reassured corporate interests that "vested rights would be protected in filling vacancies on the Supreme Court."[33] Moreover, alleged campaign contributions of some $300,000 by Gould and the West Coast railroad entrepreneur Collis P. Huntington may have influenced Garfield's decision.[34]

By the time Garfield took office, the Senate and its Judiciary Committee had changed composition. Opposition Democrats controlled the Senate when Hayes was president. Under Garfield, it was evenly split between Democrats and Republicans, and Thurman had left the Senate.[35] Organized groups renewed their opposition to Matthews. The Grange urged its members to petition senators to vote against Matthews. The Pennsylvania State Grange (representing 30,000 members) formally registered its opposition with the Senate Judiciary Committee, writing:

> We are informed and believe that the great railroad corporations of the country are endeavoring to obtain control of this court of last resort, which has heretofore been the most important bulwark in defending the public interests against the encroachment of corporations; that Mr. Matthews has been educated as a railroad attorney and naturally views railroad questions from a railroad stand-point; that his action while a member of the United States Senate proves this, and in this important respect renders him unfit for the position of a Judge of the Supreme Court.[36]

Others who registered their opposition with the Judiciary Committee included the New York Board of Trade and Transportation (representing 800 business firms) and the National Anti-Monopoly League.[37] Both stressed Matthews' role as an advocate for the railroads. The Judiciary Committee files also contain individual petitions, such as one from a "humble clerk" from Kentucky, who asked that his "feeble voice" be added "to the petition of many others" that the committee stand firm in its opposition to "Mr. Corporation Stanley Matthews' confirmation."[38]

Railroad interests came to Matthews' defense. Jay Gould personally took part, wiring senators, like Preston Plumb from Kansas, to ask for their support. So, too, did Collis Huntington.[39] Judiciary Committee files contain an array of petitions in support of Matthews, mostly from Ohio bar associations. Undoubtedly, the bulk of the petitions for and against Matthews were sent directly to individual senators.

On May 9, 1881, after weeks of wrangling, the Senate Judiciary Committee reported the Matthews nomination to the floor with an adverse recommendation. Nonetheless, the full Senate confirmed Matthews three days later by a vote of 24 to 23, with roughly equal support from both Democrats and Republicans.[40] In fact, a Republican (George Edmunds of Vermont) led the fight against Matthews, and a Democrat (Lucius Lamar of Mississippi) helped to lead the fight for him. At least two factors account for the lack of partisan unity on the Matthews vote.

First, regional concerns played an important role. This was particularly true in the post–Civil War South. During the negotiations between Matthews and southern Democrats that led to the Compromise of 1877, Matthews showed himself to be a friend of the South, assuring them of Hayes's commitment to end Reconstruction. Supporters reminded the Judiciary Committee that Matthews was "a *states' rights man.*"[41] He appeared to be as good a nominee as could be expected from a Republican president. Of the eight southern Democrats who did vote against Matthews, three had been electors for Tilden and two had had their own elected positions annulled by Republican-dominated Reconstruction governments.

Second, group pressure by the National Grange appears to have affected the vote. The Republican chairman of the Judiciary Committee, George Edmunds, had strongly supported the Thurman Act. Sympathetic to the concerns of the Grange and other groups who opposed Matthews, he led the opposition to Matthews. Republicans from states with strong Grange organizations joined him. Statistical analysis using Grange membership data by state shows that the size of the Grange within a state correlates with Republican opposition to Matthews: the larger the Grange, the more likely that Republican senators from that state would oppose Matthews.[42] In the end, only nine Republicans voted for Matthews, while thirteen voted against. Of those, one, Senator Roscoe Conkling of New York, opposed Matthews because of a patronage dispute with President Garfield.

The efforts of the Grange to block Matthews' confirmation were unsuccessful—but just barely. The historical record shows that the Grange waged a well-coordinated effort to defeat Matthews, and the evidence suggests that the Grange influence in fact mattered. Indeed, events surrounding the Matthews nomination seem to belie the standard assumptions that, in the latter part of the nineteenth century, party control of legislative voting was all but monolithic and interest group representation before Congress was unorganized and insubstantial.[43]

Matthews returned to Washington the day after the Senate confirmed him. He confided to his old friend Hayes that he was "mortified at the narrowness" of his victory, adding: "I could not understand how any one could vote against me."[44] It appeared that the railroad interests had won. As the *New York Sun* put it: "Mr. Jay Gould, under the name of Stanley Matthews of Ohio, has been confirmed by the Senate as a Judge of the

Supreme Court of the United States."[45] But Matthews, perhaps shaken by the opposition, proved to have an open mind on the bench. Less than two weeks after joining the Court, he stunned corporate interests by indirectly voting against them in his first decision as a justice.[46] In the coming years he often sided against the corporate interests that his foes had claimed he would so slavishly vote for, proving that people do not always get what they expect from Supreme Court nominees.[47]

Group Involvement after Matthews

Economic interests did not come so directly to the fore in the next few confirmation battles, although a conservative economic philosophy became an increasingly important prerequisite for securing a Supreme Court nomination. In varying degrees, all Supreme Court nominees for the next twenty years were probusiness (often having served as corporate lawyers). Few, however, faced the opposition that Matthews had encountered.

When Grover Cleveland, the first Democratic president since the Civil War, nominated Lucius Lamar in 1887, some opponents charged that the nominee had been too closely allied to railroad interests when he served as secretary of the interior and as chairman of the Senate Committee on Pacific Railroads.[48] Opponents also charged that he was too old (at sixty-two years he was the second oldest person ever nominated to the Court) and had too little judicial experience.[49] But much of the controversy over Lamar stemmed from the fact that he was the first true Confederate to be nominated to the Court since the Civil War. Lamar was an ex-general who fought in the Confederate army, served as the Confederacy's envoy to Russia, and drafted Mississippi's ordinance of secession.[50]

Chairman Edmunds of the Republican-controlled Judiciary Committee (a foe of Lamar during the Matthews fight) waged a full-scale battle to prevent Lamar's confirmation. As Lamar wrote on January 4, 1888: "I do not think that my prospects of being a Supreme Court Judge are the best," noting that the Senate Judiciary Committee was "drawing its coils so close around me that I begin to breathe with some difficulty."[51] Still, many of Lamar's colleagues in Washington held him in high regard. He had returned there as a member of the House of Representatives in 1873 and served in the U.S. Senate from 1877 to 1885 before becoming interior secretary under Cleveland. The Senate Judiciary Committee finally sent Lamar's nomination to the floor with an adverse recommendation, but the full Senate narrowly voted to confirm by a vote of 32 to 28 (with sixteen abstentions). Ironically, Lamar's reputation as a railroad man may have helped to secure the important votes of two prorailroad western Republicans, William M. Stewart of Nevada and Leland Stanford of California.[52]

Subsequent appointments consolidated the probusiness outlook of the Court. President Cleveland nominated Melville W. Fuller in 1888, a one-time railroad lawyer who numbered prominent businessmen such as Marshall Field and Jesse Hoyt as his clients.[53] Cleveland's Republican successor, Benjamin Harrison, had the opportunity to make four appointments to the Court during his one term in office: David J. Brewer in 1889, Henry B. Brown in 1890, George Shiras in 1892, and Howell E. Jackson in 1893. As Henry J. Abraham notes, David Brewer "became the leader of the ultraconservative economic laissez faire advocates on the Court," embracing a form of "judicial activism on behalf of vested property rights based on the 'freedom of contract' doctrine."[54]

Henry Brown, who as an attorney had specialized in commercial and maritime law, also embraced a laissez-faire economic attitude, generally holding that business should be free from government regulation, although he was more open-minded in his views than Brewer.[55] George Shiras had the requisite railroad endorsement when Harrison nominated him, but he also had the strong backing of steel manufacturers. As an attorney in Pittsburgh, Shiras had long represented the steel interests, and when Harrison was faced with his third Court vacancy, the general manager of the American Iron and Steel Association wrote the president suggesting that he nominate Shiras.[56] Like Brown, Shiras showed some flexibility, although he generally joined his conservative brethren on the Court in adopting a laissez-faire approach to economics.[57]

Economics per se played no role in the final Republican nomination—that of Howell Jackson, a southern Democrat. Harrison appointed him in January 1893, while President-elect Grover Cleveland waited in the wings to start his second term of office. As a replacement for Lucius Lamar, the Court's only southern justice, Jackson was a compromise choice by the Republican president to placate sectional interests and to win Democratic votes for confirmation. Once on the Court, Jackson had little opportunity to influence it. He promptly contracted tuberculosis and died after only two years on the bench. Nonetheless, Harrison had significantly shaped the outlook of the Court. Under the direction of Chief Justice Fuller, the Court steered a doctrinally conservative economic course from which the majority only occasionally deviated. This majority provoked a new set of interest groups to enter the Supreme Court selection process in the early twentieth century.

Organized Labor and the Confirmation Process

Since 1880 or so, Congress and various state legislatures had occasionally attempted to improve the working conditions of laborers by passing a variety of laws regulating business. These included child labor laws, minimum wage and maximum hours legislation, and a variety of other health and safety regulations. Business objected to these regulations and challenged them through litigation. The composition of the Supreme Court was such that it almost always struck down such legislation. Critics have argued that economic conservatives on the Court engaged in a form of judicial activism that read into the Constitution various economic liberties that shielded business from government regulation.[58] Using a broad interpretation of the due process clauses of the Fifth and Fourteenth Amendments (which the Court's majority said protected the "liberty of contract" between employer and employee to set whatever wages and working conditions they wanted) and a narrow interpretation of the commerce clause (which the Court maintained allowed Congress to regulate only the actual transportation of goods, not their manufacture), the Court effectively stymied progressive legislation at both the state and national level.

The Court's laissez-faire approach to economic regulation reached its zenith in the 1905 case of *Lochner v. New York,* which declared unconstitutional a New York state maximum hours law for bakers. The 5-to-4 majority called such legislation a "meddlesome" interference that violated fundamental economic liberties supposedly protected by the due process clause of the Fourteenth Amendment. "The right to purchase and sell labor is part of the liberty protected," the majority declared.[59] No matter that employer and employee were not in equal bargaining positions and that laborers often had to endure horrendous working conditions and staggeringly long work hours or else risk unemployment. In dissent, Justice Oliver Wendell Holmes Jr. declared that the majority's opinion rested upon "an economic theory that a large part of the country does not entertain."[60]

Theodore Roosevelt had appointed Holmes to the Court in 1902. Roosevelt, who had succeeded assassinated president William McKinley in 1901, was a progressive Republican who supported efforts to regulate business. In his three appointments to the Supreme Court, Roosevelt sought men who would support labor. He was impressed by Holmes's previous record on that score as chief justice of the Supreme Court of Massachusetts. When considering the possibility of nominating Holmes, Roosevelt wrote to Senator Henry Cabot Lodge (R-Mass.) that Holmes's labor decisions, "which have been criticized by some of the big railroad men and other members of large corporations," were actually "a strong point in Judge Holmes' favor." "The ablest lawyers and greatest judges are men whose past has naturally brought them into close relationships with the wealthiest and most powerful clients," Roosevelt continued, "and I am glad when I can find a judge who has been able to preserve his aloofness of mind so as to keep his broad humanity of feeling and his sympathy for the class from which he has not drawn his clients."[61]

As a Supreme Court justice, Holmes generally voted to sustain government regulation of business, as did another of President Roosevelt's nominees, William H. Moody, whom he appointed in 1906. But once, when Holmes voted against TR's antitrust policy, Roosevelt exclaimed in anger that he "could carve out of a banana a judge with more backbone than that!"[62] Of Roosevelt's three appointees, only William Rufus Day came out solidly against government regulation of business, much to the president's dissatisfaction.[63]

William Howard Taft succeeded Roosevelt in 1909. Although Taft had been Roosevelt's vice president and initially had Roosevelt's blessing, Taft was more conservative than TR and was determined to "save" the Supreme Court from progressives.[64] But, with a narrow majority ruling against them, organized labor also took a strong interest in the Supreme Court confirmation process. Labor knew that, short of amending the Constitution, changing the composition of the Court was the only way to prevent the judiciary from striking down regulatory legislation designed to protect workers. Thus, when Justice Wheeler Peckham (the author of the *Lochner* majority) died in 1909, labor took an active interest in Taft's selection of a replacement. Taft chose Horace H. Lurton to replace Peckham, but labor, concerned by Lurton's record as a judge on the Sixth Circuit Court of Appeals, feared that he would simply perpetuate the *Lochner* legacy.

Taft did not nominate Lurton until December 13, 1909, some two months after the death of Justice Peckham; but it was an open secret that Lurton was at the top of Taft's list of potential nominees. Taft badly wanted to appoint Lurton but delayed his decision because of Lurton's age (sixty-six). Taft had earlier spearheaded a drive to populate the bench with younger justices, and he did some soul searching before nominating his dear friend and former colleague with whom he had served for eight years on the Sixth Circuit bench.[65] In the meantime, Lurton, who could almost taste the nomination, waged a lobbying campaign to convince the president that his nomination was appropriate.[66] When opposition arose in the Senate because of Lurton's age, his daughter wired the president: "Give my father the chance of a confirmation. We are willing to risk the vote of the Senate."[67]

Labor organizations, which were well aware that Taft was seriously considering Lurton, began their own lobbying effort to prevent his nomination. The American Federation of Labor (AFL) registered its protest with the president, as did the Firemen and Enginemen's Brotherhood, the Brotherhood of Railroad Trainmen, and the Order of Railway Conductors. So, too, did Edward A. Moseley, secretary of the Interstate Commerce Commission.[68] H. B. Peckham, chairman of the Railroad Employees Department of the AFL, wrote the president that those he represented knew "from experience that matters have not been going right for the working people in the Sixth Circuit where Judge Lurton has been presiding."[69] But Taft was unmoved by the protests. In response to the charge of A. B. Garretson (president of the Order of Railway Conductors) that Lurton was "biased" and "not of an open mind" on labor issues,[70] Taft wrote that there was nothing in Lurton's "character or views of things that would make him unjust to the laboring man or to organized labor."[71] Taft concluded with some anger: "I think I know him better than those who by picking out one opinion may find something not to their liking."

In the meantime, Lurton lined up support on the other side of the aisle. Secretary of War John M. Dickenson led the campaign to secure Lurton's nomination, and on November 25, Lurton wrote to Dickenson that the president of the New York Life Insurance Company had promised "to put every influence" of his organization behind Lurton. Lurton also noted that he had friends throughout the country who were hard at work on his behalf. One had taken on the progressive prolabor Republican senator from Wisconsin, Robert M. LaFollette; another had gone to Washington "to look after the Radicals" who opposed Lurton. Despite attacks against him because of his "supposed leaning toward corporations," Lurton assured Dickenson that all his sources insisted that "there will be no serious objection" to his confirmation within the Senate if Taft nominated him.[72] He proved to be correct: the Senate debate on the nomination was secret and proceeded swiftly. The Senate gave interest groups no opportunity to voice their objections at public hearings, and it confirmed Lurton by voice vote only one week after receiving the nomination. Moroever, senators still were not directly accountable to the popular electorate. Thus, despite the opposition of noted labor leaders such as Samuel Gompers, interest groups were thwarted at the confirmation stage. The Senate easily confirmed Lurton on December 20.

Labor entered the fray again in 1912 when Taft nominated Mahlon Pitney to replace the elder Justice John Marshall Harlan. One newspaper reported that the president was forced to reject two potential nominees— U.S. Circuit Court Judge William Hook of Kansas and Secretary of Commerce and Labor Charles Nagel—because of opposition from organized labor.[73] But Pitney was no great friend of labor either. Critics paid particular attention to a decision that he had handed down during his tenure on the New Jersey Supreme Court. In the so-called Glass Bottle Blowers' Case, Pitney had ruled that a strike by bottle blowers at the Minocola plant was unlawful and sustained an injunction to stop the strike. At the time, New Jersey law held that strike organizers could be prosecuted for conspiracy.[74]

The president of the Iowa Federation of Labor informed the Senate of its opposition to Pitney, citing additional antilabor decisions. However, several senators discounted the opposition because some of those decisions had actually been decided by Pitney's father, who also served on the New Jersey bench.[75] Prolabor senators delayed the floor vote and led a lengthy assault against Pitney (based almost entirely on the Bottle Blowers' case), but in the end the Senate confirmed Pitney by a vote of 50 to 26.[76]

Unhappy with Taft, former president Roosevelt entered the 1912 presidential election as a third-party candidate. Taft and Roosevelt split the Republican vote, allowing Woodrow Wilson to win the White House. Although President Wilson was eager to appoint progressive justices who would sustain government regulations of business, his first appointment, James C. McReynolds, proved to be anything but progressive. To the dismay of the president, McReynolds quickly became the most reactionary (and by all accounts, the most boorish and bigoted) member of the Court.[77] Wilson vowed not to repeat his mistake. When Justice Lamar died in 1916, many lawyers and politicians urged Wilson to appoint former president Taft to the Court. But organized labor strongly opposed Taft, and Wilson was certainly not predisposed to nominate his Republican predecessor. Instead, Wilson turned to Louis D. Brandeis, a choice that he knew would create a "tempest," and one that shocked almost everyone.[78]

Brandeis was a progressive crusader, a trust-busting reformer who actively supported trade unionism. He had lobbied on behalf of labor in magazine articles, in testimony before Congress, and as a lawyer before the Supreme Court. His famed brief in the 1908 *Muller v. Oregon* case is credited for having convinced the Supreme Court to sustain an Oregon maximum-hour law for women.[79] That so-called Brandeis brief helped to revolutionize American law. Rather than basing the brief on constitutional arguments (which he dealt with in only two pages), Brandeis amassed over one hundred pages of evidence and statistics to show that long hours had deleterious health effects on women. Thus, he convinced the Court to sustain the Oregon law by the weight of social facts, a novel approach that helped usher in an acceptance of sociological jurisprudence.[80]

By 1916, Brandeis had developed a strong reputation as a leading force in the progressive movement, acting as a close adviser to Senator Robert M. LaFollette, the progressive Republican who also championed the cause of labor. As A. L. Todd writes, "Brandeis and La Follette were twin targets of the reactionaries' hatred. Both represented to men of privilege and property the same kind of menace. Both were dedicated, as their opponents saw them, to breaking down the traditional American way of life under which the freedom to accumulate was sacred in the eyes of those who worshipped property." Quite simply, the propertied class looked at Brandeis as a radical revolutionary. "If a man like Brandeis, with his wild ideas of a shorter day for [workers] and higher pay to go with it, his advocacy of the income tax, his schemes to break business into ruinously competitive units, his tight-control plans for public utilities—if such a man should come to a position of real power, then America would never be the same again."[81] Melvin I. Urofsky adds that what especially angered the Boston Brahmins was "that Brandeis, a graduate of Harvard Law School and a man who had given every indication of becoming a fine—and trusted—corporate lawyer, had broken away to become a reformer, and the targets of his reforms had frequently been Boston's own social and economic elite."[82]

Before submitting the nomination, President Wilson contacted AFL president Samuel Gompers to make sure that Brandeis would receive the full support of labor. Gompers assured Wilson that he would. Wilson also sent a secret missive to Senator LaFollette, asking him if the White House could count on Republican progressives to support Brandeis. LaFollette replied, yes.[83] With those assurances, Wilson nominated Brandeis on January 28. The news stunned Capitol Hill. "When Brandeis' nomination came in yesterday, the Senate simply gasped," Gus J. Karger, the Washington correspondent for the Cincinnati *Times-Star*, wrote to his friend, former president Taft, on January 29. "There wasn't any more excitement at the Capitol when Congress passed the Spanish War Resolution."[84]

Taft, who himself desperately wanted a seat on the Court, was incensed, writing to Karger on January 31 that the Brandeis nomination was one of the "deepest wounds" that he had ever received (though it is hard to imagine that Taft could really have expected the Democrat who ran against him in the 1912 presidential campaign to appoint him to the Court). "Wilson has projected a fight," Taft continued, "which with master art he will give the color of a contest, on one side of which will be arranged the opposition of corporate wealth and racial prejudice, and on the other side the downtrodden, the oppressed, the uplifters, the labor unions, and all the elements which are supposed to have votes in the election. This will lead to the confirmation because of the white-livered Senators that we have. The Senate has been LaFollettized and Gomperized so that it has ceased to be the conservative body it was."[85] Brandeis's prominent role in exposing a plan by Taft's secretary of the interior to allow big business to take over public lands in Alaska for the purpose of coal mining only exacerbated Taft's bitterness. The exposé had shown that the Taft administration had turned its back on the conservation policy that Theodore Roosevelt had championed and had prompted Roosevelt to enter the presidential race against Taft in 1912.[86]

Just as the Grange had pounced on Stanley Matthews in 1881, arguing that he was an advocate of the railroads and would not decide cases with an open mind, big business pounced on Brandeis, arguing that he was an advocate of labor—"a contender," as the *New York Times* put it, "a striver after change and reforms."[87] Such a man, opponents argued, did not have the "judicial temperament" necessary for a seat on the High Court. Anti-Semitism tinged the opposition to Brandeis (he was the first Jew ever appointed to the Court), but at root, ideology caused the fight. And what a fight it was: a no-holds-barred battle that included the first public hearings on the fitness of a Supreme Court nominee.

The Senate Judiciary Committee hearings, the publicity, and the interest group involvement were precursors to a new era of Supreme Court confirmation proceedings. Significantly, the hearings took place after the ratification of the Seventeenth Amendment to the Constitution, which called for the popular election of U.S. senators rather than their selection by state legislatures. Senators now had a new constituency to answer to, and the public hearings reflected the new trend toward popular accountability.

But in many parts of the country, a large part of the popular electorate viewed Brandeis as a hero. Thus, some senators who had once depended upon conservative state legislators to re-elect them now had to weigh mass sentiment before taking a stand on Brandeis, especially since the nomination took place in an election year. While many senators were willing to state off-the-record that they were unhappy with Brandeis, almost no one would go public with such a view.[88] Even Henry Cabot Lodge, the conservative Republican senator from Massachusetts who despised Brandeis, refused to lead a public battle against the nominee. Rather, he encouraged others (notably lawyers and bar associations) to denounce Brandeis for him.[89]

Unlike modern-day confirmation hearings, interest group representatives did not line up to testify about Brandeis and his potential impact on the voting patterns of the Court. Such representatives did submit letters and petitions to the committee urging it to take a stand one way or the other, but those who testified were individuals whom the committee summoned to discuss the nominee's previous conduct as a lawyer. Opponents, many of them from the losing side of legal battles that Brandeis had waged against them, tried to convince the committee that Brandeis had engaged in improprieties that revealed his lack of "judicial temperament," thereby disqualifying him from sitting on the Court. But supporters of Brandeis successfully defended him against the charges, and it became increasingly apparent that Brandeis "had a hold on the popular imagination" unprecedented in Wilson's appointments.[90]

On May 24, the Judiciary Committee voted along strict party lines to confirm Brandeis by a vote of 10 to 8. On June 1, with no debate, the full Senate approved the nomination by a vote of 47 to 22. Organized labor had won.

||| INTERESTS VERSUS NOMINEES

||| THE DEFEAT OF JOHN J. PARKER

Interest groups had participated sporadically in the Supreme Court confirmation process since 1881, when opposition by the National Grange and the Anti-Monopoly League helped to block Rutherford Hayes's nomination of Stanley Matthews. Although interest groups clearly wanted to influence the process during the late 1800s and early 1900s, they focused most of their lobbying at the prenomination stage. Through letters, petitions, and other forms of more direct lobbying, they urged presidents to nominate particular individuals. But once the president sent his nomination to the Senate, interest groups were relatively powerless; the Senate confirmation process was normally closed to public view, and senators were not popularly elected. Often the Senate did not even produce roll-call votes on Supreme Court nominees. Without knowing who voted for and against nominees, and without the threat of electoral retaliation, interest groups had little leverage in the process.

This changed in the twentieth century. The ratification of the Seventeenth Amendment to the Constitution in 1913 provided for the direct election of senators. This clearly had an impact on the Brandeis nomination in 1916, which took place in an election year. With an eye to popular accountability, the Senate voted to open its proceedings on the controversial nominee. Opponents called witnesses whom they hoped would raise doubts about Brandeis's character and judicial temperament. But Brandeis had widespread popular support, and many senators realized that a vote against Brandeis might hurt them at the polls. Brandeis won confirmation by a partisan vote of 47 to 22. There is little doubt that the vote would have been closer without the newly instituted electoral connection.

The opening of Senate confirmation proceedings proved to be rare until 1929, when Senate rules changes opened floor debate on all nominations on a regular basis. Herbert Hoover's 1930 nominations of Charles Evans Hughes and John J. Parker were the first to take place in the new environment, in which senators both debated nominations in public and were accountable to a popular electorate. As such, they were the first truly "modern" Senate confirmation proceedings for Supreme Court nominees. In fact, organized labor and the National Association for the Advancement of Colored People (NAACP) used the threat of electoral retaliation to convince enough senators to vote against Parker to defeat the nomination. Labor also opposed Hughes, but its efforts to defeat him came too late.

This chapter focuses on the nominations of Hughes and Parker to demonstrate the increasingly important role that interest groups came to play in the Supreme Court confirmation process. In fact, interest groups succeeded in defeating Parker.

The Hughes Nomination

President William Howard Taft appointed Charles Evans Hughes as an associate justice to the Supreme Court in 1910. Hughes served on the Court until 1916, when he resigned to run as the Republican nominee for president against Woodrow Wilson. When Hughes lost the presidential race, he went to work as a corporate lawyer. In 1920, President Warren Harding appointed Hughes as his secretary of state. The following year, Harding appointed former president Taft chief justice of the Supreme Court.

In 1930, Taft was forced to resign as chief justice due to illness, and President Herbert Hoover nominated Hughes to take his place. Although Hughes had been a relatively moderate associate justice, his abandonment of the Court for politics, coupled with his subsequent foray into the lucrative world of corporate law, led to charges that he was too much of an advocate of—and too closely tied to—corporate interests to be an impartial chief justice. Moreover, labor leaders were miffed that President Hoover had not consulted them before nominating Hughes, especially since early in his term Hoover had appeared to be a friend of organized labor.[1]

In fact, Hoover had already decided to nominate Hughes when Chief Justice Taft resigned on February 3, 1930. Unaware that this was the case, William Green, the president of the American Federation of Labor, sent a telegram to President Hoover from Toledo, Ohio, as soon as he heard reports of Taft's resignation. "I just learned of the resignation of Chief Justice Taft," Green wired, "and because the membership of the American Federation of Labor is deeply interested in the selection of his successor I hope I may be permitted to confer with you before a final decision is reached. Trust I may see you on or about February tenth."[2]

Such a request was not unusual. Typically, a period of time elapsed between the resignation of a justice and the announcement of a successor, during which the president solicited names of potential nominees. Prior to the development of public hearings, this was the one opportunity that the public had to voice their opinions, and it was often the only point in the process where real lobbying took place. Green had every expectation that Hoover would listen to him.

Unlike the rest of the country, the president had known for some time that Taft planned to resign. Although Hoover's personal preference for chief justice appears to have been his close friend Associate Justice Harlan Fiske Stone, Taft preferred the more conservative Hughes. Attorney General William D. Mitchell also supported Hughes, and Hoover owed a political debt to Hughes for his active support of the Republican ticket in the 1928 presidential election.[3] Thus, Attorney General Mitchell arranged for Justices Willis Van Devanter and Pierce Butler to dine with Hughes in New York on January 28, 1930, a week before the Taft resignation, to sound out Hughes's interest in returning to the Court. Van Devanter and Butler reported that Hughes seemed willing to accept the nomination. Two days later, the president contacted Hughes in New York and asked him to come to Washington. They met for breakfast the next morning, Thursday, January 31, at the White House, and Hughes agreed to accept the nomination when Taft resigned.[4]

A widely circulated and much debated story suggests that Hoover offered Hughes the post with the expectation that he would refuse. Then, the story goes, Hoover would have elevated the more progressive Justice Stone to be chief justice and appointed the renowned Judge Learned Hand to fill Stone's associate justice seat. Had the plan worked, Hoover could have placated Taft, repaid his campaign debt to Hughes, and still have gotten his first choice (Stone) in the chief justice post.[5] Whether or not that is true, the question of a successor had already been decided when Taft announced his resignation the following Monday. As a result, Green's efforts to lobby the president were futile; Hoover nominated Hughes less than five hours after receiving Taft's official resignation. Green's telegram did not even reach the president until the next day.

On February 10, the Senate Judiciary Committee made public two letters from citizens opposing Hughes, but it quickly dispensed with any further public hearings. By a vote of 10 to 2, the committee favorably recommended the nomination to the full Senate, which began debating the nomination that afternoon. The two senators voting against Hughes in the committee were its chairman, George W. Norris of Nebraska, and John J. Blaine of Wisconsin. Both were progressive Republicans. But neither had resorted to a speech against Hughes in the committee, and most observers expected that the full Senate would quickly endorse the nomination with little debate. That expectation was wrong.[6] The Hughes nomination was the first at the Supreme Court level since the 1929 Senate rules changes guaranteeing open floor debate on a nominee. Opponents had saved their ammunition for a highly visible floor fight, played out in front of the press gallery.

Senator Norris set off the first volley that afternoon when he stood up on the Senate floor and attacked Hughes for his close association with big business. Suggesting that "no man in public life so exemplifies the influence of powerful combinations in the political and financial world as does Mr. Hughes," Senator Norris noted that in the past five years Hughes had argued dozens of cases before the Supreme Court on behalf of corporate interests. Hughes "looks through glasses contaminated by the influence of monopoly," Norris intoned. Having failed in his political ambition to win the presidency in 1916, Hughes had "succeeded beyond the imagination in his financial ambition" and now wanted to return to the Court as its leader. How, Norris asked, could such a man be impartial?[7] Opponents further argued that Hughes put property rights before human rights and would do so through the broad stroke of judicial activism.[8]

The Senate debate over Hughes became a media sensation, continuing nearly nonstop for the next three days. The Senate gallery was packed. Even House Speaker Nicholas Longworth (R-Ohio) joined the gawking onlookers. On the fourth day, the debate lasted seven hours. As the day drew to a close, opponents of the nomination tried to send it back to the Judiciary Committee for further investigation, but the Senate rejected the motion to recommit by a vote of 49 to 31. Had the motion been successful, labor organizations and other interests would no doubt have mobilized against Hughes. Public hearings might well have rivaled those of Brandeis fourteen years earlier. Numerous letters and telegrams opposing the nomination were already being received by senators, and extended public hearings could have galvanized public opinion against Hughes.[9] As it stood, however, opposition senators knew that they did not have the votes either to reject the nominee or to carry out a filibuster. Thus, late on February 13, the Senate confirmed Hughes by a vote of 52 to 26, with eighteen senators abstaining.[10]

Even then, the debate continued. America had entered the Great Depression, and many liberals were convinced that government regulation of the economy was needed more than ever. The Supreme Court stood in the way of such legislation. Liberals called this a usurpation of power and argued that the Court had entered the field of judicial legislation. As Senator LaFollette put it, the Court consistently defeated the popular will as expressed in legislation, siding with "organized greed" rather than with the interests of the people.[11] Aware that they had hit upon a salient issue, liberal senators took the floor again the day after the Hughes confirmation. Taking aim at what they called the activist conservative majority of the Supreme

Court, they threatened to end "judge-made law" by curbing the power of the Court through a constitutional amendment.[12]

With this rhetoric ringing in their ears, representatives of organized labor were ready to take an active stance on the next Supreme Court nominee. They did not have to wait long. In March, Associate Justice Edward T. Sanford died, and President Hoover nominated Judge John J. Parker from North Carolina to replace him. Labor quickly identified Parker as its foe. As a court of appeals judge for the Fourth Circuit, Parker had upheld a lower court injunction that prevented efforts by the United Mine Workers to unionize coal workers in West Virginia. In the process, he sanctioned "yellow dog" contracts, which prohibited employees from joining a union. That was all labor had to hear. They had started their fight against Hughes too late. Now, confident that they would have the support of a solid contingent of liberal Democrats and progressive Republicans in the Senate, they set their sights on Parker.

The Parker Nomination

At the age of forty-four, John Johnston Parker was the youngest man to be nominated to the Supreme Court in one hundred years. President Hoover chose him partly as a reward to the South. Parker's home state of North Carolina had voted for Hoover in the 1928 presidential election, the first time the state had gone Republican in a presidential election since Reconstruction. Although the Deep South remained a Democratic stronghold, Hoover had won Tennessee, Virginia, West Virginia, and Florida, in addition to North Carolina in 1928 (partly as an anti-Catholic vote against Democratic nominee Alfred E. Smith). Hoover, whose political strength was rapidly being sapped by the Great Depression, knew that the South would play an important role in his 1932 re-election efforts. Thus, the Parker nomination may be viewed as part of a strategy to retain southern support for the upcoming election.

While Hoover focused on regional considerations, labor focused on Parker's opinions as a federal court of appeals judge. The case that caught their eye was *United Mine Workers v. Red Jacket Coal and Coke Company* (1927).[13] The case grew out of the violent conflict that had erupted in West Virginia in 1921 when the United Mine Workers attempted to organize unions in coalfields where workers had signed yellow dog contracts. In one county alone, some seven thousand armed miners held a protest march to unionize the local coal companies. They were met by armed forces, including airplanes, which had been organized by the coal operators. The ensuing battle culminated in a declaration of martial law and the dispatch of federal troops.[14] In the wake of the violent disturbance, 316 nonunion companies, including Red Jacket, sought a permanent court injunction to prevent any union attempts to organize their workers. Federal District Court Judge George W. McClintic granted the injunction, and the United Mine Workers appealed. Judge Parker sat on the three-man panel that reviewed the case, and it was he who wrote the court of appeals decision upholding the injunction.[15]

Ironically, Parker's political outlook was quite progressive. He had received his undergraduate training at the University of North Carolina, where he was president of his class and a Phi Beta Kappa. He went on to get a law degree from UNC in 1908, establish a private practice, and become actively involved in Republican politics in North Carolina. He ran tirelessly for public office, but his bids for the U.S. Congress in 1910, the state attorney general's office in 1916, and the governor of North Carolina in 1920 all ended in failure. They were, however, respectable failures. Indeed, he polled more votes in the 1920 gubernatorial election than any other Republican candidate for governor had ever received in North Carolina.[16] As Kenneth W. Goings writes, these campaigns demonstrated that Parker was "a New South progressive." During the campaigns, Parker "called for women's suffrage, strong support for public education, industrial development, safeguards for labor, a state income tax, and better public roads."[17] Labor leaders, however, saw only the cold reality of Parker's *Red Jacket* decision.

Parker and the Labor Issue

Parker later claimed that he had no choice in the *Red Jacket* opinion: he was merely following settled law as handed down by the Supreme Court in *Hitchman Coal & Coke Company v. Mitchell*.[18] *Hitchman* had upheld yellow dog contracts and allowed a similar court injunction against unions. Had he ruled otherwise, Parker later wrote, he would "not only have been reversed but rebuked by the Supreme Court."[19] Even the counsel arguing the case for the United Mine Workers did not challenge the validity of yellow dog contracts. Instead, the United Mine Workers confined its argument to the issue of the injunction. The Justice Department concluded that this was a tacit admission on the part of the United Mine Workers that it considered *Hitchman* to be conclusive on that point. "Whatever reasons might have been advanced for assailing such contracts on grounds of public policy," Attorney General Mitchell wrote, "Judge Parker and his associate judges were constrained by the decision of the Supreme Court in the *Hitchman* case to disregard them."[20]

Hoover accepted the argument that Parker was bound by the *Hitchman* precedent, but labor was not assuaged. In a letter to Hoover, AFL president William Green wrote that it was not so much that Parker followed the decision in the *Hitchman* case that bothered labor. Rather, it was the tone of Parker's opinion. Nowhere in the opinion, Green pointed out, did Parker express any reservations about *Hitchman* or indicate that he was following Supreme Court precedent reluctantly. On the contrary, Green argued that there was "not one single word, sentence or paragraph in his written opinion that would justify the conclusion that [Parker] was not in sympathy and in accord with the *Hitchman* decision." To Green, *Hitchman* was an abrogation of human rights. It was labor's *Dred Scott* decision, he told Hoover. "The effect of the Dred Scott decision was to perpetuate human slavery," he wrote. "The effect of the Hitchman decision is to establish and perpetuate industrial servitude. No inferior court could follow the Dred Scott decision merely because of precedent and no enlightened jurist, who appreciates the character of human relations in modern industry, would follow the decision in the Hitchman case without expressing his disapproval of the rule laid down in the famous decision."[21]

In a letter to Chairman Norris of the Senate Judiciary Committee, Green made a similar argument. He reminded Norris that the injunction that Parker "approved and confirmed" was still in effect and acted as the law of the land in southern West Virginia. "The operation of the injunction has served to make serfs of the miners," Green wrote. "Their condition is hopeless. Their wages are below a subsistence level and their conditions of employment are un-American and intolerable. The officers and members of organized labor would help them through organization and cooperation, but they dare not because if they did they would be punished for violating, not the law of the land, but a judge-made law confirmed and approved by Judge Parker."[22]

President Hoover, who was sympathetic to the interests of organized labor, had written to Green earlier to try to convince him that the *Red Jacket* decision did not mean that Parker was antilabor. Hoover sent Green a copy of a Justice Department memorandum defending Parker's decision. In his terse cover letter, Hoover told Green that labor had been "entirely misled" about Parker and was "doing a great injustice" by opposing Parker.[23] Green shot back: "I assure you, Mr. President, [that] no one has misled me and that I am not conscious of doing any one an injustice. . . . In fighting against the confirmation of Judge Parker, Labor is fighting to make and keep men free—free from the sort of industrial servitude which injunctions, such as Judge Parker approved, impose upon them."[24]

On March 25, the AFL asked the Senate Judiciary Committee to consider Parker's *Red Jacket* opinion when considering the nomination.[25] Three days later the labor organization announced its formal opposition to Parker and asked for an opportunity to testify before the subcommittee investigating the nomination.[26] It would be the first time that an organized group would testify before a Senate committee about a Supreme Court nominee.

The North Carolina chapter of the AFL had not objected to Parker when Hoover nominated him. Once the national organization made its views known, however, Parker's home state chapter fell into line.[27] In so doing, North Carolina labor joined a united and highly organized campaign to defeat Judge Parker. Telegrams from labor organizations around the country began streaming in to the Senate. These petitions urged senators to vote against the judge, using the *Red Jacket* opinion as their prime piece of evidence that Parker was antilabor. For instance, the general chairman of the Brotherhood of Railroad Trainmen wired that Parker's decisions "clearly indicate that he is unfair to organized labor and holds property rights as being superior to human or personal rights."[28] The argument was a strong one, since many senators were themselves pushing for legislation to outlaw yellow dog contracts and the use of court injunctions in labor disputes.[29]

Parker and the Race Issue

Organized labor was soon joined by the National Association for the Advancement of Colored People in opposition to Parker. For some fifteen years, the NAACP had used the Supreme Court to advance the cause of African Americans and thus took particular interest in who was nominated to the Supreme Court. Walter White, executive secretary of the NAACP, had sought information about Parker as soon as Hoover announced the nomination. On March 24, White received a copy of an article from the April 19, 1920, issue of the *Greensboro Daily News*.[30] The article was written when Parker was running for governor of North Carolina, and it included quotations from one of Parker's campaign speeches in which he stated that "the negro as a class does not desire to enter politics" and that "the participation of the negro in politics is a source of evil and danger to both races and is not desired by the wise men in either race or by the Republican party of North Carolina."

Although Parker's words were damning on their face, they were spoken in an apparent effort to mute the racial animosity that the race baiting of his Democratic opposition had enflamed. Racial tension was high in 1920; race riots in 1919 in several cities had kindled overt racial fear and hatred, and membership in the Ku Klux Klan had surged. North Carolina Democrats played on that fear and hatred in the 1920 gubernatorial campaign by reminding white voters that the Republicans were the party of Reconstruction and by suggesting that Parker was not only courting black votes but actively supporting the political empowerment of African Americans.[31] The acceptance of such charges meant certain defeat in the context of 1920 North Carolina politics. Thus, Parker felt compelled to respond to the charges. The "attempt of certain petty Democratic politicians to inject the race issue into every campaign is most reprehensible," Parker said in the same public speech that was reported by the *Greensboro Daily News*. "I say it deliberately, there is no more dangerous or contemptible enemy of the state than the man who for personal or political advantage will attempt to kindle the flame of racial prejudice or hatred."

But in his attempt to deflect the Democratic charges, Parker incorporated a racist rhetoric that the NAACP would use against him during his Supreme Court confirmation hearings and that troubled even many of his supporters. For instance, Parker went so far as to say in 1920 that the Republican party still accepted the "spirit" of the grandfather clause to the North Carolina state constitution, even though the United States Supreme Court had struck it down as unconstitutional in 1915.[32] The grandfather clause had exempted white voters from literacy tests and other devices used to keep blacks from voting if the fathers or grandfathers of those white voters had been qualified to vote before 1867. "We recognize the fact that [the black man] has not yet reached that stage in his development when he can share the burdens and responsibilities of government," Parker concluded.[33]

Walter White read the statements in the *Greensboro Daily News* with concern, and on March 26 he sent a telegram to Parker asking if the newspaper account accurately conveyed his remarks—and if it did, whether Parker still held those views. Although Parker received the telegram the same day, he did not reply.[34] Thus began a series of tactical mistakes that helped to doom the nomination. Parker felt that his own statements could be excused because of the context of the 1920 campaign; after all, the Democrats were the ones fanning the flames of racial hatred. In Parker's mind, the spirit of his own remarks should be clear to the NAACP and other black leaders. However, he knew that a direct repudiation of his statements would raise the ire of southern Democrats whose support was essential to his confirmation. Moreover, Parker appeared to believe that it was inappropriate for a Supreme Court nominee to comment on any charges made against him.[35] Given these reasons, Parker did not reply to White's telegram. To White, however, this was proof of Parker's racism: the judge would not even dignify the telegram with the courtesy of a response.

Convinced that Parker was hostile to the goals of the NAACP, White launched that organization's opposition to the nomination. On March 28, he sent letters to 177 local branches of the NAACP urging them to let their senators know of their opposition to Parker. At the same time, the NAACP directly announced its opposition to Parker in letters to U.S. senators, and White requested permission to testify against Parker in public hearings.[36] In yet another tactical error, Parker discounted the impact of this opposition. Despite rising opposition from labor and blacks, Parker continued to assume that his confirmation remained secure.[37] Had such opposition arisen prior to the constitutional amendment providing for the direct election of U.S. senators, Parker would probably have been correct. But the electoral landscape was such that a united black vote could determine the outcome of upcoming midterm elections in several northern and border states. Besides, African Americans were still a Republican constituency in 1930. The NAACP made the most of this. Thus, even a number of GOP senators who would normally have supported President Hoover eventually found themselves in the position of having to oppose Parker or face the prospect of defeat at the polls.[38]

Arthur Vandenburg, a conservative Republican senator from Michigan who had stood up against his prolabor colleagues and staunchly defended Hoover's nomination of Charles Evans Hughes earlier in the year, was a prime case in point. Despite considerable pressure from Hoover, Vandenburg ultimately voted against Parker because of the potential strength of the black vote in Michigan.[39] Vandenburg cited Parker's 1920 campaign speech as the basis for his opposition and said that blacks had "a right to be suspicious" of the nominee.[40] The opposition of senators like Vandenburg, who would have supported Parker had it not been for the black vote, coupled with the opposition of prolabor senators, ultimately proved to be a decisive blow to the White House.

The Parker Hearings

Despite their mutual interest in securing the defeat of Judge Parker, organized labor kept its distance from the NAACP. On the day of the hearings by the Subcommittee of the Committee on the Judiciary, White of the NAACP and Green of the AFL entered the hearing room at the same time, but White later wrote that Green "conspicuously" avoided speaking to him "lest senators on the committee, newspapermen, or spectators believe that we were fighting in a common battle."[41] Donald Lisio writes that, although both the AFL and the NAACP "were considered to be liberal, the unions would not admit blacks and refused to support their rights, either in general or as workers."[42] Thus, Green did not address the race issue at all in his testimony against Parker.

The three-member Senate Judiciary subcommittee also deferred to labor, letting it testify first, while the NAACP waited to speak until the end of the session. Senator Lee Overman (D-N.C.) chaired the subcommittee. The other two members were Republicans—William Borah of Idaho and Felix Hebert of Rhode Island. Green's testimony took up twenty-two pages in the published record (not including an additional sixteen pages of information submitted for the record during his testimony), while White's testimony took up only five and a half pages.[43]

White stressed Parker's statements about blacks during the 1920 gubernatorial campaign and said that it was "a reasonable certainty" that a Supreme Court Justice holding such views could not approach cases involving the civil rights of black Americans with a "dispassionate, unprejudiced, and judicial frame of mind." White also argued that Parker's statement that the Republican party of North Carolina accepted the "spirit" of the state's grandfather clause, even though it had been declared unconstitutional by the United States Supreme Court, amounted to "an open, shameless flouting of the fourteenth and fifteenth amendments to the Federal Constitution." As he put it, "Twelve million American negroes and all white Americans who have a regard for law and order cannot help condemning an attitude which indicates a willingness to support some laws and to disregard others when political expediency dictates."[44]

White admitted that he had no other evidence besides the *Greensboro Daily News* report to substantiate Parker's racism, and he added that the NAACP had no personal animosity against Parker. However, White stressed that the NAACP had made an investigation into the newspaper report and had given Parker an opportunity to explain or repudiate the statements. The NAACP had concluded that Parker did, in fact, say what the newspaper had reported and that Parker's failure to respond to them was a clear indication that his views had not changed over the past decade. That was reason enough to oppose the nomination, White argued, since it was essential that blacks receive "even-handed justice," and since the Supreme Court would clearly be hearing more cases involving the civil rights of black Americans in the near future.[45] White concluded that it was a "well-accepted fact that judges, like all other human beings, even justices of the United States Supreme Court, have their opinions colored by their social, economic, political, and other views."[46]

The Parker hearing was short and relatively uneventful. The hearing convened at 10:30 A.M. on Saturday, April 5, and was over in just two hours and forty-five minutes. In addition to Green and White, the subcommittee heard testimony from four other individuals. But the extensive lobbying campaign against Parker, of which the public testimony was a part, was paying off. Although the subcommittee voted 2 to 1 on April 14 to recommend Parker's approval by the full Judiciary Committee, the nomination was clearly in trouble. As the *New York Herald Tribune* reported on April 12:

> As a result of the opposition from Negro voters, Senators are being flooded with more letters and telegrams than they have had from labor. In consequence, Republican Senators from Northern and border states

which have large numbers of Negro voters are alarmed. They have made it known to President Hoover that they feel Judge Parker's name should be withdrawn.

Vice-President [Charles] Curtis has conferred with President Hoover on the matter and has advised him of the strong opposition in the Senate. It was declared in Senate circles today he had advised the President to withdraw the name, but the Vice-President denied he had made such representations.[47]

The Republican majority leader of the Senate, James E. Watson of Indiana, publicly stated on April 11 that he had spoken with the president, advised him of the "formidable opposition" to Parker among the president's own party, and urged that he investigate the situation.[48] The White House sought to stifle the rumors by issuing a categorical denial on April 12 that the president would withdraw the nomination.[49] But the White House statement did nothing to alleviate the fears of many senators, and Hoover (tainted by the October 1929 stock market crash and the ensuing economic depression) did not wield great power over Senate Republicans. For instance, John M. Robinson, a Republican senator from Kentucky who was up for re-election, paid a visit to the White House on April 12 and expressed his fear to the president about the power of the black vote in his state (where some 200,000 blacks were registered). Under the circumstances, he simply could not support Parker.[50]

The Parker Defense

In a belated attempt to mute the opposition to Parker, the White House circulated among senators a written defense of Parker's statements concerning blacks. But no matter how honorable Parker's intentions may have been when he made the statements, the White House rationalization of them fell flat. In fact, it seemed to perpetuate the very racism that it was trying to deny:

> In [Parker's] Greensboro speech, it was not proposed to deny the colored people any rights under the law or to discriminate against them in any way. After the adoption of the suffrage amendment they [blacks] had not attempted to participate in the political life of the state and no attempt had been made to organize them for political purposes. They were going along quietly attending to their own business. They were apparently following the advice of some of their leaders who counseled them to let politics alone. Nevertheless, in almost every campaign the Republican party had been denounced as intending to put them in power in North Carolina and restore the evils of the Reconstruction period. In 1920 certain adversaries of the party raised the same false issue and sought to stir up racial prejudice by charging that the Republicans intended to organize the

Negroes and turn the state over to them. The Greensboro speech was merely an answer to this attempt to inject the race issue into politics. It called attention to the fact that the colored people were not trying to enter politics in North Carolina, that the Republican party of the state was not trying to organize them or restore them to power in the state, and deplored the attempt to stir up racial prejudice and hatred against them.[51]

The White House also took pains to note that, as a federal court of appeals judge, Parker had not denied blacks their constitutional rights. As proof, it pointed to *City of Richmond v. Deans*, in which Parker ruled that a residential racial segregation ordinance was unconstitutional.[52] However, the administration's rationalization for Parker's antilabor ruling in the *Red Jacket* case undermined the administration's argument that the *City of Richmond* case demonstrated Parker's commitment to racial equality, since the administration had argued that the *Red Jacket* case did not represent Parker's true views on labor because he was obligated to follow Supreme Court precedent on the matter—and the *City of Richmond* case was also based on Supreme Court precedent.[53] Why not, then, interpret Parker's *Richmond* ruling the same way as the *Red Jacket* ruling? By that interpretation, Parker had to rule the way he did in the *Richmond* case, and the ruling could not be assumed to reflect Parker's true views on racial segregation. The administration suggested that, as a Supreme Court justice, Parker would have ruled differently in the *Red Jacket* case. Wasn't it just as likely that as a Supreme Court Justice, Parker would have ruled differently in the *Richmond* case? The possibility that Parker would vote against the rights of African Americans if he made it to the Supreme Court was just what the NAACP and other black leaders feared.

As opposition grew, Parker became more active in defending himself. Rumors circulated that during his gubernatorial race Parker had said that, if he was elected due to one black vote, he would immediately resign. Furious at the charge, Parker issued a categorical denial through his friend David H. Blair.[54] A group of the judge's close supporters in North Carolina also tried to counter the lobbying of the NAACP by securing endorsements of Parker from state bar associations and by mobilizing other forms of support from various states.[55] The White House, after a slow start, tried to secure an endorsement of Parker from Robert R. Moton Jr., principal of the Tuskegee Institute in Alabama and a strong supporter of President Hoover. Moton, however, was deeply disturbed by Parker's statements and by his failure to distance himself from them. If Parker had handled the situation differently, and if Moton had been asked sooner, the black leader might have come to Parker's defense. But in a letter to Walter H. Newton, President Hoover's personal political secretary, Moton refused to lend an endorsement.

"If the statements attributed to Judge Parker are true," he wrote, "there is only one position that my own self-respect will permit me to take and that is unyielding opposition to his confirmation."[56] Moton did not accept the White House rationalization of Parker's statements; even "the exigencies of politics" did not warrant the remarks attributed to Parker. "Personally I can forgive a great many things that are the reflection of our common human weakness, but when a man sets himself up to publicly attack, revile or express his contempt for my people for no other reason than that they belong to another race, he places himself in a position where I can have nothing less than an uncompromising and everlasting hostility." Although Moton said that he was planning no public attack on Parker, he nonetheless made it clear that he would express his views if asked. He also warned of the political repercussions for the Republicans if they continued to push the nomination: "I know of nothing that would so effectively turn the tide of Negro support against the President and the party . . . [than] deliberately to place on the Supreme Court a man who has openly declared his contempt for them."

President Hoover, himself a Quaker, also attempted to get an endorsement from the Society of Friends, a Quaker organization that had long supported black rights. But on April 17, Robert Gray Taylor, secretary of the society's Committee on Race Relations, told the president that they could not do so given Parker's failure to answer the inquiries posed by the NAACP. Two days later, Parker, now willing to talk, invited Taylor to his office. During the meeting, Parker agreed to mail a public letter concerning his 1920 statements about blacks to Senator Henry D. Hatfield of West Virginia, and Taylor came away from the meeting convinced that Parker was not a racist.[57]

In his letter to Senator Hatfield, Parker sought to dispel "the slightest anxiety on the part of any person, of any race or creed," and firmly stated that he acknowledged "the Constitution and all its amendments as the fundamental and supreme law of the land. . . . The effort to interpret some statements made some ten years ago in a speech in a political campaign in North Carolina as indicating a contrary disposition is not justified."[58] He concluded by promising to pronounce the law "according to its spirit and letter, to all alike." Taylor told Parker that, based on the letter, he would recommend that the Society of Friends reverse its position and support the nomination. But Walter White of the NAACP, whom Taylor telephoned, felt that the letter was insufficient to merit a change in the Society of Friends' position. As a result of White's strong objections, the society invited him to meet with its Committee on Race Relations the next day. After a three-hour session on April 20, all eight members of the committee decided to continue its fight against the Parker nomination.[59] Again, an effort to build support for Parker had failed.

Aware that the possibility of confirmation was slipping away from them, Parker's supporters decided that he should directly respond to the charges in unprecedented public testimony before the Senate Judiciary Committee. Mabel Walker Willebrandt, Hoover's assistant attorney general, strongly supported the idea. She pointed out that the charges against Parker had created the impression that he was "very unjudicial." She felt that his testimony would offset that impression because of his "very calm, judicial, reasonable demeanor."[60] Senate Majority Leader Watson and Senator Overman, the Democrat from North Carolina who was Parker's prime sponsor on the Judiciary Committee, agreed, but the liberal Republican chairman of the full committee, Senator Norris, was less enthusiastic. In the end, Norris would break with the White House (as he had done on Hughes) and lead the opposition against Parker on the Senate floor.

On April 18, Willebrandt had a long conversation with Norris. Norris said that Parker could volunteer to appear if he liked, but that the committee should not call for his appearance. By then, Parker's supporters had concluded that they should " 'leak out' to the papers" that they were "perfectly willing to have him appear before the committee."[61] The story made it into the newspapers that evening.[62] The next day Senator Overman made public a telegram from Parker. It read: "If the Judiciary Committee of the United States Senate desires my presence and requests it, I shall, of course, be glad to come."[63] But when the full committee met on April 21, it rejected a motion to invite Parker to testify by a vote of 10 to 4 and proceeded by a vote of 10 to 6 to report the nomination adversely to the full Senate. The action was "swift and unexpected."[64] During the committee vote, President Hoover was on the south lawn of the White House listening to a performance of the black Tuskegee Choir.[65]

Unable to testify, Judge Parker, at the urging of President Hoover, sent, on April 24, an open letter to Senator Overman defending his positions on race and labor.[66] "From a reading of the record there seems to be only two protests," Parker wrote, "one by the American Federation of Labor criticizing my decision in the *Red Jacket Coal* case, and the other by the National Association for the Advancement of Colored People, criticizing statements made in my campaign for Governor of North Carolina ten years ago, and expressing the fear that I might not enforce the provisions of the Constitution guaranteeing the rights of Colored People." His response to the charge of labor was that he had "followed the law as laid down by the Supreme Court" in *Coppage v. Kansas*[67] and the *Hitchman* case. In view of those precedents, Parker concluded, "it must be obvious to anyone that, as a member of the Court in the *Red Jacket* case, I had no latitude or discretion in expressing any opinion or views of my own, but was bound by these decisions to reach the conclusion and to render the decision that I did." He then turned to the protest of the NAACP:

> The protest of the Colored People seems to be based upon the fear that I might not enforce the provisions of the Constitution in so far as same guarantees their rights. Needless to say, such fear is entirely groundless. I regard the Constitution and all its amendments as the fundamental and supreme law of the land, and I deem it the first duty of a judge to give full scope and effect to all of their provisions. In the discharge of my duties as Circuit Judge, I have never hesitated, I hope and believe, to meet this obligation in the fullest degree.
>
> The effort to interpret some statements alleged to have been made ten years ago in a speech in a political campaign as indicating a contrary disposition, is wholly unjustified. My effort then was to answer those who were seeking to inject the race issue into the campaign. . . . I knew the baneful effects of such a campaign and sought to avoid it. . . . While I made it clear that my party was not seeking to organize the Colored People of the state as a class, I at no time advocated denying them the right to participate in the election . . . nor did I advocate denying them any other of their rights under the Constitution and the laws of the United States. Any charge or intimation that I appealed to race prejudice is most unjust. I deplored that appeal to race prejudices and did my utmost to eliminate it from the campaign.
>
> In conclusion let me say that I have no prejudice whatever against the Colored People and no disposition to deny them any of their rights or privileges under the Constitution and the laws. I think that my record as a Judge of the United States Circuit Court of Appeals, in a circuit where many of them reside, shows that I have no such prejudice or disposition.

The letter did no good; it actually hurt Parker among those who had expected a more forceful repudiation of his statements from the 1920 campaign. In fact, Parker omitted some stronger language from an earlier draft of the letter, apparently out of fear of alienating southern senators, whom he was counting on for a favorable confirmation vote.[68] As it stood, the NAACP promptly denounced the letter as a "disingenuous piece of sophistry."[69]

The Parker Defeat

Senate debate on the Parker nomination began on April 28. The gallery was packed with onlookers and the debate droned on until May 7, but few senators came to Parker's defense. The most excitement came when Senator Henry F. Ashurst (D-Ariz.) falsely accused the Hoover administration of offering federal judgeships and other political appointments to senators in exchange for voting for Parker.[70] If anything, Hoover probably should have used patronage and other lobbying tactics more aggressively than he did. But as one presidential adviser, French Strother, told Hoover's military aide, Col. Campbell B. Hodges, Hoover was "handicapped because he didn't understand playing the political game well enough—trading and swapping one thing for support on another later on."[71] The president attempted, belatedly, to win the support of usually friendly senators, but to no avail.[72]

Parker's chances for confirmation were further undermined during the Senate debate when Senator George McKellar (D-Tenn.) introduced a letter dated March 13 from Joseph M. Dixon, first assistant secretary of the interior, to Walter H. Newton, one of Hoover's personal aides. The letter urged the president to nominate Parker because it would be "a major political stroke" to solidify support for the president in the South, where he had made gains in the 1928 presidential election.[73] The letter helped to portray the selection of Parker as a political ploy by the president to shore up his chances for reelection in 1932. This was largely true, but it led to the erroneous implication that Hoover chose Parker in part because he *was* a racist and to shore up the "lily-white" image of the Republican party and thereby lure traditional southern Democrats into voting for him.

When the vote finally came on Monday, May 7, the Senate defeated Parker by a vote of 41 to 39. Eight southern Democrats crossed party lines and voted for Parker, but seventeen Republicans opposed him. Most of the Republicans opposing Parker were progressive midwesterners with strong ties to labor, but fear of retaliation from black voters clinched the opposition of several other Republicans. The black vote was particularly important in Illinois, Indiana, Kentucky, Maryland, Massachusetts, Michigan, Missouri, New Jersey, New York, Ohio, Pennsylvania, and Tennessee.[74] Of the sixteen Republicans from those states, only nine voted for Parker. In the end, a shift of just one vote would have allowed Vice President Charles Curtis to break a 40 to 40 tie in favor of Parker.

The White House responded to the Senate defeat with stony silence. Hoover apparently wanted to issue a statement decrying the defeat, but after meeting with Senator Henry Allen (R-Kan.), who had voted for Parker, and Undersecretary of State Cotton, the president decided to put off making any statement.[75] During the next day and a half, the president drafted at least four versions of a public statement. In a May 7 draft, Hoover wrote:

> Judge Parker's confirmation was opposed by a vigorous nation-wide propaganda from different groups among our citizens resulting in numbers of protests to senators from their constituents. These groups, in advancing the causes to which they are devoted, have carried the question of confirmation into the field of political issues rather than personal fitness. . . .

These activities have placed many senators in the position of appearing to vote for or against an issue with which Judge Parker has little to do.

There is no one in a democracy who does not uphold the vital importance of public opinion. But public opinion as a whole cannot function in this manner.[76]

In an undated draft, Hoover was even more pointed. "It is deplorable that an issue of such fundamental importance as this has been confused by nationwide propaganda based on misunderstanding in relation to labor questions and wicked misrepresentations in connection with the eminent rights of the colored people of the United States to participate in citizenship. . . . I have no regrets at the presentation of Judge Parker's name."[77] Ultimately, Hoover decided not to issue a public statement about Parker's defeat and simply nominated Owen J. Roberts to fill Justice Sanford's post on the Court.[78]

Hoover maintained for the rest of his life that Parker was unfairly defeated. In the final draft on his unissued public statement, Hoover wrote that "Judge Parker was mistakenly and I believe unintentionally made a symbol of opposition" to the causes of labor and civil rights and that "neither his character nor his actions" warranted his rejection.[79] In his memoirs, Hoover displayed bitterness at his fellow Republicans for deserting him on the Parker vote. He noted that a number of Republican senators "ran like white mice" as a result of pressure from organized interests. "This failure of my party to support me greatly lowered the prestige of my administration," he concluded.[80]

After the defeat, Parker remained on the court of appeals, where he established a distinguished record that repudiated the concerns of both African Americans and labor. Walter White, who led the NAACP fight against Parker, wrote in his memoirs that Parker's "decisions on both Negro and labor cases" in the years since his Senate defeat were "above reproach."[81] Admired by his colleagues, including liberals such as Harlan Fiske Stone, Parker came to be regarded as one of the country's most distinguished federal judges. Sixteen years after his defeat, the American Bar Association concluded that Parker's rejection was one of the "most regrettable combinations of error and injustice that has ever developed as to a nomination to the great court."[82]

||| INTERESTS VERSUS NOMINEES

THE DEFEAT OF CLEMENT HAYNSWORTH

The nomination of Clement F. Haynsworth Jr. had a good deal in common with that of John J. Parker. Both Haynsworth and Parker served on the Fourth Circuit Court of Appeals when they were nominated to serve on the United States Supreme Court (Parker was still on the court when Haynsworth joined it in 1957, and the two became close friends). Both were opposed by organized labor and civil rights leaders. Both were rejected by the Senate but continued to serve on the court of appeals and to solidify their reputations as distinguished jurists after their defeat. And both defeats have come to be regarded by many as a mistake.

The two presidents who nominated them also had much in common. Both Herbert Hoover and Richard Nixon were Republicans. Both were Quakers. Both made their nominations as part of a "southern strategy" to solidify regional political strength and thereby increase the likelihood of reelection. Like Hoover in 1928, Richard Nixon in 1968 had won North Carolina, Tennessee, Virginia, and Florida and had also picked up South Carolina. Moreover, both Hoover and Nixon were politically vulnerable when they made their nominations. Hoover's political strength was sapped by the Great Depression. Nixon, though still in his first year in office, was an unusually weak first-year president. He had narrowly defeated Democrat Hubert Humphrey and the third-party candidate George Wallace in the 1968 presidential election, winning the presidency with only 43.4 percent of the popular vote. Moreover, Nixon was the first newly elected president since Zachary Taylor in 1849 to take office with both houses of Congress controlled by the opposition.[1] And, as Nixon liked to point out, the nation was badly divided—more so, he later claimed, than at any point since the Civil War.[2] Political assassinations, race riots, student uprisings, and antiwar demonstrations shook the status quo.

President Nixon nominated Haynsworth on August 18, 1969, to fill the seat of Associate Justice Abe Fortas. Just as the Parker battle has to be viewed in the context of the Hughes nomination, the Haynsworth battle cannot be understood without knowing something about the circumstances surrounding the departure of Justice Fortas from the Supreme Court.

The Trouble with Fortas

Abe Fortas resigned from the Court on May 14, after revelations that as a justice he had signed a contract to receive $20,000 a year for life from the Wolfson Family Foundation for "consulting," a yearly fee that would continue to be paid to his wife in the event of his death. The revelation provoked outcry, because the fee (which was more than half of Fortas's $39,500 salary from the Supreme Court) looked like a payoff. Louis Wolfson, the millionaire director of the foundation, was under investigation by the Securities and Exchange Commission. Fortas was aware of the investigation. Indeed, his law firm had represented Wolfson in 1965, the year before Fortas signed the financial contract with the Wolfson Foundation. In fact, Wolfson was eventually convicted on charges of stock manipulation and served nine months in prison, but not before asking Fortas for help in securing a presidential pardon (which Fortas declined).[3] Fortas severed his contract with the Wolfson Foundation after less than six months and returned his initial payment of $20,000, but that did not diminish the appearance of wrongdoing when *Life* magazine exposed the financial contract in 1969.[4]

Although Fortas had broken no law, the revelations prompted conflict of interest charges and questions concerning Fortas's judgment and integrity. The matter was further complicated by the fact that Fortas had withdrawn his nomination to be elevated to the chief justice post after a successful Senate filibuster against his nomination in 1968. Although the opposition to Fortas in 1968 was largely political (he was nominated by a lame duck Democratic president only four months before a presidential election that seemed would be won by the Republican candidate), his opponents justified their opposition by charging that Fortas was guilty of judicial impropriety. They made much of the fact that, after joining the Court, Fortas continued to counsel President Lyndon Baines Johnson personally, talking with the president at least eighty-seven times about everything from Vietnam policy and the Detroit race riots to the drafting of presidential speeches and President Johnson's re-election strategy.[5] They argued that such close contact with the president undermined the justice's judicial independence by breaching separation of powers and raised questions about a possible conflict of interest. Thus, when *Life* published the new conflict of interest charges in May 1969, they seemed particularly damning. Major newspapers, including the *Chicago Tribune*, the *Los Angeles Times*, the *New York Daily News*, and the *Washington Post* called for Fortas's resignation.[6] Facing the possibility of an impeachment proceeding against him in the House of Representatives, Fortas resigned.

President Nixon accepted Fortas's resignation with pleasure. His Justice Department, headed by Attorney General John Mitchell, had helped to orchestrate Fortas's downfall.[7] When Nixon ran for president in 1968, he espoused a strict "law and order" philosophy and promised to nominate "strict constructionists" to the Supreme Court, people who would not use "their interpretation of the law to remake American society according to their own social, political, and ideological precepts."[8] Nixon's nomination of Warren Burger as chief justice had sailed through the Senate earlier in 1969, and the president was eager to appoint another strict constructionist. He also wanted to appoint a southerner to the Court to reward a region of the country that had supported him in 1968 and whose support he needed to win re-election in 1972. Haynsworth fit both of Nixon's criteria. But by nominating a conservative southerner to the Court, Nixon promptly drew fire from liberals, who feared that Haynsworth would undermine the rulings of the Warren Court. Both the AFL-CIO and the NAACP immediately announced their opposition to the Haynsworth nomination and were soon joined by other organized interests.

Interest Group Opposition to Haynsworth

Black leaders objected to Haynsworth because of his court of appeals votes in a number of civil rights cases in the 1950s and early 1960s. Although Haynsworth joined opinions upholding the claims of minorities against discriminatory practices in at least eighteen cases, he also joined three rulings against desegregation (later overruled by the Supreme Court) and dissented from at least three other opinions that upheld civil rights claims.[9] Critics charged that those opinions demonstrated Haynsworth's insensitivity to claims of racial discrimination and were evidence that he was a foot-dragging segregationist.[10] Likewise, the AFL-CIO argued that the seven labor cases in which Haynsworth's position had been reversed by the Supreme Court demonstrated that Haynsworth was antilabor and predicted that its opposition to the nomination would be "one of our biggest fights on the Hill this year."[11]

Had the opposition to Haynsworth rested solely on the way he voted on the Fourth Circuit on cases dealing with race and labor, his confirmation would have been secure. Unlike Parker, Haynsworth had made no public statements that could be used as evidence that he held biased views against labor or minorities, and Haynsworth's supporters could easily argue that his opinions were a reflection of judicial self-restraint rather than a reflection of his personal policy predilections. Even some liberal Democrats defended Haynsworth and called opponents' claims exaggerated. What killed the Haynsworth nomination were charges of conflict of interest. At any other time, the charges would probably have had little impact. But given the Senate's opposition to Fortas on conflict of interest grounds the year before and Fortas's forced resignation from the Court because of conflict of interest charges—and the fact that Nixon nominated Haynsworth to fill the vacancy left by Fortas—any hint of conflict of interest was damning. Opponents were well aware of this and made the most of the charges.

In and of themselves, the charges were relatively insubstantial. The most serious involved Haynsworth's relation with a vending machine firm called the Carolina Vend-A-Matic Company, which he was a director of when he joined the court of appeals in 1957. When the Judicial Conference of the United States adopted a resolution in 1963 that no judge should serve as an officer or director of any business corporation organized for profit, Haynsworth resigned his directorship.[12] Nonetheless, he still owned stock in the company and, subsequently, joined a court of appeals ruling favoring another company (Deering-Milliken) that had a business relation with Carolina Vend-A-Matic.[13] Haynsworth did not know of the business relation, which amounted to only 3 percent of Vend-A-Matic's total business, and thus did not disqualify himself from the case. But the appearance of possible impropriety remained. Moreover, critics raised questions about Haynsworth's ownership of stock in other companies whose cases appeared before him, although none of his holdings were large.[14] Haynsworth, like Fortas, was guilty of no crime. Still, the Senate was in an awkward position. As Henry J. Abraham puts it: "How could the Senate confirm Haynsworth when it had played such an admirable activist-moralist role in causing Fortas's resignation?"[15] The problem was particularly acute for Republicans, who had led the fight against Fortas.

The death of Senate Republican leader Everett Dirksen further undercut Haynsworth's position by delaying the start of the confirmation hearings until September 16. This gave Haynsworth's opponents time to marshall their forces. Birch Bayh, a liberal Democrat from Indiana, led the fight against Haynsworth in the Senate. It was a fight infused with politics. By the time the Senate Judiciary Committee voted on the nomination, labor and civil rights organizations had generated a "wave of anti-Haynsworth mail and telegrams" that poured into Senators' offices.[16] The committee approved the Haynsworth nomination by a vote of 10 to 7 on October 9, but the full Senate rejected it by a 45-to-55 vote on November 21. Among the Republicans voting against Haynsworth were "strict constructionists" like minority whip Robert Griffin (R-Mich.) and Jack Miller (R-Iowa). Both had led the fight against Fortas in 1968.[17] (Nixon was furious at his fellow Republicans for opposing Haynsworth. He told his chief of staff, H. R. Haldeman, that he would "destroy Griffin as Whip" because of his opposition to Haynsworth.)[18]

At the outset, the White House maintained a low profile regarding the Haynsworth nomination. Nixon's nomination of Warren Burger had proceeded without a hitch, and the White House expected the same with Haynsworth. Although members of the administration, particularly Attorney General John Mitchell, had played an active behind-the-scenes role in ousting Abe Fortas, they initially decided against a vigorous lobbying campaign on behalf of their nominee to replace him. Even when allegations against Haynsworth began to surface, Nixon and Haldeman instructed members of the administration, including the Justice Department and White House Press Secretary Ronald Ziegler, to refuse to comment on specific allegations made against Haynsworth. In retrospect, this was a major mistake—one very similar to the ill-fated approach taken by Parker and the Hoover White House in 1930.

The Nixon administration's only categorical defense of Haynsworth appears to have been a statement by Assistant Attorney General William Rehnquist on September 5 and that dealt only with the charges relating to Haynsworth's association with Carolina Vend-A-Matic.[19] Thus, even Republican senators who had questions about the charges against Haynsworth had difficulty getting answers from the administration.[20] This proved to be particularly problematic during the Senate Judiciary Committee's public hearings on the nomination, which began on September 16. Quite simply, Republican senators on the committee who wanted to help Haynsworth received little or no guidance or support from the administration. Haynsworth received coaching from Assistant Attorney General William Rehnquist on how to testify, but he had no staff to help him respond to the charges leveled against him. Moreover, his shy demeanor and a minor speech impediment hurt him during aggressive questioning. One newspaper reported that Haynsworth "appeared edgy and stuttering under hours of questioning," leaving the impression that the stuttering was a sign that Haynsworth was overwhelmed by the charges and must therefore be guilty.[21]

The White House Responds

The White House did not swing into action until the beginning of October, after the completion of the Senate Judiciary Committee hearings. By that time, Republican Whip Griffin had predicted that Haynsworth would be defeated by a vote of 52 to 48, and Nixon's Congressional Liaison Director

Bryce Harlow had recommended that Nixon withdraw the nomination; Nixon blamed the Justice Department, but Assistant Attorney General Rehnquist convinced him that White House inaction was to blame.[22] The president then ordered a major White House offensive on behalf of Haynsworth: "We can stimulate mail too. There should be letters and wires from the Farm Bureaus, Southern bar associations, the National Rifle Association and our other friends; they have got to be energized. Get pro-Haynsworth speeches into the record; we've got to build a wave of support for our man."[23]

The White House strategy was, first, to convince voters to put pressure on their senators to vote for Haynsworth and, second, to publicly declare that those who opposed Haynsworth were engaging in brute political tactics. The efforts began in earnest during the week the Senate Judiciary Committee voted on Haynsworth's confirmation, when Clark Mollenhoff wrote a detailed twenty-five-page report rebutting the charges against Haynsworth.[24] Mollenhoff, a former investigative reporter for the *Des Moines Register* and *Tribune,* served as counsel to the president. His job was to discover and alert Nixon to mismanagement and wrongdoing in the administration. Mollenhoff, having questioned Haynsworth at length in the presence of William Rehnquist, had concluded that there was nothing illegal or unethical about Haynsworth's conduct.[25] At the same time, the White House Congressional Liaison Office researched the Brandeis and Hughes nominations to show how opponents to those nominees had infused politics into the confirmation process. The point was to show that two of the most distinguished members of the Court had faced fierce opposition similar to that being faced by Haynsworth. Even Chief Justice Warren Burger entered the process, contributing information about justices whose nominations had been controversial but who went on to great success.[26]

Nixon used this information at an informal press conference held in his office on October 20. He reviewed the charges against Haynsworth and echoed Mollenhoff's rebuttal of those charges. Then, claiming that Haynsworth had become the target of "vicious character assassination," he turned to the research that Harlow had provided. "If you want to go back and read what really can happen in cases of this sort," he said, "I would suggest that you read the debate over Louis Brandeis and also the confirmation of Charles Evans Hughes in which they poured on [them] all the filth they could possibly amass."[27]

After that press conference, the White House Office of Communications sent a mass mailing to three thousand editors, publishers, and broadcasters. In states with a wavering senator, the mailings were sent to the editors of every daily newspaper. In the remaining states, the mailings went to editors of dailies with a circulation of over twenty-five thousand. Included in the mailing were a cover letter signed by Herbert Klein (director of the Communications Office), a condensed version of Mollenhoff's report, a transcript of the president's press conference, and excerpts from a book concerning the controversy over the nomination of Charles Evans Hughes.[28]

When the White House mailed the packages, Klein met with a group of Nixon advisers to discuss strategy for promoting Haynsworth. The group included the president's speechwriter, Patrick Buchanan, who prepared the president's Daily News Summary, Lyn Nofziger of the Congressional Liaison Office, who provided speech material to proadministration representatives and senators, and Alvin Snyder of the Office of Communications, who was responsible for placing administration (and proadministration) spokespeople on radio and television. To generate favorable comment, they followed up the mailing with personal phone calls to editors and broadcasters. The Office of Communications spelled out the plan in a memo, with specific instructions for White House aides to initiate press contacts in various states. For instance:

> Pat Buchanan will contact Bill Buckley, James J. Kilpatrick, William White, John Chamberlain, Vic Lasky, and Nick Thimmesch. Clark Mollenhoff . . . will initiate contacts with the Dover [Delaware] newspaper, and also with John Cauley of the Kansas City *Star*. Mr. Klein will reach Cruise Palmer of the *Star* and also the Emporia *Gazette*. Paul Costello in our shop [the Office of Communications] will work on New Hampshire and Vermont. In Illinois, Pat will contact the *Globe Democrat*, and Lyn [Nofziger] the Rockford newspaper. Al Snyder will work with broadcasters in Illinois.[29]

The Hoover administration had made some ad hoc efforts to build newspaper support for Parker in 1930 and had even compiled a thirteen-page list of newspapers that supported Parker,[30] but nothing that it did even remotely rivaled the efforts of the Nixon administration. Pat Buchanan later wrote a report on his contacts with various columnists in 1969:

> I drafted personal letters along with back-up material to some 10 of the nation's top conservative columnists, including the Human Events and National Review crowd. Everyone I have seen has responded favorably— De Toledano, Buckley, Kilpatrick, White, Lasky, Human Events and National Review. Their support on this issue is as good as it was on ABM [the antiballistic missile system]—which was the best to date. Some of them are using the Brandeis thing; others take a different tack; the fact that the President is pushing a "conservative" for the Court is the reason behind their unanimous support.[31]

The last phrase reveals the gap between Nixon's private political goal and his public face. Contrary to his claim that opposition to Haynsworth's judicial philosophy was not "proper ground" for the Senate to consider in its debate over Haynsworth, judicial philosophy was precisely why Nixon nominated Haynsworth in the first place. Shortly after Nixon came into office, Tom Huston, a young White House aide who received widespread attention during the Watergate investigations for devising a plan for domestic spying that had been approved by President Nixon, wrote a memo for Nixon in which he set out a strategy for making judicial appointments in a way to support Nixon's political philosophy. As Huston put it to Haldeman, his memo to Nixon discussed "the function of the federal courts and the role of the President in influencing their action through appointments" and offered "a point of view that I doubt [the president] will get elsewhere."[32] John Ehrlichman forwarded the memo to Nixon with a cover memo, which read: "Huston's memorandum is well done and raises some interesting points." Underneath, Nixon scrawled some comments of his own. "To [Deputy Attorney General Richard] Kleindienst: RN *agrees*," Nixon wrote in his typical third person. "Have this analysis in mind in making judicial nominations."[33]

In fact, Nixon's opposition to the judicial philosophy of Earl Warren and Abe Fortas had led to his behind-the-scenes maneuvers to oust them from the Court, and opposition to the judicial philosophy of Justice William O. Douglas would soon prompt Nixon to urge the House minority leader, Gerald R. Ford of Michigan, to push for impeachment proceedings against Douglas. Thus, despite the president's public rhetoric, the lobbying tactics used by the administration to secure Haynsworth's nomination were the same as those it would have used to advance a pet policy initiative. At times, however, the White House lobbying effort degenerated into strong-arm tactics that ultimately did more harm than good. The White House recognized this too late. On the day the Senate voted to reject Haynsworth, Haldeman wrote in his private diary: "At the end [Nixon] overplayed, with excess pressure on some, which backfired, was too heavy-handed. So we learned something and politically probably came out ahead."[34]

Efforts to bring pressure on senators to vote for Haynsworth took several forms. First, members of Nixon's Political Affairs Office, headed by Harry S. Dent, personally contacted state Republican chairmen in key states to enlist their help in lobbying targeted senators.[35] In addition, the Political Affairs Office mailed the Mollenhoff report to Republican organizations and all state chairmen with the request that they assist the White House in a letter-writing campaign on behalf of Haynsworth.[36] Many responded wholeheartedly. For instance, James E. Holshouser Jr., chairman of the North Carolina Republican party, sent a memo to all county and district chairmen asking them to "generate a letter and telegram campaign in favor of the confirmation of Judge Haynsworth," a campaign to be directed at twenty-six undecided or wavering Senators.[37] Likewise, Ronald C. Romans, chairman of the Young Republican National Federation, urged Young Republicans around the country to join in the campaign.[38]

The White House also asked state Republican chairmen in the South "to contact friendly newspapers and start letter-writing campaigns stressing the point that Haynsworth is being attacked because of his geographical origin."[39] The day after his press conference, Nixon personally instructed Dent that "Southern chairmen, as well as other chairmen, who are willing to do so, should make statements praising RN for coming out fighting in defense of Haynsworth. Will you see that this is implemented."[40] Dent later reported good responses from state chairmen. Most had "reacted favorably" and were "issuing press releases in behalf of the President and working on target Senators." Dent also reported that he had stressed to newspapers the "Southern angle": the argument that Haynsworth was being attacked because of his geographic origin. In a memo to Attorney General Mitchell and Bryce Harlow, Dent wrote:

> A group of eight of the leading Washington correspondents from Southern newspapers met with me in my office the day after the President's press conference. I briefed them on how to best play this up down South and all agreed to help out on the "Southern angle." Several of the correspondents have been cooperative above and beyond the call of duty, namely Frank van der Linden, who represents several leading Southern papers, and Lee Bandy of the Columbia, S.C., *State*.[41]

White House attempts to influence senators also included asking the "top federal appointees from Oregon, Kansas, Illinois, Delaware, Vermont, Pennsylvania, Ohio, and Idaho . . . to generate home-state opinion with influential people," such as heads of the American Bar Association, judges, and lawyers. The point was "to get pressure from 'legal ethics' people in the home states to say that Haynsworth did nothing bad."[42]

The administration's most notable lobbying effort to generate pressure on senators was through campaign contributors. Ohio serves as a case in point. By October 15, the directors of nine corporations (including Lubrizol, Republic Steel, L. M. Berry, and General Tire and Rubber) had "indicated a strong willingness to help out" the White House. Representatives of the administration reported that the support of such corporations seemed to be as much a result of "their discontent with [Ohio Senator William B.] Saxbe as [of] any particularly strong interest in Haynsworth. Uniformly, these people seemed almost eager to pin Saxbe down."[43] By October 24, the list of major contributors in Ohio willing to lobby Saxbe had increased to fifteen. A report on the contacts indicated that the "effect to date has been an indication that if we are unable to persuade Saxbe, he may be prevailed upon to leave town for a few days [during the Senate vote on Haynsworth]."[44]

An aide to Saxbe said at the time that the senator had received "tens of hundreds of threatening letters from people in the state who have contributed to his campaign. It's as strong as anything we've seen."[45] The White House also enlisted major contributors from Pennsylvania, Illinois, Tennessee, Oregon, Idaho, Kansas, Missouri, Washington, Iowa, Delaware, and Arkansas to pressure senators.[46] The National Rifle Association joined the effort in instances where it "had made substantial contributions to target Senators."[47] These tactics backfired. For example, Clark Mollenhoff recalls Senator John J. Williams (R-Del.) telling him that "nothing in Haynsworth's record troubled [him] as much as the tactics being used by the White House in its efforts to force a united Republican front on the appointment."[48]

Ultimately, Senator Williams, along with many of those who had received the most pressure from contributors—including Senators Saxbe, Hugh Scott (R-Pa.), and Charles Percy (R-Ill.)—voted against Haynsworth. Senator Williams later said that the reason he voted against Haynsworth was not because of anything in Haynsworth's record but because of a conversation he had with Attorney General Mitchell and another undisclosed Republican political figure. According to Clark Mollenhoff, Mitchell had argued that "Judge Haynsworth was a conservative and could be counted upon to vote for his political friends on the Supreme Court." Mollenhoff concluded: "It was the wrong argument to use with Senator Williams, who wanted only the assurance that the appointee was an able man who would vote his conscience."[49]

The directives to play "hardball" with Senate opponents appear to have come directly from the president. The day after his press conference, Nixon met with Haldeman and expressed his desire to put heat on those in the Senate who were opposing Haynsworth. He instructed Haldeman to tell Bryce Harlow that they needed "a murderer's row in [the] Senate—need to kick Bayh around." He also ordered Haldeman not to leave "Haynsworth PR to Harlow" and to see that Lyn Nofziger got "people on [the Senate] floor to speak up." Nixon was angry that arrangements had not been made for four or five senators to praise him immediately after his press conference "for defending an honest man." They must "keep [the] offensive going," Nixon said, "esp. rip Bayh."[50]

The White House had already attempted to discredit Senator Bayh. On October 15, Dent had informed the president that the Columbia (S.C.) *State* would break a story the next morning "showing that Senator Bayh collected $70,000 in campaign contributions from unions in 1968." He also said that Scripps-Howard papers would pick up the story that afternoon.

Labor unions were vocally opposing Haynsworth, and Dent noted that "the stories will point out that the union leaders got Bayh to launch the campaign against Haynsworth."[51] Two days later, Dent reported that the union contributions to Bayh were "being publicized" to show *his* "conflict."[52]

In addition to placing pressure on senators through lobbying and negative publicity, the White House tempted senators with favors. On October 17, Harry Dent wrote: "We are gathering together the list of favors the target Senators have been asking the Administration for—jobs, projects, grants, etc., and are trying to use this as leverage with the Senators, usually using the State Chairmen as the intermediary parties."[53]

Finally, the administration attempted to mobilize public support for Haynsworth through public appearances by administration and proadministration officials. By the end of October, the administration made concerted efforts to speak with one voice on behalf of Haynsworth. Cabinet secretary John C. Whitaker distributed a one-page summary of Mollenhoff's report called "The Truth about Judge Haynsworth" to members of the cabinet with the request that they use it in their "speeches, television appearances, press conferences and so forth." Whitaker also suggested to cabinet members that they send copies of the summary to any "Assistant Secretaries who you feel can beneficially use this information."[54] The Office of Communications distributed the summary to members of the White House staff and other administration spokespersons.[55]

In the Senate, Lyn Nofziger fed pro-Haynsworth speech materials to senators such as Roman Hruska (R-Neb.) and Marlow Cook (R-Ky.) for use on and off the Senate floor. Hruska, in particular, became the administration's foil to Birch Bayh. Whenever Bayh made a public statement against Haynsworth, the White House urged Hruska to come out swinging. The networks often gave coverage to Hruska. For instance, an ABC News report included footage of Bayh followed by Hruska charging Bayh with "going on a fishing expedition." Patrick Buchanan, who prepared Nixon's Daily News Summary, took note of such appearances. "Hruska did a good job," Buchanan reported. Nixon circled Buchanan's comment in the News Summary, and wrote in the margin: "Harlow—call [Hruska] & tell him RN noted it."[56] Nixon also observed when the networks neglected Hruska or some other pro-Haynsworth senator. In the margin of a Daily News Summary on one such occasion, Nixon ordered Herbert Klein to "Demand [underlined four times] equal time for Hruska & Cook on Haynsworth."[57]

Klein was the administration's "soft voice" toward the press.[58] He opposed the "hardball" tactics that other members of the administration (including the president) liked to use against the media and the administration's excessive emphasis on public relations.[59] In response to Nixon's demand for "equal time," Klein cautiously explained: "The law does not provide for equal time demands on news shows. I did talk with John Chancellor and his superiors in very direct terms and, as a result, I think we should not have Hruska, Scott and others on TV countering the Birch Bayh–type argument."[60]

The fact that Klein contacted Chancellor was consistent with his philosophy of letting news organizations know when he felt that their coverage was, in fact, biased. For instance, on October 27, he complained to Benjamin Bradlee, executive editor of the *Washington Post*, about the its relative placements of pro- and anti-Haynsworth stories. Klein was particularly concerned that the *Post* had "buried" deep in an article on page 4 the news that sixteen past presidents of the American Bar Association had publicly urged the Senate to confirm Haynsworth. On the other hand, Klein noted that when the Trial Lawyers Association came out against Haynsworth, it "resulted in a three column head on page one."[61] Bradlee responded:

> Yes, I think the Haynsworth endorsement by 16 former ABA presidents was seriously underplayed. I think it should have been the lead, but at least the second paragraph.
>
> I think the Trial Lawyers story was probably overplayed, but it was a dull news day, if you remember.
>
> I *don't* [think] there is a trend toward downplaying Haynsworth support in our paper. We have had page one stories in defense of Haynsworth on October 10, October 11, October 13, and October 21, when we led the paper with the President's defense.[62]

The Nixon administration always stressed the importance of placing proadministration voices on television to support its causes. The Haynsworth situation was no different. Alvin Snyder of the Office of Communications helped to schedule those appearances. For instance, he scheduled senators such as Cook and Ernest Hollings (D-S.C.) on the NBC morning program, *Today*, to talk on behalf of Haynsworth.[63] Herbert Klein even spoke up for Haynsworth on the *Tonight Show with Johnny Carson*. Clark Mollenhoff, one of the most frequently used spokesmen, championed Haynsworth's cause on numerous local television news and talk programs as well as Mutual Radio's program *World Today*.[64] In his Daily News Summary, Pat Buchanan summarized an interview with Mollenhoff by Martin Agronsky and Earl Mazo on Washington's local CBS news program:

> The finest defense of Haynsworth we've seen yet. . . . Mollenhoff said the Administration had underestimated the irresponsibility of the critics and he expressed regret that GOP Senators' opposition was based on misinformation and propaganda of the critics. He called Bayh's Bill of Particulars [against Haynsworth] "Hogwash" and explained the background of several of the ten cases cited by Bayh. Each of them, individually, examined, adds up to a "zero"; Bayh is trying to take 10 "zeroes" and make

them add up to 10. Forcefully, Mollenhoff said 10 zeroes adds up to—zero. "You sound convinced, Clark," said Mazo. "I am convinced, Earl," responded Mollenhoff to conclude the interview.[65]

In the margin, Nixon wrote "Good!!"

On November 3, Nixon delivered his successful "Silent Majority" speech to the American people. In it, he sought support for his administration's policy toward the Vietnam War. In the coming days, Nixon tried to channel some of the support he had received from that speech toward Haynsworth's confirmation. On November 12, Nixon wrote to Harlow, "I think we may not be adequately using the Presidential popularity angle on the [wavering Senators]—the support we have on the Vietnam speech should be a good launching pad for Haynsworth, but we have to use it effectively with Senators so that they realize that a vote against the President might prove to be very unpopular, clearly apart from what the issue is."[66]

The Haynsworth Defeat

Despite all the efforts by the White House, it was obvious by November that there was not sufficient support in the Senate to confirm Haynsworth. Several days before the final vote, Herbert Klein, White House aide Charles Colson, and Lyn Nofziger met with Jeb Stuart Magruder. Magruder was a young aide to H. R. Haldeman who dealt with public relations matters and later became deputy director of the Office of Communications. Together, the four men devised a public relations strategy for defeat.[67] On the morning of the Senate vote, Magruder outlined the tactics to Bryce Harlow in a memorandum. State Republican chairmen in the South and selected border states would be asked to make public statements emphasizing "the political nature of the defeat." Favorable columnists would be contacted to "talk up the fact that . . . [Haynsworth] was defeated only by politics and labor." The American Bar Association and other outside groups would be contacted to issue press releases condemning the way Haynsworth was defeated. Magruder even suggested that Republican senators who had *opposed* the nomination, such as Robert Griffin, speak out "about how well the President handled the situation." A copy of the memo was sent to H. R. Haldeman, who wrote margin notes asking exactly who had acted, what columns had been produced, and so forth.[68]

The Senate defeated Haynsworth by a vote of 45 to 55 that afternoon. Eighteen Southern Democrats voted for Haynsworth, but sixteen Republicans voted against Haynsworth. These included virtually all "liberal" Republicans, senators like Edward Brooke of Massachusetts, Mark Hatfield of Oregon, Jacob Javits of New York, Charles Mathias of Maryland, Charles

Percy of Illinois, and Bob Packwood of Oregon, all of whom were more likely to sympathize with labor and civil rights concerns than their more conservative Republican colleagues. But Nixon also lost several "moderate" Republicans, most notably Senate Minority Whip Robert Griffin from Michigan. Labor played a role in securing Griffin's opposition. So, too, did Griffin's earlier opposition to Democratic nominee Abe Fortas on conflict of interest charges. To support a Republican nominee facing similar charges would reveal the political nature of his earlier opposition to Fortas.

After the Senate defeat, President Nixon released a statement to the press. "I deeply regret this action," he said. "I believe a majority of the people in the nation regret it. Especially I deplore the nature of the attacks that have been made upon this distinguished man. His integrity is unimpeachable. The Supreme Court needs men of his legal philosophy to restore the proper balance to that great institution." And Attorney General John Mitchell complained: "If we'd put up one of the Twelve Apostles it would have been the same."[69]

Soon thereafter, the president wrote a memo about "how we ought to handle the Senators who voted against us on both ABM and Haynsworth." The memo was sent to Haldeman, Ehrlichman, Harlow, and National Security Adviser Henry Kissinger. In it, Nixon wrote:

> With regard to all those who opposed, I want one general rule followed without deviation. You are undoubtedly going to have instances where [Republican Senators who opposed us] may contact members of the White House staff indicating their willingness to support us in the next nomination or on some other issue which may be coming up. . . . I want the answer in each case to be along these lines: "Thank you very much but the President wants you to feel free to vote your politics on this issue. He doesn't need you on this one." This will be quite effective and very hard for them to respond to.

The president also wrote, "Since several Senators like [Len B.] Jordan [R-Idaho], Saxbe, [Richard S.] Schweiker [R-Pennsylvania], et al. have complained about 'White House pressure' I think the best line to follow in the future with them is not to discuss anything with them and if they complain simply say we didn't discuss it with them because we wanted to honor their request that we not exert White House pressure." Quite simply, the president "froze out" Senate opponents. He concluded: "It goes without saying that those who are in this group should be given completely proper treatment so they cannot have anything obvious to complain about but none of them should get in to see me until I have gone through the list—one by one—of seeing all of those who supported us on these issues. I anticipate that this will take me several months."[70]

Under other circumstances, Haynsworth might well have won a place on the Supreme Court. Many compared his defeat with that of John J. Parker. Nixon himself suggested that comparison to Haynsworth when he invited the judge to meet with him at the White House on December 4, less than two weeks after the Senate rejected his nomination.[71] Sitting in wingback chairs by the fireplace in the Oval Office, the president reminded Haynsworth that Judge Parker had grown in public estimation after his defeat. Indeed, Nixon pointed out that Parker had become better known than some of his contemporaries on the Supreme Court. Haynsworth replied that his association with Parker was closer than the president may have realized. He explained that Parker had been in law practice with his father and grandfather and that he himself had served with Parker for a year on the court of appeals. In fact, Haynsworth said, "I held Judge Parker's hand when he died."

The president said that he realized that Haynsworth had been subjected to "brutal and vicious and unfair" attacks but that he hoped Haynsworth would put the ordeal behind him and remain on the Fourth Circuit. He reminded him of the thousands of letters that had come to the White House supporting Haynsworth after the defeat. "You can't let these folks down," Nixon said.

Haynsworth replied that he was interested in "doing what I can now to serve my country." He also said that he was grateful for those senators who had stood by him through the battle. The president pointed out that the White House had made the tactical decision to let a few senators "off the hook" once it was obvious that the nomination was lost. Senator Thomas J. Dodd (D-Conn.), facing heavy opposition to the nomination from labor, was one such example. Nonetheless, he said, they had fought a good battle. Never before had a president of the United States "put the efforts of the White House staff so earnestly behind a nominee for the Court." They had fought for what was right. Judge Haynsworth expressed his appreciation.

As he prepared to leave, Haynsworth smiled and said that press coverage of his nomination had been "very interesting." Why, one day while reading about his "wrongdoings" in the *New York Times*, he was convinced himself that anybody as bad as that didn't deserve to be on the Supreme Court. The judge appeared to have accepted his loss. The wounds are "pretty well healed," he said, "pretty well healed." "Only gratitude lingers."

The defeats of John J. Parker and Clement Haynsworth demonstrate the increasing power that interest groups came to play in the confirmation of Supreme Court justices. In the days when Senate proceedings were closed to public view and senators were less accountable to popular opinion and electoral retaliation, it is unlikely that groups such as the AFL and the NAACP could have prompted such defeats. We turn next to the changes that took place in the thirty-nine years between the Parker and Haynsworth defeats.

SPEAKING OUT

INTEREST GROUPS, NOMINEES,

AND PRESIDENTS

The Supreme Court nominations examined in the previous two chapters had much in common, but the Senate confirmation process had changed considerably over the years between John Parker's nomination in 1930 and Clement Haynsworth's in 1969. Most of those changes are related to the increasingly public nature of the process. This chapter looks at these changes and examines how three participants in the Supreme Court selection process—organized interests, the nominees themselves, and the presidents who choose them—have responded to the opening of the Senate confirmation process.

As we shall see, interest groups and nominees have increasingly used public testimony and other types of public appeal to influence senators and to mobilize broader public support for their cause. Since the 1980s, presidents have also made it a routine practice to make public appeals on behalf of their nominees. In short, all three participants pay much more attention to the mobilization of public opinion than participants ever did in the nineteenth century.

Herbert Hoover's nominations of Charles Evans Hughes and John J. Parker in 1930 were the first ones made after a Senate rules change in 1929 that opened floor debate on nominations as a matter of course. This, together with the popular election of U.S. senators (brought about by the 1913 ratification of the Seventeenth Amendment), increased senators' public accountability for their actions. Public opinion now mattered. This increased the potential leverage of interest groups; they could now mobilize public opinion and use the threat of electoral retaliation as a weapon in confirmation battles. Likewise, other participants began making public appeals to influence the Senate confirmation vote.

Public confirmation hearings were virtually nonexistent prior to the

1916 Brandeis nomination. Even after that, it took many years for the Senate Judiciary Committee to routinely hold full-fledged public hearings on nominations. Instead, committee proceedings were usually pro forma affairs that were closed to the public. A few witnesses testified when Warren Harding nominated Pierce Butler in 1922, and reporters were present when Harlan Fiske Stone testified before the committee in 1925, but the first full-scale public hearings after Brandeis did not come until the Parker nomination in 1930.[1] The Parker hearings were the first Supreme Court nomination hearings to have testimony by representatives of organized interest groups. Moreover, Parker was the first nominee kept off of the bench by interest group pressure. (Organized interests played a role in blocking Rutherford Hayes's nomination of Stanley Matthews in 1881, but they were unable to block Matthews' confirmation when James Garfield renominated him that same year.) Thus, the Parker proceedings were the first to take on many of the characteristics of "modern" confirmation proceedings.

Still, the Parker proceedings were quite different from today's norm. By today's standards, the Parker hearings were perfunctory. A subcommittee, rather than the full Judiciary Committee, held them. The hearings took place on one day and lasted less than three hours. Only two organized interests testified. The nominee himself did not appear, nor did President Hoover make any public statements on behalf of his beleaguered nominee. The published record of the committee's proceedings totaled only eighty-three pages.

In comparison, the full Judiciary Committee held hearings on Haynsworth. They took place over a period of eight days. Representatives from twelve organized interests testified, and several others submitted written material for the public record. Haynsworth testified before the committee, and President Nixon spoke on his behalf at a press conference designed to rally support for the nomination. The length of the published record of the committee's proceedings was 762 pages.

In terms of the length of the hearings, the array of interests testifying, the nominee's testimony, and the White House efforts to bolster public support for its nominee, the Haynsworth proceeding may be characterized as the first truly modern one. The proceedings for Lyndon Johnson's nominations of Thurgood Marshall in 1967 and of Abe Fortas to be chief justice in 1968 also contend for that distinction, but the array of interest group testimony was limited in both cases (one group testified at the Marshall hearings and four testified at the Fortas hearings), and by today's standards the White House engaged in only paltry efforts to build public support for its nominees.

Comparisons with more recent confirmation proceedings are useful. Hearings for Robert Bork lasted twelve days. Representatives from over twenty groups testified (with written material submitted for the record by over a hundred other groups). Bork himself testified for five days. The published record of the committee proceedings filled 6,511 pages. President Ronald Reagan made over thirty public statements on Bork's behalf, and the White House waged a major (though largely unsuccessful) public relations offensive to build support for its nominee. Even the relatively uncontroversial nomination of David Souter in 1990 resulted in five days of committee hearings, testimony by representatives from twenty-six interest groups, three days of testimony by Souter, 1,119 pages of proceedings, and ten public statements by President George Bush on behalf of his nominee.

Public opinion is a key ingredient in modern Supreme Court confirmation battles. Through testimony before the Judiciary Committee and a variety of other public appeals, a wide range of actors attempt to mold public opinion in hopes of influencing the outcome.

The Emergence of Public Hearings

Our knowledge of pre-1929 Supreme Court confirmation proceedings is far from complete. It is especially difficult to delineate the role of the Senate Judiciary Committee in the first forty or so years of its existence. Although the Senate created the Judiciary Committee in 1816 (along with eleven other standing committees), surviving records of committee proceedings relating to Supreme Court nominees date back only as far as the mid-1800s.[2] Even in the years since then, there are substantial gaps in the committee's records. For instance, with the exception of the Brandeis nomination, committee records from 1900 to 1922 are almost completely lost.[3] Moreover, newspaper accounts of early confirmation proceedings are often scanty since, of course, reporters were not allowed to cover the closed proceedings.

The first public hearings for a Supreme Court nominee appear to have been for Brandeis in 1916, although the Senate Judiciary Committee held closed hearings (complete with testimony from witnesses) as early as 1873, when President Ulysses S. Grant nominated his attorney general, George H. Williams, to succeed Salmon P. Chase as chief justice. Prior to the Williams nomination, the committee had often met and offered its recommendation on nominees to the full Senate, but there is no evidence that the committee had previously called witnesses or otherwise engaged in thorough investigative hearings on nominees.[4]

After the Brandeis hearings in 1916, the Senate Judiciary Committee did not hold another round of full-fledged public hearings for a Supreme Court nominee until Parker in 1930 (although subcommittee questioning of nominee Harlan Fiske Stone was open to reporters in 1925). A subcommittee of the Judiciary Committee conducted the Brandeis and Parker hearings, and the practice of a subcommittee holding public hearings continued until 1941. No published records of committee proceedings exist for the Rutledge (1943), Burton (1945), or Vinson (1946) nominations (see table 5). Since 1949, the full Judiciary Committee has held public hearings on all Supreme Court nominees; before that year, public hearings were almost always perfunctory affairs. For instance, public hearings on Franklin Roosevelt's nomination of William O. Douglas in 1939 lasted five minutes. Even the Parker hearings in 1930 lasted less than three hours. Only the Brandeis hearings in 1916 rivaled today's public hearings in terms of length. But no organized interests testified at the Brandeis hearings. Instead, the committee summoned individuals who had business dealings with Brandeis. Through such testimony, the committee attempted to determine Brandeis's "judicial temperament."

Speaking Out: Interest Groups

The Parker hearings were the first in which organized interests testified about a Supreme Court nominee. Of the thirteen nominations after Parker (through Vinson in 1946), organized interests testified in public hearings for only two (Reed in 1938 and Frankfurter in 1939). It is only since Nixon's nominations of William Rehnquist and Lewis Powell in 1971 that organized interests have testified at public hearings for every Supreme Court nominee (see table 5).

Prior to Haynsworth in 1969, only a smattering of interests testified about Supreme Court nominees. Although Harry Truman's nomination of Tom Clark in 1949 attracted testimony from representatives of ten groups, few hearings attracted more than one or two, and several did not attract any. Of the twenty-nine nominations from Hughes through Burger (1930–69), representatives for an average of only 1.2 groups testified per nominee. Haynsworth's hearings in 1969 attracted testimony from representatives of 11 groups. The fifteen public hearings for Supreme Court nominees from Haynsworth through Breyer have elicited testimony from an average of 13.1 groups. With regard to the array of groups testifying, Haynsworth's nomination was a turning point.

With the emergence of televised proceedings in 1981, public testimony became a way for interest groups to obtain free exposure to a mass audience. But testimony before the Judiciary Committee is now only one of the ways that interest groups make public their stand on Supreme Court nominees. They use public opinion polls to help target their appeals and focus group sessions to help fashion their messages. For instance, groups opposing the nomination of Robert Bork in 1987 formed a Media Task Force to plan and coordinate public appeals against Bork.[5] Using polling data, the

TABLE 5. Public Hearings on Supreme Court Nominees, 1930–1994

Nominee and Year of Nomination	Length of Hearings (in days)	Transcript Length (in pages)[a]	Number of Organizations Testifying[b]
Charles Evans Hughes (c.j.), 1930	1	[c]	0
John J. Parker, 1930	1	83	2
Owen Roberts, 1930	1	[c]	0
Benjamin Cardozo, 1932	1	[c]	0
Hugo Black, 1937	1	[c]	0
Stanley Reed, 1938[d]	1	26[e]	1
Felix Frankfurter, 1939[f]	2	128	3
William O. Douglas, 1939[d]	1	3[e]	0
Frank Murphy, 1940[f]	1	[c]	0
Harlan Fiske Stone (c.j.), 1941	1	2[e]	0
James F. Byrnes, 1941	0	0	0
Robert Jackson, 1941[f]	4	70	0
Wiley Rutledge, 1943	0	0	0
Harold Burton, 1945	0	0	0
Fred M. Vinson (c.j.), 1946	1	[c]	0
Tom Clark, 1949	3	359	10
Sherman Minton, 1949	1	23	1
Earl Warren (c.j.), 1954	2	104[e]	2
John Harlan, 1955[f]	2	182	7
William Brennan, 1957[f]	2	40	0
Charles Whittaker, 1957[f]	1	34	0
Potter Stewart, 1959[f]	2	146	0
Byron White, 1962[f]	1	26	2
Arthur Goldberg, 1962[f]	2	103	0
Abe Fortas, 1965[f]	1	58	1
Thurgood Marshall, 1967[f]	5	198	1
Abe Fortas (c.j.) and Homer Thornberry, 1968[f]	16[g]	1,404[g]	4 / 0
Warren Burger (c.j.), 1969[f]	1	116	1
Clement Haynsworth, 1969[f]	8	762	11
G. Harrold Carswell, 1970[f]	5	467	5
Harry Blackmun, 1970[f]	1	134	0
William Rehnquist and Lewis Powell, 1971[f]	5[g]	492[g]	13 / 8
John Paul Stevens, 1975[f]	3	229	3
Sandra Day O'Connor, 1981[f]	3	414	15
William Rehnquist (c.j.), 1986[f]	4	1,165	16
Antonin Scalia, 1986[f]	2	369	10
Robert Bork, 1987[f]	12	6,511	17
Douglas Ginsburg, 1987	0	0	0
Anthony Kennedy, 1987[f]	3	1,119	14

TABLE 5. *Continued*

Nominee and Year of Nomination	Length of Hearings (in days)	Transcript Length (in pages)[a]	Number of Organizations Testifying[b]
David Souter, 1990[f]	5	1,198	25
Clarence Thomas, 1991[f]	11	3,300	43
Ruth Bader Ginsburg, 1993[f]	4	681	8
Stephen Breyer, 1994[f]	3	[h]	9

a. Includes material submitted for the record.
b. Does not include individuals not representing organizations.
c. No transcript.
d. Nominee present at hearing but not testifying.
e. Transcript is unpublished, double spaced.
f. Nominee testified.
g. Combined hearings.
h. Transcript not published when this book went to press.

task force pinpointed the salient issues in different parts of the country. It then targeted different anti-Bork messages at different parts of the country based on those polls. Thus, anti-Bork activists stressed his threat to environmental protection in the West but in the South stressed that Bork would "turn back the clock" on civil rights.[6] Senators from southern and border states who were dependent upon black votes for reelection were particularly sensitive to the civil rights issue. Thus, southern Democrats who had previously voted for the "strict constructionist" nominees of Republican presidents did not vote for Bork. In fact, only one southern Democrat, Ernest Hollings of South Carolina, voted for Bork.

Groups opposed to Bork took the then unusual approach of running television, radio, and print advertisements against Bork. The most famous was a television spot narrated by actor Gregory Peck. The camera focused on a traditional four-person nuclear family standing on the steps of the Supreme Court, the father pointing to the words Equal Justice Under Law while his two children looked on. Over this picture, Peck narrated: "There's a special feeling of awe people get when they visit the Supreme Court of the United States, the ultimate guardian of our liberties." But, Peck continued, Robert Bork "defended poll taxes and literacy tests, which kept many Americans from voting. He opposed the civil rights law that ended Whites Only signs at lunch counters. He doesn't believe the Constitution protects your right to privacy. And he thinks freedom of speech does not apply to literature and art and music."[7] The camera showed the family in profile, looking in awe at the Supreme Court, then moved to the face of the youngest child. "Robert Bork could have the last word on your rights as citizens, but the Senate has the last word on him," Peck concluded. "Please urge your senators to vote against the Bork nomination, because if Robert Bork wins a seat on the Supreme Court, it will be for life—his life and yours."[8]

The anti-Bork coalition also set up press briefings, arranged interviews, and mailed information packets to reporters covering the "Bork beat." Its database could print out mailing labels for some two thousand journalists and an additional seventeen hundred editorial writers.[9] It also made prepackaged radio stories ("actualities") available to local radio stations around the country for use on their news programs.

Radio actualities are the audio equivalent of a written press release. They contain a sound bite (a brief spoken statement by a prominent individual) surrounded by a voice wrap (a narrative that sounds like a news report that sets up the sound bite). Radio stations could then broadcast the actuality in its entirety, leaving the impression that it was an independently produced news story. Or they could edit it and use just the sound bite as part of their own reporter's story. Actualities containing anti-Bork sound bites of the Reverend Jesse Jackson and NAACP director Benjamin Hooks were targeted at black radio stations in the South. Actualities with sound bites from Sierra Club officials were targeted at radio stations in the West, while those with sound bites of Antonia Hernandez of the Mexican-American Legal Defense and Education Fund were targeted at the Southwest.[10]

Since the Bork nomination, interest groups have routinely coordinated public campaigns for and against Supreme Court nominees. Speaking out through testimony at Senate Judiciary Committee hearings is an important part of that process.

Speaking Out: Nominees

For three days in October 1991, millions of Americans sat riveted to their television screens by the emotional testimony of Anita Hill and Clarence Thomas before the Senate Judiciary Committee. Hill, a professor of law at the University of Oklahoma, charged that Thomas, George Bush's nominee to replace Justice Thurgood Marshall on the United States Supreme Court, had sexually harassed her when she worked for him in the Department of Education's Office of Civil Rights and, later, when she served as his personal assistant when he became chairman of the Equal Opportunity Employment Commission (EEOC). The EEOC is a government organization that deals with sexual harassment claims. As its chairman, Thomas effectively served as the nation's chief enforcement official on sexual harassment.[11]

No congressional hearings since Watergate so captured the interest of the American people. Clarence Thomas's testimony on Friday night, October 11, captured higher ratings than baseball's American League playoff game between Toronto and Minneapolis for the World Series.[12] Hill had testified throughout the day, and Thomas began his rebuttal testimony at 9:00 P.M. eastern time. Ratings for the earlier Hill testimony were about 15 percent higher than for normal viewing during the morning and afternoon hours. Thomas's Saturday morning testimony produced a "dramatic" increase in the normal size of the television audience. Average ratings for the Thomas hearing on Saturday morning were about 16.6. Average Saturday morning ratings are normally about 9. Even on Sunday night, after both Hill and Thomas were through testifying and after the three major networks stopped televising the hearings, viewers remained interested. In New York City, for example, PBS coverage of the hearings gained a 13.3 rating and a 20 percent audience share, beating out part 1 of NBC's Jackie Kennedy miniseries (11 rating and 17 percent of audience), ABC's showing of the movie *Captive* (7.8 rating and 12 percent), and the National League Pittsburgh-Atlanta playoff game on CBS (11.2 and 17).[13] Such public fascination with the Senate Judiciary Committee proceedings was unprecedented. Even the hearings for Robert Bork paled by comparison. In fact, the ratings for the Bork hearings were so low that ABC, CBS, and NBC stopped televising them after the first day.

In the wake of the Thomas-Hill hearings some felt that the process had become *too* public. For instance, President George Bush, complained that the sexually explicit testimony of Hill and Thomas should have been heard behind closed doors.[14] In fact, the overtly public nature of nominee testimony is a distinctly modern phenomenon. Supreme Court nominees have testified before the Judiciary Committee on a regular basis only since 1955, and that testimony has been televised only since 1981. Indeed, the norm through the nineteenth and much of the twentieth centuries was for Supreme Court nominees to maintain absolute silence until they were confirmed. Most nominees went so far as to stay out of Washington until Senate deliberations had concluded.

In 1925, Harlan Fiske Stone became the first Supreme Court nominee to testify. However, earlier nominees occasionally communicated with the committee in some other fashion, the earliest known example being George Williams in 1873. This nomination prompted hearings because so many people felt that Williams was unqualified to sit on the Supreme Court.[15] Much like G. Harrold Carswell almost a hundred years later, opponents labeled Williams mediocre, and the press and the bar joined forces in questioning the nominee's ability. As the *Springfield Republican* bluntly put it: "The nomination surprised and disgusted every lawyer in the United States who has the honor of his profession at heart."[16]

Almost immediately, the charge that Williams was mediocre was coupled with the charge that he was corrupt. When the Judiciary Committee met to consider the nomination on December 8, one individual formally presented the corruption charge to the committee. The committee delegated responsibility for a preliminary investigation of the charge to its chairman, George F. Edmunds (R-Vt.), who informally questioned Williams the next day and examined relevant files at the Justice Department. Edmunds reported back to the committee on December 10 that no further investigation was necessary. The committee recommended that the full Senate confirm Williams.[17]

However, opposition to Williams was mounting, new charges against him were making the rounds on Capitol Hill, and the full Senate quickly recommitted his nomination to the Judiciary Committee for a more thorough investigation. What followed were closed hearings that included testimony by those leveling charges against Williams. The most damaging testimony concerned the accusation that, as attorney general, Williams had improperly borrowed Justice Department funds and that he had extravagantly used public money to purchase horses and a carriage for his own official use. Williams, however, did not appear at the hearings. The committee pointed out that Williams declined to attend the proceedings, but Williams later claimed that he did not attend because he was not allowed to state his case and cross-examine his accusers.[18]

By early January 1874, it was clear that the Senate would reject Williams. A leading Republican senator relayed this information to President Grant in a lengthy meeting at the White House on Saturday, January 3. The Judiciary Committee hearings had received no publicity, and even the president was reportedly surprised to learn the breadth of the opposition. "He had no idea that the Committee had, during its investigation, collected so much material," the *New York Herald Tribune* reported.[19] As a result of the meeting, Grant took the highly unusual step of visiting Capitol Hill on Monday, January 5. After dispensing with some business in the House of Representatives, the president sent for the Republican members of the Senate Judiciary Committee and caucused with them for nearly two hours about the Williams nomination. The Republican senators convinced the president that the nomination was doomed. Although President Grant had assured Williams that he would not withdraw his nomination, Grant authorized the secretary of state to explain the dire situation to Williams and urged him to ask for the withdrawal of his nomination.[20] Reluctantly, Williams agreed.

In a letter to President Grant dated January 7, 1874, Williams wrote that, since being nominated, "the flood-gates of calumny" had opened against him "in all directions." "My abilities have been disparaged and my integrity brought into question," he wrote. As a result of "public opinion adverse to my appointment," he asked the president to withdraw his nomination. He did so, he concluded, with "a perfect consciousness that I have performed with clean hands and an upright purpose all the duties of the various public offices to which I have been called," and with the hope that "time and a just public, when better informed," would bring about "my vindication."[21]

In fact, Williams immediately set out to secure that vindication. President Grant withdrew the Williams nomination on January 8, and on January 17 Williams sent the Judiciary Committee a lengthy statement defending himself against the charges that had forced his withdrawal. He asked that the statement be read to the full committee, argued that the charges against him were false, and alleged that the committee had violated his procedural rights in the way it had conducted the investigation. Most important, he asked that the committee preserve both his statement and the testimony that had been made against him. The committee did so in a formal report to the Senate.[22] An argument can be made that the corruption charges against Williams were exaggerated and that politics, as usual, played a prominent role in his opposition. After the forced withdrawal of Grant's next nominee, Caleb Cushing, more than a dozen Republican senators suggested that the president renominate Williams.[23] He did not—nominating Morrison Remick Waite instead. The weary Senate promptly confirmed Waite on January 21, 1874.

The importance of the Williams case for our purposes rests not only in the fact that the Judiciary Committee held full-fledged (though closed) investigative hearings but also in the fact that it is the first clearly documented instance of a Supreme Court nominee directly confronting the Senate Judiciary Committee and responding to charges in a written statement to the committee. Hearings were not held for either the Cushing or the Waite nominations; Cushing's nomination was quickly withdrawn, and Waite's was quickly endorsed by the committee and confirmed by the Senate. However, the next nomination, that of John Marshall Harlan by President Rutherford B. Hayes in 1877, was bogged down in the Judiciary Committee for six weeks.[24]

Harlan was the first southerner nominated to the Court since the Civil War, and some senators were suspicious. His supporters pointed out that Harlan had supported the Union during the war, served in the Union army, and was a Republican. Critics pointed out that he was a rather late convert to the Republican party, having voted for the Democratic presidential candidate as late as 1864. He did not formally declare himself a Republican until 1867.[25] Critics also noted that, although Harlan had served in the Union army, he had resigned his commission shortly after President Abraham Lincoln signed the Emancipation Proclamation—implying that Harlan resigned to protest Lincoln's action. Moreover, Harlan originally opposed the Civil War Amendments to the United States Constitution (although he later changed his mind). Thus, the Republican chairman of the Judiciary Committee, George Edmunds, was determined to investigate Harlan's Republicanism thoroughly.

Edmunds actively sought information about Harlan, but there is no evidence that the committee itself held any sort of investigative hearings. Nonetheless, the charges concerned Harlan enough that he responded to them in a lengthy letter to his home-state senator, James B. Beck (D-Ky.). Harlan told Beck that he could do what he wanted with the letter, and Beck turned it over to the Judiciary Committee.[26] In his letter, Harlan wrote that he was aware that "certain stories" were "being circulated in Washington" as part of an effort to block his nomination. Such stories, he added, "call for a full statement of my political record," although he was quick to add that he did not want to appear defensive. "For obvious reasons I should not like to be placed before the country as defending myself against assaults which I have no reason to believe are regarded by the Judiciary Committee as of any consequence," Harlan wrote. However, he added that if the committee *did* treat the charges seriously, he hoped that it would not act "without an opportunity being given me and my friends to be heard."[27]

In his letter, Harlan vigorously defended his Republicanism. He pointed out that his home state of Kentucky had no organized Republican party until the presidential election of 1868, and that although he had voted for the Democrat, George B. McClellan, rather than Lincoln in the 1864 election, subsequent events had satisfied him that his decision to do so had been wrong. He was later convinced, he wrote, that the defeat of Lincoln in 1864 "would have been the greatest calamity which could have befallen the country at that time." He noted that he joined the Republican party in 1867, that he had been "unanimously nominated as the Republican candidate" for governor of Kentucky in 1871, and that he had publicly stated the error of his vote for McClellan in speeches given in 1868, 1871, 1872, and 1875. He further argued that his resignation from the army was due solely to the need to attend to the estate and business of his father, who had died suddenly, and had nothing to do with the Emancipation Proclamation.

Harlan also brushed off his early opposition to the Civil War Amendments and pointed out his subsequent support of them in various speeches throughout the country. Even Lincoln's attorney general, James Speed, came to Harlan's defense on this point. In a letter to Chairman Edmunds, Speed admitted that Harlan had initially opposed the Emancipation Proclamation and the Thirteenth Amendment but that Harlan had "sloughed his old pro-slavery skin and [had] since been an earnest, open and able advocate of what he had [once] thought wrong or inexpedient."[28] The truth of this was later proven by Harlan's actions on the Supreme Court. As a justice, he was the sole dissenter in the *Civil Rights Cases* of 1883, which limited the reach of the Thirteenth and Fourteenth Amendments to state action (rather than allowing it to be used to restrict private discrimination), and again in *Plessy v. Ferguson* (1896), which endorsed racial segregation with the logic of "separate but equal."[29]

Despite his apparent willingness to appear before the Judiciary Committee, Harlan did not go to Washington to do so.[30] He did, however, send others to lobby on his behalf, among them his law partner, "Gus" Willson.[31] Another was Harlan's friend, Gen. Eli Murray. The same day that Harlan wrote Senator Beck he also wrote President Hayes and told him that he had sent Murray to Washington to "take such steps as he may deem proper for the protection of my good name against those who would assail it."[32] The efforts of Harlan and his friends were successful. The Judiciary Committee favorably reported Harlan's nomination to the full Senate on November 26, which confirmed him by voice vote on November 29, 1877.

The written statements that Williams and Harlan sent to the Senate did not set the norm for future Supreme Court nominees. For nearly fifty years after Harlan's confirmation, most nominees remained silent (and out of Washington) while the Senate considered their nomination. Melville W. Fuller, nominated for chief justice in 1888 by President Grover Cleveland, refused to respond to charges even when explicitly asked to do so by Chairman Edmunds of the Judiciary Committee. Edmunds submitted his request to Fuller in a letter of June 11, 1888. Fuller wired back: "While assuring the Committee that I intend no disrespect to them I cannot consent to reply to anonymous aspersions of the character referred to in yours of the eleventh."[33]

Typically, nominees also refused to speak to the press. When Benjamin Harrison nominated George Shiras Jr. to the Court in 1892, reporters tracked down Shiras in his hometown of Pittsburgh. But Shiras declined to comment, saying simply: "The United States Senate has not acted as yet upon my appointment and it would be indelicate of me to say anything."[34] Similarly, when reporters questioned Louis Brandeis in Washington after Woodrow Wilson nominated him to the Court in 1916, Brandeis refused to comment. "I have nothing whatever to say," he told reporters. "I have not said anything and will not." Throughout his tumultuous confirmation battle, Brandeis remained publicly silent. When pressed for a comment by the rabidly Republican New York *Sun*, Brandeis responded: "I have nothing to say about anything, and that goes for all time and to all newspapers, including both the *Sun* and the moon."[35]

Public silence by the nominees did not mean that they were above indirect (and at times even direct) lobbying of senators. For instance, both

Shiras and Brandeis countenanced the use of surrogates to make their case for them. Among those acting on behalf of Shiras were several of his former classmates from Yale University. One of them, Albert W. Bishop, wrote Shiras on July 22, 1892: "The Committee on the Judiciary [will] meet again this morning. Last evening I dined with [Senator Randall Lee] Gibson. He will take care of the Democratic members."[36]

Brandeis and his advisers decided that it would be unwise for him to testify on his own behalf at the Judiciary Committee hearings, even though many witnesses were testifying against him. To do so would give the appearance that Brandeis was on trial.[37] His advisers even convinced him to leave Washington while the Senate considered his nomination.[38] They then arranged for George Anderson, a federal district attorney, to serve as a staff member of the committee. There he would act as the nominee's chief advocate, although he did so under the guise of being a mere "fact finder" for the committee. Despite Anderson's claim at the hearings that he did "not appear for Mr. Brandeis or for the friends of Mr. Brandeis," that was precisely his function. He was in constant contact with Brandeis and his supporters and was even allowed to cross-examine witnesses who appeared before the committee.

Brandeis also received strong support from one of his law partners, Edward McClennen, who set up shop in Washington and served as a liaison between Brandeis and his supporters.[39] As witnesses appeared before the committee, Brandeis and another of his law partners, George R. Nutter, sent McClennen "a steady stream of explanatory letters and memoranda."[40] McClennen, himself, testified at length during the committee hearings, with Anderson leading off the questioning.[41] Brandeis also held frequent conferences with Anderson.[42]

After a solid month of committee hearings, Brandeis was frustrated. Critics had distorted his record and questioned his character. Some were motivated by anti-Semitism (Brandeis would be the first Jew to sit on the Supreme Court). Thus, Brandeis suggested in a letter to McClennen that perhaps he should appear before the committee after all. "I have accepted the opinion that it would be unwise for me to go down to Washington and appear [before the committee]," he wrote, "but if the proceedings continue on the lines which have been taken . . . I think I would rather go down and testify." McClennen shot back that that was a bad idea. "What you could say has been said by the papers and the witnesses," he wrote. "You would dignify the adverse claims by coming here. And your presence would surely be misconstrued to mean that you were seeking the position."[43]

For two more months, Brandeis stayed in Boston. But by early May, just over three months after leaving Washington, Brandeis briefly returned. He did not testify before the committee, but he did meet informally with two influential Democratic committee members who were likely to vote against him, James A. Reed of Missouri and Hoke Smith of Georgia. The meeting took place on May 14, 1916, at a carefully planned social gathering at the apartment of Norman Hapgood, the editor of *Harper's Weekly* and a strong supporter of Brandeis. Brandeis won over both senators and promptly returned to Boston.[44] When the Judiciary Committee voted on the nomination on May 24, both Reed and Smith supported Brandeis; the final committee vote was 10 to 8 in favor of confirming Brandeis. The full Senate voted 47 to 22 to confirm Brandeis on June 1.

The Brandeis battle was a precursor of the confirmation battles we now take for granted, complete with dramatic public hearings and full-blown press coverage. What was distinctly traditional was Brandeis's public silence, but even that tradition soon changed. On January 28, 1925, Attorney General Harlan Fiske Stone came to Capitol Hill, where the Senate Judiciary Committee questioned him for over four hours.[45] Nominated by Calvin Coolidge to fill the vacancy left by the resignation of Associate Justice Joseph McKenna, Stone became the first Supreme Court nominee ever to testify before the committee. Stone did not discuss his judicial philosophy. Instead, he responded to charges leveled against him concerning his conduct as U.S. attorney general.

The press and the bar had greeted the Stone nomination enthusiastically. None other than the great judge Learned Hand stated that Stone was "as nearly fitted for the job as a man can be by training, by experience and by character."[46] But the Senate was raring for a fight. Cleavages between the progressive and conservative wings split the Republican party. President Coolidge, representing the conservative wing, had just been elected, but a third-party Progressive ticket led Senator Robert M. LaFollette (with Senator Burton K. Wheeler as his running mate) had made a respectable showing at the polls and had drawn support from Republican progressives. Conservative Republicans retaliated. As John P. Frank writes, "Senate committee assignments were withdrawn from Republican Progressives, and President Coolidge undertook to discriminate against them in patronage distribution." As a result, "there was a strong group of Senators who were hostile to Coolidge and who would have opposed anything he did which could possibly be called reactionary."[47]

The Stone nomination quickly became part of the fight between progressives and conservatives. Stone's predecessor as attorney general, Harry M. Daugherty, had launched an investigation into Senator Wheeler that resulted in an indictment by a Montana grand jury in April 1924. The grand jury charged that Wheeler had taken $10,000 for appearing before the General Land Office of the Interior Department on behalf of oil claims made by his client, Gordon Campbell. Wheeler represented Campbell after having been elected to the Senate but before he actually took office. Although the payment was for Wheeler's legal services, Daugherty claimed that it violated a U.S. statute that prohibited members of Congress from receiving compensation in return for using their influence with U.S. departments.[48]

Wheeler claimed that the indictment was politically motivated. No doubt he was correct. President Warren Harding had chosen Daugherty as attorney general because he was a close personal friend, and in his new post, Daugherty became a model of corruption. As Alpheus Thomas Mason writes, "Lurid tales of his exploits had long concerned even the shabby politicians of Harding's administration." Such exploits included "all night poker-and-liquor parties" that served as the meeting place for "shady barons of industry" and "captains of bootleg and highjack"; "lucrative traffic in Department of Justice liquor permits, [with] the 'deals' [being] handled by Jess Smith, Daugherty's valet, chargé d'affaires, and buffer"; the " 'shadowing' of congressmen who dared expose, or had exposed, the Harding scandals; stock market speculation by the Attorney General himself under an assumed name, and so on."[49] At the time that Daugherty brought the indictment against Wheeler, Wheeler was the chairman of a Senate committee investigating Daugherty and the Justice Department. The Senate's own investigation of the charges against Wheeler exonerated him and suggested that the indictment was part of an effort by Daugherty to discredit the senator.

The same month that the Montana grand jury brought the indictment against Wheeler, Daugherty resigned as attorney general and was replaced by Harlan Fiske Stone. Stone fully recognized the political motivation of Daugherty's indictment of Wheeler, but he was not convinced that that meant Wheeler was innocent. Therefore, he ordered a new investigation. The results of that investigation convinced Stone that Wheeler was, in fact, part of a broader land fraud scheme. In early December 1924, Stone ordered that the new charges be submitted to a District of Columbia grand jury.

On January 5, 1925, President Coolidge nominated Stone to sit on the Supreme Court. One of the members of the Judiciary Committee was Senator Thomas J. Walsh (D-Mont.), who had served as Wheeler's counsel. Stone informed Walsh on January 16 that he was submitting the new evidence against Wheeler to a grand jury. Walsh evidently believed that this marked the beginning of the end of the matter. Walsh assumed that Stone would drop the Montana indictment and apparently felt that the District of Columbia grand jury would not indict. Three days later, he voted for Stone along with the rest of the Judiciary Committee. Stone, however, quickly made it clear that he had absolutely no intention of dropping the Montana indictment. Walsh met with Stone at the Department of Justice on January 22 to try to convince him otherwise, but the attorney general refused to give in. On Friday, January 24, Walsh stood up on the Senate floor and demanded that Stone's Supreme Court nomination be sent back to the Judiciary Committee.[50]

Shaken, Republican leaders went straight to the White House, where they met with Stone and the president. Stone suggested that the facts were such that the Senate could not reject him if they were properly aired. He therefore suggested that he appear before the Judiciary Committee. Everyone agreed. President Coolidge also let it be known to the press that he would not withdraw the nomination and that he had no objection to the nomination being sent back to the Judiciary Committee.

On Monday, the Senate unanimously approved the motion to recommit the nomination, and two days later Stone appeared before the committee to testify. His appearance was a resounding success. Most of the questions dealt with the Wheeler case. Unable to hurt Stone on that score, Senator Walsh implied that Stone was part and parcel of a corrupt department. An expert cross-examiner, Walsh methodically ran through a list of officials in the Justice Department that Daugherty had hired and that Stone had retained. In so doing, he implied that Stone had perpetuated the corruption of his predecessor. The tactic had little effect. Stone was unflappable. Despite questioning designed to bait him into "some indiscreet action or statement," Stone remained "forthright, courteous, and cooperative." His supporters were ecstatic and the press raved about his performance.[51] On February 2, the Judiciary Committee again approved the nomination. Three days later, the full Senate voted to confirm by a vote 71 to 6. Walsh and Wheeler abstained.

For a time, Stone's testimony before the Judiciary Committee appeared to be an anomaly. Charles Evans Hughes did not appear before the committee when President Hoover nominated him to be chief justice in 1930, nor did John J. Parker, Owen Roberts, Benjamin Cardozo, Hugo Black, or Stanley Reed, although Parker wanted to and Reed showed up at the hearings in case the committee had any questions (which it did not).[52] But, even though he did not testify, Hugo Black did go to the public in an extraordinary fashion shortly after his confirmation. Rumors that Black, a senator from Alabama, may have once belonged to the Ku Klux Klan emerged in August 1937 during Senate consideration of his nomination to be a Supreme Court justice. The Senate voted against investigating the charge by a vote of 66 to 15 on August 17 and confirmed him by a vote of 63 to 16 the same day.[53]

Then, on September 13, Ray Sprigle published the first in a series of stories in the *Pittsburgh Post-Gazette* showing not only that Black had been a member of the Klan but also that he appeared to still be a member.[54] Klan records showed that Black joined the Klan on September 11, 1923, and resigned on July 19, 1925, when he began his campaign for the U.S. Senate. But after winning the Democratic nomination (tantamount to Senate election in Alabama at that time), Black attended a statewide Klan meeting on September 2, 1926, at the great hall of the Invisible Empire in Birmingham. Bibb Graves, soon to be governor of Alabama, attended with Black. Sprigle had located an official transcript of the meeting, which he published in his stories. Two thousand Klansmen had attended the meeting, including "Exalted Cyclops from half a hundred Klans, Great Titans from the three provinces of the realm of Alabama, Kludds and Kleagles and Kladds from every city and cross roads village." There, "under the beaming smile of Imperial Wizard of the Invisible Realm Hiram Wesley Evans," Black and Graves were given the golden Grand Passport of the Alabama Klan, which accorded them life membership in the KKK.

Black then addressed the Klansmen: though stressing that he preferred to be called Hugo Black rather than the title conferred upon him by the Klan, he accepted the Grand Passport and thanked those assembled for their support. "I realize that I was elected by men who believe in the principles that I have sought to advocate and which are the principles of this organization," he said. "It is indeed pleasing to me to be present on this occasion. . . . I thank the Grand Dragon. He has stood by me like a pillar of strength. . . . I thank you, friends, from the bottom of my heart."

In the 1920s, the Klan enjoyed its peak popularity in Alabama, with up to ninety thousand members.[55] Arguably, no politician could hope to win public office without its support. But the implication that Black might still be a member was devastating. Black, on vacation in Paris with his wife, refused comment. Reports began circulating that White House aides felt Black should resign from the court, and columnists talked of impeachment.[56] President Roosevelt refused comment until Black returned to the United States. Black set sail for the United States on September 25 and scheduled an unprecedented radio address to the American people on October 1. All three national radio systems carried the speech, canceling their normal commercial programs. The speech gave Black the opportunity to present his case directly to an audience of some fifty million radio listeners. Shortwave radio carried the address around the world. Black said that he wanted the opportunity of a radio speech to ensure that his remarks would not be misquoted or otherwise distorted.[57]

In his half-hour speech, Black said that "no ordinary maneuver executed for political advantage" would justify a public response by a Supreme Court justice.[58] But because the charges against him threatened "the existing peace and harmony between religious and racial groups in our country," Black felt compelled to reply. Black insisted that the insinuations that he was prejudiced against "people of the Jewish and Catholic faiths, and against members of the Negro race" were false. "I believe that my record as a Senator refutes every implication of racial or religious intolerance," he said. "It shows that I was of that group of liberal Senators who have consistently fought for the civil, economic and religious rights of all Americans, without regard to race or creed."

Black told the American people that the insinuations of racial and religious intolerance were based on the fact that he had once joined the Ku Klux Klan. "I did join the Klan," he said. "I later resigned. I never rejoined. . . . I never have considered and I do not now consider the unsolicited card given to me shortly after my nomination to the Senate as a membership of any kind in the Ku Klux Klan. I never used it. I did not even keep it. Before becoming a Senator I dropped the Klan. I have had nothing whatever to do with it since that time. I abandoned it. I completely discontinued any association with the organization."

Black insisted that he had never preached intolerance at any meeting of any organization. Even the transcript of his 1926 speech to the Klan bears this statement out, although Black did not refer to it during his radio address. Speaking to the Klansmen, Black had stressed that "the real Anglo-Saxon sentiment" was embodied in the "heaven-born principles of liberty which were written in the Constitution of this country." "I shall endeavor with all my heart and mind and conscience to be fair to every man and every woman and every boy and every girl and every child," he told the Klan. What he liked about the Klan, he told them in 1926, was "not the burning of crosses. It is not attempting to regulate anybody." Instead, "I see a bigger vision. I see a vision of American honored by the nations of the world. Not only honored by the nations, but with a smile of the great God of the universe, beaming down upon it as it remains true to the principles of human liberty."

Black stressed his tolerance in his 1937 radio address: "I number among my friends many members of the colored race. I have watched the progress of its members with sympathy and admiration. Certainly they are entitled to the full measure of protection accorded to the citizenship of our country by our Constitution and our laws." He also stressed his

> steadfast faith in the unfettered right of every American to follow his conscience in matters of religion. I have no sympathy with any organization or group which, anywhere or at any time, arrogates to itself the un-American power to interfere in the slightest degree with complete religious freedom. . . . Some of my best and most intimate friends are Catholics and Jews. Shortly after I moved to Birmingham, more than a quarter of a century ago, I formed one of the most valued friendships of

> my life with a son of Jewish faith. . . . He stood so nearly in the place of a father to me that while in the Army in 1918 I designated this trusted Jewish friend as sole executor of my will.

Black ended his speech by saying that he would have nothing further to say on the subject. "I believe the character and conduct of every public servant, great and small, should be subject to the constant scrutiny of the people. . . . It is in this spirit that I now bid those who have been listening to me goodnight."

Editorial reaction was mixed, but the speech appears to have been very successful in influencing public opinion. Surveys taken by the Institute of Public Opinion before and after the speech showed "one of the sharpest changes ever measured in an Institute poll."[59] Before the speech, a nationwide poll conducted by the institute showed that 59 percent of those polled thought Black should resign. After the speech, only 44 percent thought he should resign. In some regions of the country, Black's support had increased as much as twenty-five percentage points (see table 6). When asked after the speech if Congress should remove Black, 75 percent of the Democrats polled and 55 percent of the Republicans said no. The speech even affected those groups most likely to be offended by Klan membership, like blacks, Catholics, and Jews. The institute concluded that their survey showed "how quickly the debate has subsided."

Black joined the Court when its 1937 term began on October 11. The Court quickly rejected a challenge to Black's right to sit and turned to other business. Black's long tenure on the Court confirmed his commitment to civil liberties.

In 1939, Felix Frankfurter became the first nominee since Stone to testify. His nomination by Franklin D. Roosevelt on January 5, 1939, was greeted with great enthusiasm in most quarters. Peers held him in high regard, and a Gallup Poll showed strong public support as well.[60] Like Brandeis before him, however, Frankfurter faced opposition from anti-Semites, who were quick to point out that Brandeis already filled the Court's "Jewish seat." "If we put another Jew on the Court, then the Jew element in the Court will represent 29 million of the population," one angry lawyer wrote to the Judiciary Committee—and that, he pointed out, was far more than the Jewish population in the United States. Then he demanded to know: "Would you put two Negroes on the Court, or two Chinese on the Court, or two Japanese?"[61]

Although the committee received many anti-Semitic letters concerning Frankfurter, much of the opposition was couched in terms of Frankfurter's foreign birth and his perceived "radicalism." Some even pointed to his membership in the American Civil Liberties Union as proof of his radi-

TABLE 6. Public Opinion on Hypothetical Resignation of Hugo Black, October 3 and 23, 1937

Respondents	Percentage saying Black should resign	
	Before Black's radio speech (October 3[a])	After Black's radio speech (October 23[a])
All	59	44
Blacks	82	68
Catholics	80	63
Jews	80	75
New England states	66	58
Middle Atlantic states	66	56
East Central states	61	42
West Central states	62	39
Southern states	35	27
Rocky Mountain states	57	32
Pacific coast states	67	46

Source: Institute of Public Opinion.
a. Date when the institute released the poll.

cal tendencies. A subcommittee held public hearings on the nomination on January 11 and 12. Elizabeth Dilling (author of *The Red Network*), insisted that Frankfurter was a communist.[62] She added that President and Mrs. Roosevelt, Supreme Court Justices Hughes, Stone, and Brandeis, and Judiciary Committee members William E. Borah and George W. Norris were, as well. "I don't want my children to live under [a socialist or communist form] of government," she told the subcommittee. "I want the kind of freedom that we have had in the past." Pushing on, she added, "I don't want the kind of colleges that Justice Brandeis was connected with, where they teach communism and have free love and nudist colonies." Taken aback, Senator Norris asked, "You have some feeling against Harvard Law School?" "Yes," Mrs. Dilling emphatically replied.

Frankfurter wanted to keep his distance from the hearings, and especially from the "crackpots" (as he later termed them) who were testifying.[63] Therefore, he sent Dean Acheson, then a lawyer engaged in private practice, to represent him at the hearings.[64] In executive session, however, subcommittee members informed Acheson that they wanted Frankfurter himself to appear. Reluctantly, Frankfurter did so the next day. Newspaper coverage of the first day of hearings stressed the inconsistencies in the testimony. The *New York Times* noted that witnesses "opposed the nominee because he was a Jew, because he was born abroad, because he was 'the fixer' for an alien conspiracy, because he was an 'incompetent lawyer,' because he was a 'brilliant lawyer' but un-American," and so forth.[65] When one witness told the committee that he had information that the senators would find "really surprising," Senator Matthew M. Neely replied with amusement, "The Committee does not want you to restrain yourself because of any fear of its being startled. The committee became shock-proof long before you appeared."[66] Dean Acheson later recalled that the witnesses "were an odd lot."[67]

By the time Frankfurter appeared, the hearings had become something of a media circus. As he entered the room, a mob of reporters and onlookers greeted him. Acheson later wrote that the large Caucus Room where the hearing was held was "jam-packed"—"so packed that police had to precede us like icebreakers to open a path to the witness table."[68] Frankfurter opened with a brief statement. He pointed out that Harlan Fiske Stone was the only previous nominee to testify, and that Stone did so only to answer charges about his conduct as attorney general. Frankfurter made it clear that he was uncomfortable appearing before the committee. "While I believe that a nominee's record should be thoroughly scrutinized by this committee," he said, "I hope you will not think it presumptuous on my part to suggest that neither such examination nor the best interests of the Supreme Court will be helped by the personal participation of the nominee himself." Although Frankfurter told the committee that he was happy to accede to its request that he appear, he stated in no uncertain terms that he would not express his "personal views on controversial political issues affecting the Court." "My attitude and outlook on relevant matters have been fully expressed over a period of years and are easily accessible," he added. "I should think it not only bad taste but inconsistent with the duties of the office for which I have been nominated for me to attempt to supplement my past record with present declarations."[69]

With that, the questioning began. It dealt with his membership in the ACLU, the validity of his citizenship papers, and whether or not he was a communist. The toughest questioning came from Senator Pat McCarran (D-Nev.), a self-proclaimed anticommunist crusader, but the assembled crowd was clearly on the side of Frankfurter. When McCarran asked Frankfurter if he believed in the doctrine of Karl Marx, Frankfurter replied that he did not believe that McCarran himself could be "more attached to the theories and practices of Americanism" than was he.[70] According to the *New York Times*, that response elicited an ovation from the audience that lasted over two minutes.[71]

Still, supporters of Frankfurter on the committee were concerned that Frankfurter was not refuting McCarran's charges directly enough. At one point during the questioning, Senator Matthew M. Neely (D-W.Va.) conferred privately with Dean Acheson. Neely told Acheson that Chairman

Henry F. Ashurst (D-Ariz.) believed that Frankfurter should respond point-blank to the question of whether he was or ever had been a communist. A negative response, they believed, would effectively halt McCarran. Acheson agreed and relayed the message to Frankfurter. He also "urged him to be sensible and not reply by asking the Chairman what he meant by 'Communist.' "[72] Thus, when the rest of the committee had finished its questions, Senator Neely asked the question for Chairman Ashurst:

> *Senator Neely:* . . . The chairman, with great reluctance, propounds one inquiry that he thinks ought to be answered as a matter of justice to you. Some of those who have testified before the committee have, in a very hazy, indefinite way, attempted to create the impression that you are a Communist. Therefore, the Chair asks you the direct question: Are you a Communist or have you ever been one?
>
> *Dr. Frankfurter:* I have never been and I am not now.
>
> *Senator McCarran:* By that you mean that you have never been enrolled as a member of the Communist Party?
>
> *Dr. Frankfurter:* I mean much more than that. I mean that I have never been enrolled, and have never been qualified to be enrolled because that does not represent my view of life, nor my view of government.[73]

With that, Acheson recalls, a "great roar came from the crowded room. People shouted, cheered, stood on chairs, and waved. The Chairman, banging his gavel, was inaudible."[74] Finally he quieted the room long enough to adjourn the proceedings. Then the audience rushed to Frankfurter and "nearly submerged him in the effort to shake his hand. The police cleared a breathing space around him and gradually got the crowd moving out. But the end was not yet. The newsreel men had missed the dramatic moment. It had to be repeated several times for their benefit by Chairman and witness."

Despite the dramatic media coverage of Frankfurter's testimony, the relative unimportance of nominees' testimony continued to be assumed for some years after the Frankfurter hearings. Of the next eleven nominees, only two (Frank Murphy and Robert H. Jackson) testified (see table 5). Hearings were not even held for James F. Byrnes in 1941, Wiley B. Rutledge in 1943, and Harold H. Burton in 1945. When Dwight D. Eisenhower nominated Earl Warren to be chief justice in 1954, the Judiciary Committee chose not even to ask Warren to testify.

During the Warren hearings, Deputy Attorney General William P. Rogers reminded the Senate Judiciary Committee Subcommittee in executive session that the Senate had never asked a nominee for chief justice to testify.[75] Members of the subcommittee agreed that Warren should not be asked to appear. "I for one would be very much embarrassed to have to ask a man of the calibre and standing of the Chief Justice questions relating to unsubstantiated charges, or relating to his professional capacity and his character," Senator Thomas C. Hennings Jr. (D-Mo.) told his colleagues. Senator Arthur V. Watkins (R-Utah) agreed, saying that "it would be an affront to the Court and to the people of this country" to call for Warren's testimony. Besides, Warren was a recess appointee and was already sitting on the Court when his confirmation hearings took place. As Rogers reminded the subcommittee: "I doubt very much if you could elicit much information which you do not have already, unless you in some way conflicted with matters now pending before the Court."

Nonetheless, William J. Brennan and Potter Stewart, both of whom were also Eisenhower recess appointees, did testify before the Judiciary Committee. Brennan had already been sitting on the Court for four months when he finally testified on February 26 and 27, 1957. He made it clear that "having taken an oath of office" as a sitting Supreme Court justice, it was his "obligation" not to discuss any matters pending before the Court.[76] He did, however, answer general questions about the proper scope of constitutional interpretation. As a Catholic, he was also asked which was greater, his allegiance to the pope or his allegiance to the Constitution. But the most remarkable aspect of Brennan's appearance was questioning by Senator Joseph McCarthy (R-Wisc.).

Like Senator McCarran before him, McCarthy was a hard-line anticommunist crusader. McCarthy was concerned because Brennan had, in various speeches, criticized the highly emotional communist investigations of that era. Brennan said in a 1954 speech that "some practices in the contemporary scene" were "reminiscent of the Salem witch hunts," that those practices "engender[ed] hate and fear by one citizen of another," thereby bringing the country "perilously close to destroying liberty in liberty's name," and that some of the procedures used at anticommunist hearings smacked of "barbarism." In a 1990 interview with Nat Hentoff, Brennan said that he had made speeches all around Monmouth County, New Jersey, calling McCarthy "all sorts of names."[77] "Hell," he added, "when I made those speeches I had no idea I would ever get to sit on the Supreme Court. . . . So when Eisenhower announced he was going to appoint me, McCarthy issued a statement saying that I was supremely unfit for the Supreme Court."

McCarthy did not sit on the Judiciary Committee, but he wanted to question Brennan anyway. "At first, there was resistance to McCarthy's sitting in on the committee," Brennan told Hentoff. "He was in decline. He had already been censured, and he died not long after my hearings." But, Brennan added, "I thought those who were against his sitting with the committee were wrong. There's absolutely nothing in the Constitution which limits the advice and consent function of the Senate. Nothing. And, because each senator has to cast his own vote on the matter, he should be able to interrogate the nominee if he wants to." According to Brennan, McCarthy asked him about "the craziest things" and that those who heard the exchanges at the hearings "did not think it was one of Senator McCarthy's finest hours."

Even fellow senators were embarrassed by McCarthy's questioning. The end of the first day of Brennan's testimony culminated in an explosion from Senator McCarthy: "I have been reading in every left-wing paper, the same type of gobbledegook that I find in your speeches [where you talk] about the barbarism of committees [and] Salem witch hunts. I just wonder if a Supreme Court Justice can hide behind his robes and conduct a guerilla warfare against investigating committees."[78] Moments later, the chairman of the committee stopped the questioning and called a recess until the next morning. When the committee reconvened, it read a letter from McCarthy. "I believe that the written record of this committee now confirms that Justice Brennan harbors an underlying hostility to congressional attempts to investigate and expose the Communist conspiracy," he wrote. "And I am doubtful that further questioning on the subject would serve any useful purpose." Later, the Judiciary Committee voted 11 to 0 to recommend that Brennan be confirmed, which the full Senate did by voice vote.

Every Supreme Court nominee since John Marshall Harlan in 1955 has testified before the Judiciary Committee. Increasingly, senators have tried to pin down a nominee's judicial philosophy. On occasion, they even ask how a nominee would vote in particular cases. This trend began in the mid-1950s, prompted largely by the Supreme Court's desegregation decision in *Brown v. Board of Education*. Conservative southern Democrats argued that *Brown* was an "activist" ruling, in which the Court changed the meaning of the Civil War Amendments to the constitution. Thus, when Dwight D. Eisenhower nominated Potter Stewart in 1959, southern Democrats on the Committee bombarded him with questions about *Brown* and his judicial philosophy.[79]

Senator Olin Johnston from South Carolina asked: "Do you consider yourself what is termed a 'creative judge' or do you consider yourself a judge that follows precedent?" "I don't really consider myself a 'creative' or 'non-creative' judge," Stewart replied. "I like to try to be a good one." Johnston then pressed him on the Civil War Amendments. Should they be applied according to their understanding when they were ratified or according to contemporary understanding? Stewart evaded the question. Johnston tried to pin Stewart down on *Brown*. How had the Court changed the constitution through the *Brown* decision? Again Stewart hedged. Then Senator John McClellan from Arkansas picked up the questioning. "Do you

agree with the view, the reasoning and logic applied . . . and the philosophy expressed by the Supreme Court in arriving in its decision in the case of
Brown v. Board of Education on May 17, 1954?" Stewart tried to get at the issue
indirectly: "I am an Ohioan. I live in a state where as a matter of state law,
since the 19th century, it has been illegal to discriminate or segregate among
school children on the basis of race. That is the law. And so . . . the basic
decision [in *Brown*] did not shock me or appear wrong to me."

But McClellan was not satisfied. He repeated his question, Did Stewart agree with the reasoning, logic, and philosophy of *Brown?* to which
Stewart finally replied: "Senator, if I may, basically the answer is 'yes.'"
Senator Thomas Hennings (D-Mo.) then interrupted with a point of order:
"I do not think it proper to inquire of a nominee for this court or any other
his opinion as to any of the decisions or the reasoning upon decisions which
have heretofore been handed down by that court." After considerable debate, in which several senators argued that they could ask whatever they
wanted and Stewart was free not to respond, Senator Hennings withdrew
his point of order.

In fact, most nominees have refused to discuss cases with members of
the Judiciary Committee. During his 1986 confirmation hearings, Antonin
Scalia went so far as to refuse comment on *Marbury v. Madison,* the 1803 case
involving the Court's power of judicial review. But Robert Bork—with an
extensive public record of law review articles, speeches, and other public remarks—took the unusual approach in his 1987 hearings of talking at
length about his judicial philosophy and about specific cases that the Court
had decided. His was the longest and most detailed public testimony of any
Supreme Court nominee. In addition, he actively courted the press, starting
with an hour-long interview with *New York Times* reporter Stuart Taylor Jr.
some two months before his confirmation hearings began.[80] "It was our
way of humanizing him and showing that he didn't have horns," according
to White House lobbyist Tom Korologos.[81] But some critics accused Bork of
undergoing a "confirmation conversion" and using his public testimony to
moderate his controversial stands on issues such as free speech and the
right to privacy.

In terms of the specificity of his testimony, Bork remains an anomaly.
In the wake of Bork's Senate rejection, presidents nominated individuals
with little in the way of a public record that interest groups and other
opponents could use against them, individuals whom the press labeled
"stealth nominees." Given the emotional debate over abortion rights, President Bush particularly sought nominees who had not taken a public stand
on abortion. During his confirmation hearings in 1991, senators asked Clarence Thomas where he stood on the abortion issue over seventy times
during his three days of testimony.[82] Thomas went so far as to say, in re-

sponse to questioning from Senator Patrick Leahy (D-Vt.), that he had never discussed *Roe v. Wade*, the 1973 Supreme Court case that extended the constitutional right of privacy to protect a woman's right to have an abortion. Even as a student at Yale Law School at the time the Supreme Court handed down the decision, Thomas claimed never to have discussed it.

Leahy was incredulous. "Have you ever had a discussion of *Roe v. Wade*, other than in this room?" he asked, provoking laughter from those assembled in the committee room. Nervously, Thomas answered: "If you are asking me whether or not I have debated the contents of it, the answer to that is no, Senator," "Let me ask you this," Leahy continued. "Have you made any decision in your own mind whether you feel *Roe v. Wade* was properly decided, without stating what that decision is?" Thomas replied: "I have not made, Senator, a decision one way or the other with respect to that important decision."[83]

A year earlier, David Souter had avoided the question with more aplomb when Senator Howard Metzenbaum (D-Ohio) pushed him on the question. Metzenbaum, in an obvious attempt to put Souter on the defensive, lectured Souter about testimony he had heard from women who had illegal abortions prior to *Roe*. "They were women about your age," Metzenbaum told Souter. "They told horrible stories." One woman, "who was poor and alone, self-aborted," he continued. "It is a horrible story, just a horrible story, with knitting needles and a bucket." "My real question to you is not how you would rule on *Roe v. Wade* or any other particular case coming before the Court," Metzenbaum concluded. "But what does a woman face when she has an unwanted pregnancy . . . ? I would just like to get your view and your own thoughts of that woman's position under those circumstances."[84]

Souter gave a masterful reply. It was an intimate narrative that deflected Metzenbaum's question, underscored Souter's sensitivity to the issue, and effectively silenced the senator. It also reinforced efforts by President Bush and other members of his administration to portray Souter as fair—a "kinder, gentler" Supreme Court nominee than Bork, who was defeated largely because of the perception that he was unfair. Yet Souter's reply achieved all that without giving any indication whatsoever of how he would vote on abortion cases.

Souter responded to Metzenbaum's question by recalling an incident that happened when he was in law school, serving as a freshman dormitory adviser at Harvard College. One afternoon, Souter recalled, a freshman came to him "in pretty rough shape." The boy told Souter that his girlfriend was pregnant and that she was going to try to have a self-abortion but that she didn't know how to do it. She was afraid to tell her parents and afraid to go to the health clinic, and the boy asked Souter to talk with her. "I will not try to say what I told her," Souter told Metzenbaum, "but I spent two hours in a small dormitory bedroom that afternoon . . . listening to her and trying to counsel her . . . and your question has brought that back to me." Souter looked Metzenbaum straight in the eye and said with conviction: "I know what you were trying to tell me, because I remember that afternoon."

The emotional impact of that reply helped to deflect questions about Souter's stand on abortion. Like many other nominees, Souter refused to state how he would rule on abortion, and his past record on the issue was unclear. Souter did not attempt to discourage abortions at Concord Hospital in New Hampshire when he served as an unpaid member of the hospital's board in the 1970s, but he had used seemingly prolife rhetoric in 1977 as New Hampshire's attorney general.[85] Although he refused to comment on abortion cases, Souter did state in his testimony that he believed in a constitutional right to privacy, even though it is not explicitly enumerated in the Constitution. "I believe that the due process clause of the 14th amendment does recognize and does protect an unenumerated right of privacy," he said.[86] But so, too, did Clarence Thomas.[87] Simply stating a belief in a constitutional right to privacy says nothing about how one would rule on the abortion question, which pits the right to privacy of the mother against the potential right to life of the fetus. In fact, Thomas voted to overrule *Roe v. Wade* in 1992, while Souter co-authored a majority opinion reaffirming (though modifying) *Roe*.[88]

Today, Supreme Court nominees are carefully coached for their televised testimony before the Judiciary Committee. Mock question-and-answer sessions, known as "murder boards," are a routine preparation for their appearances. For a nominee to refuse to appear before the committee in this day and age would be unthinkable.

Speaking Out: Presidents

Just as Supreme Court nominees used to maintain absolute public silence during Senate consideration of their nomination, presidents used to refrain from public comment on their nominees. Presidents felt that to make public comments would be to stoop to "politics" in a process that was supposed to be (but of course never was) untainted by political considerations. Besides, presidents generally refrained from overt public appeals in the nineteenth and early twentieth centuries. Scholars of the presidency, such as Jeffrey Tulis, remind us that during that period presidents avoided the practice of public appeals because they thought it would "manifest demagoguery, impede deliberation, and subvert the routines of republican government."[89] The avoidance of public appeals reflected the founders' fear of "pure" or "direct" democracy. Although the founders felt that public consent was a requirement of republican government, they nonetheless felt that the processes of government should be insulated from the whims of public opinion. In short, presidents shunned the now commonplace practice of direct public appeals because it went against the existing interpretation of the constitutional order.

That interpretation of the constitutional order changed in the twentieth century. Increasingly, public appeals became an important strategic device used by presidents to win support of their policies and influence other policymakers. Today, public support does not just elect presidents, it is a president's most visible source of ongoing political power. More than ever before, presidents and their surrogates take messages directly to the people in an attempt to mold mandates for policy initiatives. A strategy of presidential power based on such appeals is known as "going public." As defined by Samuel Kernell, this understanding of presidential power assumes that the elite bargaining community that implements policy is neither as isolated from public pressure nor as tightly bound together by established norms of elite behavior as it used to be.[90] As a result, policymakers are increasingly susceptible to the influence of public opinion.[91] A key to presidential power, then, is the ability to harness (or manufacture) that opinion. The result is a sort of unending political campaign.[92]

Even after going public became more commonplace, presidents were unwilling use the tactic overtly to promote Supreme Court nominees. Thus, Woodrow Wilson did not speak publicly on behalf of Louis Brandeis, and Herbert Hoover, although he drafted several versions of a public statement decrying the Senate's defeat of Parker, decided against issuing any of them (see chap. 4). More recently, the stormy battles over the nominations of Abe Fortas in 1968, Clement F. Haynsworth Jr. in 1969, and G. Harrold Carswell in 1970 did not provoke any appreciable number of public statements by the president. Not until Ronald Reagan did presidents personally embrace the tactic of going public on behalf of their Supreme Court nominees as a routine tool.

Before Reagan, Supreme Court nominees were lucky if the president *ever* publicly uttered their name after nominating them. Even the nomination announcement was often left to the White House press secretary or a Justice Department spokesperson. When presidents did make the announcement, it was usually done in the relative obscurity of an intimate news conference. For instance, President Harry Truman's announcement of his nomination of Senator Harold H. Burton (R-Ohio) was the last of six brief announcements that he made during a news conference in his office on September 18, 1945. Truman chose Burton to replace Owen Roberts, one of just two Republicans left on the Court. (The other was Chief Justice Harlan Fiske Stone, who had been elevated from associate justice by Franklin

Roosevelt.) Since 1837, each major party had maintained at least two members on the Court,[93] so Truman felt that he needed to nominate a Republican. But Burton was also a close personal friend of the president. When Truman announced his intention to nominate Burton, the reporters reacted with "subdued laughter and a surprised low whistle," but they did not ask the president any questions about the nomination.[94] The Democrat-controlled Senate asked no questions either. It dispensed with Judiciary Committee hearings and simply approved the nomination of their colleague by voice vote the next day.

Now presidents announce their Supreme Court nominees with great fanfare, and they follow up on the announcement with public statements aimed at eliciting popular support for the nominee. Richard Nixon went so far as to announce his 1971 nominations of Lewis Powell and William Rehnquist in a formal prime-time television address to the American people. But only since Ronald Reagan have presidents routinely spoken out on behalf of their nominees throughout the Senate confirmation process. Reagan publicly touted his first nominee, Sandra Day O'Connor, at a speech before the National Federation of Republican Women in 1981. In 1986, Reagan spoke about his nomination of Antonin Scalia in three nationally broadcast radio speeches.

With his nomination of Robert Bork in 1987, Reagan broke all records. From July 1 through October 23, 1987, he waged a full-scale public campaign on behalf of Bork, making a total of thirty-three public statements on behalf of his nominee (including his initial announcement of the nomination). Evening newscasts of the three major television networks covered twenty of those statements; two were carried "live" in their entirety on prime-time television.[95] It seemed that the president would use virtually any public forum to push his nominee, whether it be signing a proclamation for National Hispanic Heritage Week or German-American Day, speaking at an awards dinner for Minority Enterprise Development Week, or delivering remarks before groups such as the National Alliance of Business, the National Law Enforcement Council, and Concerned Women for America. Arguably, Reagan's going public was part of his broader politicization of the judicial appointment process (which is discussed in more detail in the next chapter).

Subsequent nominees have all drawn public statements of support from the president who nominated them:[96]

President Truman
  Harold H. Burton: 0   Tom C. Clark: 0
  Fred M. Vinson: 0

President Eisenhower
  Earl Warren: 0
  John Marshall Harlan: 2
  William J. Brennan Jr.: 0

  Charles E. Whittaker: 0
  Potter Stewart: 0

President Kennedy
  Byron R. White: 0

  Arthur J. Goldberg: 0

President Johnson
  Abe Fortas: 0
  Thurgood Marshall: 3

  Abe Fortas (for chief justice): 3
  Homer Thornberry: 1

President Nixon
  Warren E. Burger: 1
  Clement F. Haynsworth: 2
  G. Harrold Carswell: 3

  Harry A. Blackmun: 0
  Lewis F. Powell: 0
  William H. Rehnquist: 0

President Ford
  John Paul Stevens: 1

President Carter
  (No nominees)

President Reagan
  Sandra Day O'Connor: 2
  Antonin Scalia: 5
  William H. Rehnquist
    (for chief justice): 4

  Robert Bork: 32
  Douglas Ginsburg: 3
  Anthony M. Kennedy: 10

President Bush
  David Souter: 10

  Clarence Thomas: 24

President Clinton
  Ruth Bader Ginsburg: 5

  Stephen Breyer: 1

That President Clinton made relatively few statements on behalf of Ruth Bader Ginsburg and Stephen Breyer was probably because their confirmations were never in doubt.

As we shall see in the next chapter, presidents now use institutionalized staff units in the White House to mobilize public appeals by a wide range of individuals on behalf of their Supreme Court nominees. In fact, this is only one of several ways that modern presidents have responded to changes in the confirmation process and have attempted to increase their influence on the final Senate vote. The confirmation process is now a distinctly public affair, with all of its participants grappling with each other for public support.

CHAPTER SEVEN

THE INSTITUTIONAL PRESIDENCY

STRATEGIC RESOURCES AND THE
SUPREME COURT SELECTION PROCESS

Twentieth-century changes in the Senate made that body more accountable to the people and led to a more visible Supreme Court confirmation process. Those changes made participants in the confirmation process more responsive to public opinion, but they also prompted participants to wage their own campaigns to mobilize public opinion. Aware that mass sentiment could influence the Senate vote on a Supreme Court nomination, they attempted to direct public opinion. This resulted in the selling (and shelling) of Supreme Court nominees.

These changes transformed the Senate confirmation process. Senate Judiciary Committee hearings, once so secret that even presidents claimed not to know what was transpiring in them, could now receive higher television ratings than baseball's World Series playoffs. Interest groups, long thwarted by a secretive and relatively unaccountable Senate, emerged as major players when a constitutional amendment made senators dependent upon the electoral connection. Nominees, who had once remained silent and out of Washington during Senate deliberation on their nominations, took center stage in public testimony at the hearings. And presidents, who traditionally thought it improper to comment publicly on their judicial nominees, began stumping for them as if they were candidates for elective office.

Like the Senate, the institution of the presidency underwent major changes in the twentieth century. Notably, the president became a policy leader—the "Chief Legislator," as Clinton Rossiter puts it.[1] At the same time, a large White House staff has emerged with specialized units performing highly specific functions (screening nominees, influencing public opinion, mobilizing interest groups, and lobbying the Senate) to assist the president in policy formulation and implementation. This new White House–centered system of government is often referred to as the "institutional presidency."[2]

This chapter looks at changes in the presidency and how they have affected the president's role in the Supreme Court selection process. Particular emphasis is placed on attempts by presidents to increase their policy leadership by influencing judicial decisionmaking through Court appointments. Judicial decisions can have a direct effect on policy; by defining privacy rights, interpreting the First Amendment, setting guidelines for the treatment of criminal defendants, and exercising its power of judicial review in a host of other areas, the judiciary establishes public policy.

In theory, impartial judges who objectively apply the law according to established standards of interpretation should all reach the same "correct" decision in cases that come before them. In practice, judges hold different views about how to interpret legal texts. As human beings, judges are influenced, at least in part, by their backgrounds, personal predilections, and judicial philosophies. Quite simply, different judges often reach very different conclusions when confronted with the same case. Thus, presidents attempt to predict how their nominees will vote on key issues coming before the Court. Through careful screening, presidents attempt to use judicial nominees to influence policy—for instance, by choosing a "law and order" nominee, or one who is "prochoice"—and they use their staff units as strategic resources to influence the outcome of the Senate confirmation process.

The Rise of the Institutional Presidency

Two events are largely responsible for the rise of the institutional presidency. One was congressional passage of the Budget and Accounting Act of 1921, which created the Bureau of the Budget and required presidents to develop fiscal policy for the government. The other was congressional passage of the Reorganization Act of 1939, which, in accordance with the recommendations of the Brownlow Committee on Administrative Management, gave the president major staff resources by creating the Executive Office of the President (EOP) and the White House Office (WHO).

Congress passed the Budget and Accounting Act of 1921 as part of an effort to increase the fiscal responsibility and efficiency of government. The act created the Bureau of the Budget as a part of the Treasury Department and required the president to use the expert advice of the bureau to propose annual fiscal policy for the government. Quite simply, the legislation compelled the president to take an active role in domestic policy formulation. As James Sundquist writes:

Before 1921, a president did not have to have a program for the whole of the government, and none did; after that date, he was compelled by the Budget and Accounting Act to present a program for every department and every bureau [within the Executive Branch], and do it annually. Before 1921, a president did not have to propose a fiscal policy for the government, and many did not; after 1921, every chief executive had to have a fiscal policy, every year. That made the president a leader, a policy and program initiator, and a manager, whether he wished to be or not.[3]

There were, of course, strong presidents who exerted policy leadership before 1921. But nothing compelled presidents to act. As a result, earlier presidential efforts to direct policy had been "ad hoc, sporadic, and largely unorganized."[4] Even after 1921, Presidents Warren Harding, Calvin Coolidge, and Herbert Hoover dutifully submitted proposals to Congress but seldom exerted strong leadership to secure enactment.[5] That changed during the presidency of Franklin Roosevelt, who used the crisis of the Great Depression as a rallying cry for policy enactment.

Roosevelt surrounded himself with an ad hoc inner circle of personal staff known as the "brain trust" to help him formulate policy. Together, they actively sought to manage the economy, but several of Roosevelt's most important legislative victories (including the National Industrial Recovery Act) were struck down as unconstitutional by the Supreme Court. The president quickly realized that the current conservative majority on the Court could thwart his policies. Thus, after winning a landslide reelection in 1936, Roosevelt introduced a plan in Congress to increase the size of the Supreme Court, thereby giving him an opportunity to appoint a new majority of justices.

Roosevelt also sought to create a permanent staff of White House advisers to enhance his position as a policy leader. As part of an effort to achieve that end, he created the Brownlow Committee on Administrative Management in 1936 to study the management needs of the president and to offer recommendations for reform. Proclaiming that "the President needs help," the Brownlow Committee Report recommended "salvation by staff" through the creation of the Executive Office of the President.[6] Roosevelt forwarded the report to Congress in January 1937 with the recommendation that it transform the recommendations into law.

Congress rejected Roosevelt's court-packing plan, but natural attrition on the Court soon solved the president's problems. By the time Roosevelt died in 1945, he had appointed all but one justice. Roosevelt's reorganization proposal also faced strong opposition, but Congress passed a modified version of the Brownlow Committee recommendations in 1939. The Reorganization Act of 1939 made a distinction between "institutional" and "personal" staff resources. Institutional staff would serve in the Executive Office of the President, which was designed to be a politically neutral organization consisting of civil servants who would serve as expert advisers to successive presidents. The EOP currently includes such advisory units as the National Security Council, the Council of Economic Advisers, and the Office of Management and Budget (previously called the Bureau of the Budget).

Personal staff, on the other hand, would serve in the White House Office, which, unlike the EOP, was designed to contain political staff dedicated to the interests of the particular president in office. As a result, personal staff would be much more responsive to the incumbent president, and its personnel would change from one administration to the next. Not surprisingly, all of the units designed to help the president in the Supreme Court selection process are a part of the White House Office. These include the Office of Communications, the Congressional Liaison Office, the Office of Public Liaison, and the Office of White House Counsel.

In the years following the passage of the Reorganization Act of 1939, presidential staff became institutionalized. In 1947, the first Republican House and Senate since 1931 took power. This Eightieth Congress quickly appointed its own commission to reexamine executive management. Congress was clearly eager to trim presidential staff and, not coincidentally, to flex its muscle against the incumbent Democratic president, Harry Truman.[7] The chairman of the new commission was former Republican president Herbert Hoover, the last president to serve before the full emergence of the bureaucratic state. Yet the Hoover Commission reaffirmed the earlier recommendations of Roosevelt's Brownlow Committee. Rather than providing an opportunity for congressional oversight and control of the executive branch, the commission called for the consolidation of executive authority and led to the creation of additional staff assistance for the president.[8]

The growth of staff continued under Truman's Republican successor, Dwight Eisenhower, who created a number of new posts in the White House Office, including the chief of staff and the Congressional Liaison Office.[9] Another Republican president, Richard Nixon, further expanded the White House Office, partly in an effort to increase his power over what he called the "Democrat-infested" executive bureaucracy.[10] In sheer numbers, presidential staff had grown exponentially since Franklin Roosevelt. During FDR's first term the entire White House staff (including the grounds crew and the White House police force) numbered forty-seven. By the end of the Nixon administration (1974), it had grown to well over 500; by 1969, total presidential staff (including the EOP) numbered 5,167.[11]

These staff resources increased the president's ability to formulate and implement policy. Not surprisingly, presidents began utilizing these resources on behalf of their judicial nominees. President Nixon was the first to take full advantage of these resources—with mixed success.

The Screening and Selection of Federal Judges

Lower Federal Court Nominees

In a memorandum to President Richard Nixon in 1969, White House aide Tom Charles Huston noted that judicial appointments were perhaps "the least considered aspect of Presidential power." "In approaching the bench," he wrote, "it is necessary to remember that the decision as to who will make the decisions affects what decisions will be made. That is, the role the judiciary will play in different historical eras depends as much on the type of men who become judges as it does on the constitutional rules which appear to [guide them]." If the president "establishes *his* criteria and establishes *his* machinery for insuring that the criteria are met, the appointments will be *his,* in fact, as in theory."[12] Nixon was impressed with Huston's memo. "RN agrees," the president responded. "Have this analysis in mind when making judicial nominations."[13]

Of course, presidents since George Washington have nominated Supreme Court justices who reflect their ideological views, but presidents once accorded considerably less attention to the appointment of lower federal judges. The Constitution does not specify how lower federal judges should be appointed. In fact, the Constitution does not even require that there be a federal judiciary below the Supreme Court, leaving it to Congress to create lower federal courts at its discretion. (Each state has the power to create its own court system, which is distinct from federal courts.) Congress created a system of lower federal courts in 1789, and they have existed ever since.

The appointment process for lower federal court judges has always followed the process for appointing Supreme Court justices: the president nominates and the Senate confirms. However, senators have traditionally had broad power to offer advice to the president about whom to nominate for these posts, especially at the district court level. Each judicial district, in which the federal trial courts operate, falls within the boundaries of a single state. By tradition, judges for these district courts come from the state in which the district falls. Starting with George Washington, presidents have turned to senators of their own political party from the state in which the district court vacancy occurred to suggest a nominee. This practice assumed that home-state senators were better able to select qualified individuals than the president (who, before the age of easy communication, was both literally and figuratively distant from the various states). It also accorded these home-state senators a virtual veto power over nominations they disapproved. By the practice of senatorial courtesy, fellow senators would reject a nominee opposed by a home-state senator. Thus, presidents were bound to clear their district court nominees with these senators.[14] Herbert Hoover's attorney general, William D. Mitchell, noted the special role that senators played in the selection of district court nominees. In a 1929 radio speech discussing judicial selection, he said: "It would be futile, of course, for the President to nominate a United States District Judge who could not be confirmed because of the determined opposition of the Senators from his state."[15]

Senators thus came to treat the judgeships largely as a patronage tool. As former attorney general Robert F. Kennedy once put it, the practice amounted to "senatorial appointment with the advice and consent of the Senate."[16] Senatorial courtesy also applied to appointments to U.S. courts of appeals but in a more diluted fashion, since judicial circuits (in which the federal appeals courts fall) cross state lines (thereby weakening the influence of any one home-state senator).

In 1977, President Jimmy Carter undermined senatorial courtesy by creating, through an executive order, the Circuit Court Nominating Commission, whose establishment was part of an effort to institute merit selection of federal judges. Thus, the power to screen nominees for the courts of appeals and suggest whom to nominate was taken away from senators and given to the nominating commission (which was appointed by the White House).[17] In a separate executive order, President Carter urged senators to create, voluntarily, nominating commissions to advise him on the selection of district court judges. By 1979, senators from thirty-one states had complied with Carter's request to establish district court nominating commissions.[18] This further diluted the power of home-state senators to choose nominees.

When Ronald Reagan became president in 1981, he abolished Carter's commission system and seized control of the lower federal selection process by creating the President's Committee on Federal Judicial Selection as part of WHO. Representatives from the White House and the Justice Department staffed the committee. As David O'Brien writes, the committee "concentrated power within—and institutionalized the role of—the White House" in the selection of federal judges.[19] Thus, President Reagan succeeded in creating the type of formal machinery for screening judicial nominees that Tom Charles Huston had urged President Nixon to create in 1969.

President Reagan also expanded the power of the Justice Department by giving its Office of Legal Policy broad responsibility for judicial selection. The Justice Department had assisted presidents in screening judicial nominees since the 1800s. As Attorney General Mitchell put it in 1929, the Justice Department aided the president "by obtaining for him information about the qualifications of those suggested for [federal judicial posts]."[20] But until Reagan, this task was primarily a responsibility of the attorney general, the Justice Department's director, and was limited by the practice of senatorial courtesy. Under Reagan, the Justice Department created staff resources designed solely to screen judicial nominees. As Sheldon Goldman says:

> The screening process was systematized and, for the first time in the history of judicial selection, all leading candidates for judicial positions were brought to Washington for extensive interviewing by Justice Department personnel. If a candidate had previous judicial experience, that person's record would be carefully examined. Articles and speeches of candidates likewise were scrutinized. Arguably, the Reagan administration was engaged in the most systematic judicial philosophical screening of candidates ever seen in the nation's history.[21]

Stephen J. Markman, who, as Assistant Attorney General for Legal Policy from 1985 to 1989, coordinated judicial screening for the Reagan administration, described the process this way:

> When a candidate arrived at the Department of Justice, he would go through a series of interviews, coordinated by the Office of Legal Policy, with a battery of attorneys of widely varying backgrounds. . . . Each interview generally ran between 30 minutes and one hour, and candidates generally averaged between four and five hours of interviews during their visit to the Department. . . . Department interviewers sought to learn more about a candidate's background and professional experience and to determine whether he or she appreciated that the source of law for a self-governing citizenry is the consent of the people themselves as expressed in the Constitution and legislatively-enacted statutes, and not the judiciary; in other words, whether a candidate reasoned from constitutional premises.[22]

To "reason from constitutional premises" was shorthand language for adherence to what Reagan's attorney general Edwin Meese III called "a jurisprudence of original intent," a controversial approach to constitutional interpretation that bound judges to the framers' understanding of constitutional language. Its proponents argue that adherence to original intent limits judicial policymaking by promoting fidelity to the text of the Constitution. But critics call the approach anachronistic and argue that it would bind twentieth-century judges to the eighteenth-century notion of "cruel and unusual punishment" or the nineteenth-century interpretation of the Fourteenth Amendment's equal protection clause. Critics further argue that determining original intent is often impossible, since the Constitution was a jointly drafted document based on compromise, with only sketchy notes of the debates surviving. Moreover, the Constitution was ratified by each of the states, often with differing understandings of constitutional language.

In such a case, whose intention counts? Finally, critics contend that the jurisprudence of original intent is, itself, politically motivated—aimed at undoing many of the rulings of the liberal Warren Court that the conservative Reagan administration disagreed with.[23]

Many of these same critics charge that Reagan's new selection units were responsible for administering an ideological "litmus test" to potential nominees.[24] Fred Fielding, Reagan's White House counsel, admitted that the reforms were designed to choose "people of a certain judicial philosophy." Attorney General Meese was even more candid, saying that Reagan's judicial appointments were designed to "institutionalize the Reagan revolution so it can't be set aside no matter what happens in future presidential elections."[25]

Of course, future presidents can appoint judges who reflect their own ideology, so presidential elections will, in time, undermine the judicial legacy of a particular president. But because federal judges have life tenure they can influence policy long after a president leaves office. Fielding called Reagan's judicial appointments his "best legacy"; and Huston reminded Nixon in his memorandum that through judicial appointments a president "has the opportunity to influence the course of national affairs for a quarter of a century after he leaves office."[26] Control over the selection of lower federal judges gives the president considerable leverage over judicial policymaking because the lower courts are where most legal decisions are made. The Supreme Court decides a mere fraction of 1 percent of all the cases heard in federal courts (roughly 150 cases a year, compared with some 275,000 cases decided by district courts). Thus, the composition of these lower federal courts matters.

By the time Bill Clinton became president in 1993, his immediate predecessors, Republicans Ronald Reagan and George Bush, had appointed more than 60 percent of federal judges below the Supreme Court (389 of 645 district court judges in active service, and 102 of 167 courts of appeal judges in active service).[27] Just as Reagan and Bush had nominated judges who reflected their conservative ideology, Clinton began to nominate judges who reflected his more liberal ideology. In his first year in office, Clinton had the opportunity to fill 119 vacancies on federal courts, but he and the Senate were slow to act. By March 1994, President Clinton had nominated only 58 judges and the Senate had confirmed only 34.[28]

White House control of judicial selection continues into the Clinton administration. President Bush retained the President's Committee on Federal Judicial Selection in the White House, and screening units (which interviewed candidates) continued to exist in the Justice Department.[29] President Clinton abolished the formal President's Committee on Federal Judicial Selection, but an ad hoc version of the committee continues to meet.

He gave White House responsibility for overseeing judicial nominations to the office of White House Counsel. In the Justice Department, Clinton transferred the responsibility for judicial screening to the Office of Policy Development.[30] Thus, despite some minor jurisdictional changes, presidential control of the federal judicial selection process remains firmly in place.

Supreme Court Nominees

Since 1853 the Justice Department has had the formal responsibility for collecting the applications and recommendations of potential nominees, who also undergo a background check by the Federal Bureau of Investigation, a unit of the Justice Department.[31] Although the attorney general and other Justice Department staff play an important role in screening nominees, the growth of presidential staff has complicated the picture. The Office of White House Counsel, created as part of the president's personal staff in WHO during the Truman administration, now plays an important role as well. So too does the White House chief of staff and other close confidantes of the president. These overlapping responsibilities can lead to internal power struggles. For instance, when Lewis Powell resigned from the Court in 1987, Attorney General Edwin Meese and other Justice Department officials immediately pushed for the nomination of conservative stalwart Robert Bork. But the strong conservative views of the Justice Department were not matched by White House aides. President Reagan's chief of staff, Howard Baker—hired just months earlier to bring order to the White House in the wake of the Iran-contra scandal—was a moderate Republican with a distinctly pragmatic outlook. Democrats had just won control of the Senate. Why provoke a fight with a controversial nominee, especially given the sour relationship with Congress brought about by Iran-contra investigations? Thus, Baker and White House Counsel Arthur B. Culvahouse pushed for a consensus nominee.[32]

Meese, a close friend of the president, won. Reagan nominated Bork. The nomination provoked a storm of controversy, and the Senate ultimately rejected Bork's nomination. The defeat would probably have occurred anyway, but moderates in the White House such as Baker, Culvahouse, and White House Communications Director Thomas Griscom may have added to Bork's problems by waiting too long to wage an aggressive campaign on his behalf.

Traditionally, an array of considerations have gone into a president's choice of a nominee, the most obvious being party affiliation. With rare exceptions, presidents nominate individuals from their own political party to sit on the Supreme Court (although Republicans have sometimes nominated conservative southern Democrats). In the early days, geographical balance was also an important consideration, especially since Supreme

Court justices were then responsible for the onerous task of riding circuit—traveling around the country to preside over appeals in federal courts of a particular judicial circuit. Until the Civil War, presidents made appointments with an eye toward having a justice from each of the circuits (which had grown from three in 1789 to ten in 1863). But Congress radically curtailed the practice of circuit riding in 1869 and abolished the requirement altogether in 1891 (while leaving justices eligible to hear cases in the circuits).[33]

Although the underlying necessity of geographical balance vanished with the demise of circuit riding, some degree of sectional representation continues to be of importance for political reasons. With an eye toward reelection, Abraham Lincoln selected two justices from Ohio and one each from Illinois and Iowa.[34] Three more recent Republican presidents—Herbert Hoover, Richard Nixon, and George Bush—attempted to reward the South with appointments, since all three needed southern support to help secure reelection.

Various other representational considerations go into the selection of a Supreme Court nominee, such as religion, race, gender, and ethnicity.[35] Of these, religion has been a factor the longest. For most of its history, there has been at least one Roman Catholic justice on the Court. This "Catholic seat" began by happenstance when Andrew Jackson appointed Roger Taney in 1836. After Taney's death in 1864, no Catholic sat on the Court until 1894, when Grover Cleveland appointed Edward D. White. Since then at least one Catholic has sat on the Court except for the seven years between the death of Frank Murphy in 1949 and Dwight Eisenhower's appointment of William Brennan in 1956. Currently, two Catholics sit on the Court: Antonin Scalia and Anthony Kennedy. A "Jewish seat" has existed since 1916, when Woodrow Wilson appointed Louis Brandeis. Wilson did not appoint Brandeis to create a Jewish seat, but, like the Catholic seat, it took on symbolic importance to subsequent presidents. Thus, the Jewish seat continued without interruption until the resignation of Abe Fortas in 1969. It remained vacant until Bill Clinton appointed Ruth Bader Ginsburg in 1993. The vast majority of Supreme Court justices have been Protestant.

Race and gender representation on the Court began only recently. No African American sat on the Court until Lyndon Johnson appointed Thurgood Marshall in 1967. When Marshall resigned in 1991, George Bush appointed another African American, Clarence Thomas. Although an African American had been admitted to practice before the Supreme Court as early as 1865, the American Bar Associated excluded African Americans until the early twentieth century.[36] Moreover, legal training was largely unavailable to blacks until the 1960s. Even liberal Democratic presidents prior to Johnson gave little thought to the appointment of African American judges. Franklin Roosevelt did not appoint any African American to a life-time federal judgeship during his twelve and a half years in office, and Harry Truman appointed only one. Things began to change in the 1960s. John Kennedy appointed four African American judges and gave serious consideration to appointing William H. Hastie, the former dean of Howard University, to fill the Supreme Court vacancy left by Charles Whittaker in 1962. Kennedy reportedly passed over Hastie because he was too conservative. Instead, Kennedy nominated Byron White, who proved to be no flaming liberal either.[37]

The first woman to be admitted to practice before the Supreme Court was Belva Lockwood in 1879 (forty-one years before women won the constitutional right to vote), but no president appointed a woman to the federal judiciary until 1928, when Herbert Hoover appointed Genevieve Cline to the U.S. Customs Court (a lifetime position). An editorial in the *Christian Science Monitor* urged Herbert Hoover to appoint a woman to the Supreme Court in 1930, suggesting Florence E. Allen, a judge on the Ohio state supreme court, and Mabel Walker Willebrandt, Hoover's own assistant attorney general. A woman by the name of Rena Smith clipped the editorial and sent it to the White House to make sure the president saw it. It "seems to be a very good editorial," she wrote, "at least from the woman's point of view."[38]

Later, supporters of Florence Allen waged campaigns on her behalf when Supreme Court vacancies occurred during the administration of Franklin Roosevelt. Roosevelt appointed her to the U.S. Court of Appeals for the Sixth Circuit instead, making her the first woman appointed to a lifetime position on a federal court of general jurisdiction (and the only woman that FDR appointed to the courts). She knew she was there to stay; shortly after her 1934 appointment, she wrote that a woman would never be appointed to the Supreme Court in her lifetime.[39] She was correct. She died as senior judge of the Sixth Circuit in 1966. No president appointed a woman to the Supreme Court until 1981, when President Reagan appointed Sandra Day O'Connor (Reagan had promised to name a woman to the Court during his 1980 presidential campaign). Ruth Bader Ginsburg became the second woman on the Court in 1993, when President Clinton appointed her.

Region, race, and gender have all become important symbolic aspects of Supreme Court appointments, ways for presidents to build or reward support among their constituency. Ethnicity can be used in the same way. Ronald Reagan appointed the first Italian American justice, Antonin Scalia, in 1986. Scalia was an outstanding jurist, but the president and his party also saw the appointment as a way of building capital among the many Italian American voters in this country. Similarly, George Bush and Bill

Clinton gave serious consideration to appointing the first Hispanic to the court. Such an appointment would curry favor with the large Hispanic population in key electoral states such as Texas, Florida, and California.

The growth of personal presidential staff, whose job is to further the political interests of the president, may increase the pressure to nominate politically expedient candidates. But such considerations can take on too much importance. Rather than choosing the most qualified individuals, presidents can become sidetracked by pragmatic political concerns. Will the nominee vote the way the president wants on key issues? Will the nomination add to the president's political capital? Is there a paper trail of speeches and writings that interest groups could use against the nominee? These questions may be important, but there is a danger that the substantive abilities of potential nominees will be given less consideration than their stylistic appeal.

A final consideration that goes into current Supreme Court nominations is the rating of potential nominees by the American Bar Association. The ABA, an association of lawyers founded in 1878, has long taken an interest in the selection of Supreme Court justices. In its early years, the ABA's membership consisted mostly of corporate lawyers, who fought the "downgrading of property rights."[40] The conservative makeup of the ABA led it to take an active role in opposing Woodrow Wilson's nomination of Louis Brandeis in 1916, and this conservative tenor continued for many years. The ABA remains an exclusive organization (only 12 percent of America's lawyers belonged to the organization in 1920; fewer than half belonged as late as 1985), and the association barred African Americans from membership for many years. Indeed, the ABA did not lift its formal vestiges of racial discrimination until 1956 (two years after the Supreme Court's *Brown v. Board of Education* ruling that struck down racial segregation in public schools).[41]

Not surprisingly, the ABA had little influence on judicial selection when Democrats Franklin Roosevelt and Harry Truman were president. But Republican Dwight Eisenhower formalized a relationship between the ABA and the Justice Department during his presidency. Starting in 1956, the administration gave the names of potential Supreme Court nominees to the ABA at the same time that the FBI began its background check. The ABA then ranked the nominee as "qualified" or "unqualified" (later, the ratings were changed to "highly qualified," "not opposed," or "not qualified," then to "well qualified," "qualified," or "not qualified").[42]

Democratic presidents after Eisenhower deemphasized the role of the ABA in judicial selection, but by the 1980s, as membership expanded, the ideological makeup of the ABA was changing. Thus, Republicans Ronald Reagan and George Bush had their own run-ins with the ABA and its rating system. In 1987, the fifteen-member ABA committee on the federal judiciary split in its ranking of Robert Bork. While ten of the committee members voted Reagan's nominee "well qualified," four voted him "not qualified," and one voted "not opposed." Moreover, the ABA angered the Reagan administration because of its ranking of lower federal court nominees. Reagan sought out young nominees, ones who would sit on the bench for many years—but ABA rules required twelve (previously fifteen) years of post–law school experience for potential nominees. Earlier, this requirement had worked against President Carter's attempts to place women and African Americans on the judiciary (who tended to be younger than their white male counterparts, since they had entered the legal profession more recently); now it hindered President Reagan's efforts to appoint young conservatives. Moreover, the ABA released the names of potential nominees to liberal organizations, such as the Alliance for Justice and People for the American Way, to obtain a broad range of views about the candidate.[43] This infuriated conservatives because they felt it gave these organizations a head start in opposing nominees.

In 1985 and 1986 the conservative Washington Legal Foundation sued the ABA, charging that its confidential "star chamber" process of evaluating nominees ran afoul of the Federal Advisory Committee Act of 1972, which requires most presidential advisory committees to maintain public records and minutes of their proceedings. In 1988, the Supreme Court unanimously upheld lower court rulings that the act did not apply to the ABA.[44] In 1991, after President Bush threatened not to seek the ABA's recommendation on judicial nominees, the association agreed to stop sharing names of potential nominees with other groups.[45] In short, presidents of both political parties, increasingly reliant on their own personal staffs for screening nominees, have found the role of the ABA to be a hindrance to their control over the selection of Supreme Court nominees and lower federal judges. But the selection of nominees is only half the process. Presidents now rely on other White House staff units to help secure confirmation once the nomination has been announced.

Securing the Confirmation of Supreme Court Nominees

Presidential power is measured by more than constitutional provisions. Such provisions mean little if the president cannot persuade others to follow his lead. As Richard Neustadt succinctly puts it, "presidential power is the power to persuade."[46] Thus, modern presidents use staff units to promote their policy goals through various types of persuasion. Many of these units are used to help secure the confirmation of Supreme Court justices.

The Office of Communications: Building Public Support

Presidents since Reagan have made it standard practice to "go public" on behalf of their Supreme Court nominees. Although earlier presidents usually refrained from any personal participation in publicly promoting their Supreme Court nominees, they often relied on surrogates to make their case for them. This was true as early as 1916, when President Wilson nominated Brandeis. Neither Wilson nor Brandeis publicly commented about the nomination, but they fought back against the campaign waged by opponents with a behind-the-scenes public relations offensive of their own, using Norman Hapgood, editor of *Harper's Weekly,* to employ "aggressive publicity" on the nominee's behalf.[47]

In 1969, President Nixon created the Office of Communications as part of his personal staff within the White House Office. Since then, it has served as a formal public relations apparatus to coordinate the news flow from the entire executive branch, to set the administration's "line of the day," and to target public appeals.[48] Nixon quickly used this public relations apparatus on behalf of his Supreme Court nominees. For instance, the office pursued a strategy of getting the entire administration to "speak with one voice" about Nixon's nominees. Thus, it distributed a fact sheet, titled "The Truth about Judge Haynsworth," to members of the cabinet and other administration spokespersons in 1969. The office asked recipients to use the material to tout Haynsworth whenever possible, whether it be in a speech, broadcast interview, or comment to a reporter.[49] At the same time, the Office of Communications actively scheduled television appearances to support the nominee. Thus, administration officials and pro-Haynsworth senators could be found speaking out on everything from *The Tonight Show with Johnny Carson* to the Sunday morning talk shows.

Nixon also recognized the importance of local newspapers as a means of bypassing the influential "Eastern establishment" media and taking messages directly to the people. When Nixon nominated Warren Burger as chief justice in 1969, the Office of Communications hired the services of a direct mail firm and inundated some thirty thousand publications with a fact sheet about the nominee. Jeb Stuart Magruder, an aide to White House Chief of Staff H. R. Haldeman and, later, deputy director of the Office of Communications, wrote that "hundreds of editors wrote to express their thanks for this attention, and thousands of small newspapers carried more information on Burger than they otherwise would have. From a political point of view, we had to assume that this kind of publicity helped generate a favorable climate for Senate confirmation, although in Burger's case confirmation was never in doubt."[50] The office sent a similar mailing on behalf of Clement Haynsworth later that year.[51]

During the 1970 Carswell nomination, the White House even generated letters to be published in letters-to-the-editor columns of newspapers
and other publications to demonstrate support for the nominee. The letters
themselves were written by professional writers at the administration's
behest and then sent around the country to Republican loyalists, who cop-
ied them and added their own signatures. Some of the letters were written by members of the White House staff, including speechwriter Patrick
Buchanan. Later, the letter-writing operation was transferred to the Republican National Committee, where it generated fifty to sixty letters a
week, 15 to 20 percent of which were published.[52] Ron Baukol, a White
House fellow who was assigned to the letter-writing operation in early
1971, described the program as "a true under cover operation." He said that
the cost was about $100 per letter published. The operation targeted influ-
ential publications such as the *Washington Post, New York Times, Christian
Science Monitor,* and *Newsweek.* Baukol concluded that "a $100 tab for a good
letter in the *Washington Post* is pretty cheap compared to what we spend on
our other public efforts."[53]

The Office of Communications continues to play an active role in
Supreme Court nominations. During the Bork fight in 1987, the office actively generated public statements on behalf of the nominee. Reagan's communications director, Thomas Griscom, said that promoting Bork was "a
very broad-based effort." Secretary of Education William Bennett and Attorney General Edwin Meese III were "very much out on the circuit," he
recalled, "but you'd also try to find . . . senators who might be helpful
who'd go out and talk for you."[54] According to Martha Joynt Kumar, the
White House used administration officials to promote Bork through sat-
ellite interviews with local television stations, particularly in the South;
through radio interviews; and through op-ed articles.[55] During the five-
week public relations offensive, Kumar reports, the Office of Communications arranged an average of fifteen radio interviews a week dealing with
Bork and published twenty op-ed articles in newspapers "under the signa-
ture of administration officials."

As we saw in the last chapter, Bork himself went public. He participated in the longest and most detailed public testimony of any Supreme
Court nominee, and he took the unusual step of actively courting the press,
starting with an hour-long interview with the *New York Times* reporter Stuart Taylor Jr. on July 7.[56] Nonetheless, Bork's opponents were able to set the
agenda. As Thomas Griscom put it, the opposition created a "perception" of
Bork that "became a reality." Those who win in politics, Griscom noted, are
those who have "the ability to control and manage the agenda—control and
manage public perception."[57]

Thus, the administration of George Bush went out of its way to set the terms of the debate after the president nominated David Souter in 1990. In public statement after public statement, White House Chief of Staff John Sununu, White House Legal Counsel C. Boyden Gray, and other administration officials repeated the White House line: there should be no "litmus test"—"no condition in exchange for confirmation." Such a test would be unfair, they argued. Indeed, that line dovetailed neatly with the other point the administration was stressing: Souter's "fairness," his judicial temperament.

A year later, the Bush White House criticized others for carrying out a public "high-tech lynching" of nominee Clarence Thomas and at the same time aggressively spoke out on behalf of the nominee. Again, Bush stressed that the White House had used "no litmus test" in the selection of Judge Thomas, but he accused liberal interest groups of unfairly attacking Thomas for failing their own litmus test. When such a litmus test is failed, Bush told reporters, "some groups are going to rant and rave and go after [the nominee] with anything they can bring to bear on the process."[58] At the same time, the president attempted to tap public support for Thomas. He urged the American people to express their support for Thomas to the Senate. The judge, he reminded one audience, "has tremendous support from a broad . . . cross-section of America . . . [including] overwhelming support in minority communities. . . . So when you hear about opposition to Judge Thomas from one beltway group or another, it's clear that they are simply out of touch with mainstream America."[59]

The White House tactic of going public does not necessarily imply the sound and fury associated with the Bork fight or the Anita Hill–Clarence Thomas confrontation, nor does it necessarily detract from the decorum of the confirmation process. In fact, Bush's use of the tactic for Souter and Clinton's use of the tactic for Ginsburg may have increased decorum by defusing the opposition. However it is employed, going public is now part and parcel of the Supreme Court appointment process, which is ever more grounded in public opinion.

The Congressional Liaison Office: Building Senate Support

Since the administration of Dwight D. Eisenhower, presidents have had a formal Congressional Liaison Office as part of their personal staff in WHO. That office, often working together with a special ad hoc unit, plays an important role in the confirmation process of Supreme Court nominees. The tactics used to lobby senators are often similar to those associated with bareknuckled political fights. For instance, when President Johnson nominated Abe Fortas to be chief justice in 1968, Johnson's congressional liaison unit enlisted cabinet members and other departmental officials to draw "on political capital accumulated over time with senators they had worked closely with." Since Senator Henry Jackson (D-Wash.) was a member of the Armed Services Committee and interested in defense and weapons procurement, the White House had Defense Department officials lobby him on the Fortas nomination. The liaison unit also "systematically organised interest groups to bring additional pressure on senators," prepared speeches and other written material for use by friendly senators, and even resorted on occasion to the leverage of patronage and politics. "Try to soften [Senator] Russell Long [D-La.] on Abe Fortas," Johnson wrote. "He is interested in Camp Polk—I'm helping him; he wanted Buffalo NY building—I helped him; I need his quiet help."[60] Despite the prodding, Long did not listen.

Similar tactics were employed by President Nixon's liaison unit. Like Johnson, Nixon supplemented the activities of the Congressional Liaison Office with that of special ad hoc units. During the Carswell nomination, that unit included Congressional Liaison Director Bryce Harlow and Deputy Attorney General Richard Kleindienst as co-chairs; William Rehnquist and John Dean of the Justice Department; Senators Robert Dole (R-Kan.) and Howard Baker (R-Tenn.); and White House aides Charles Colson, Herbert G. Klein, Jeb Magruder, and Lynn Nofziger. According to Magruder, the group met "at eight each morning to plan the day's pro-Carswell activities."[61] In preparation for nominations to fill the vacancies left by Hugo Black and John Harlan in 1971, White House aide Egil Krogh recommended to Nixon's chief domestic affairs adviser John Ehrlichman that a similar group be formed:

> There should be a White House unit directly charged with seeing these proceedings through. I think it will require the attention of the best people here, and an *integrated* effort is mandatory. Therefore, I think a Confirmation Committee—on a very secret basis—should be established which would meet ad hoc beginning right away. Members would include:
>
> Clark MacGregor, Bill Timmons: Congressional relations. They should be asked to prepare a general and then a specific congressional relations plan which would be daily updated. I would encourage this type of Congressional Relations be undertaken directly by them.
>
> Dick Moore, Bill Safire: Press plan / announcements / statements. They should develop a precise plan for announcing the nominees and, working with the Congressional Relations team, work out timing. Both are very sensitive to questions of tone.
>
> Chuck Colson: Public support / PR / interest group support. I think it's clear that some of the muscle—if it's necessary—will have to come through Chuck's operation. . . .
>
> John Dean: Committee coordinator. He knows the Hill, the confirmation business, the Court, and possesses good judgment. He should be entrusted with the daily—even the hourly—watchdog responsibility for the work of the Committee. . . .

David Young: I think one independent mind, very facile and penetrating, should be brought to bear on this. David would be excellent.[62]

As it turned out, little orchestration was needed for the nominations of William Rehnquist and Lewis Powell to fill these vacancies. Nonetheless, Charles Colson recalls that the Confirmation Committee did meet.[63]

Some have argued that the Reagan White House spent too little time courting senators during the Bork nomination fight in 1987.[64] According to Ethan Bronner, the former Supreme Court reporter for the *Boston Globe*, Reagan did not make any telephone calls to lobby senators to vote for Bork until September 30, 1987, "after most senators had made up their minds." Reagan "did not call most southern Democrats," Bronner continues. "His first meeting with Republican Senate leaders took place on the day [confirmation hearings] began, September 15." Bronner also argues that Howard Baker, the White House chief of staff and former Senate majority leader, waited too long to mount a lobbying effort. Baker "called all the southern Democrats on July 21 and 22 but did not do more personal lobbying until mid-September," Bronner concludes.[65] White House officials have since argued that they simply were not prepared for the intensity of the lobbying against Bork. As communications director Griscom put it: "We thought it was going to be a coast job, to tell you the truth—that it was going to be easy. . . . [We had] never seen somebody run the type of effort they ran [against Bork] and we let it get away from us."[66] It is also the case that many of those in charge of White House staff units designed to promote Bork were not enamored of the nominee.

Unlike Reagan, both Johnson and Nixon closely supervised the congressional lobbying efforts on behalf of their Supreme Court nominees. For instance, Nixon frequently issued orders and demanded to be kept informed of his lieutenants' activities. On March 25, 1970, William Timmons, of the Congressional Liaison Office, sent Nixon a memorandum outlining the office's activity on behalf of Carswell:

1. Friendly reporters are trying to get "soft" Democrats to publicly commit.
2. The "Conscience of the Senate" John Williams [R-Del.] is planning to make a public statement in support.
3. Justice Department is preparing a detailed, item by item speech for [Sen.] Bob Griffin [R-Mich.] to use to refute opponents.
4. We have duplicated favorable articles and editorials for Senate distribution each day by a different Carswell supporter.
5. Bill Rehnquist of Justice Department is spending time with the undecided and weak Senators.
6. Jeb Magruder is redoubling efforts to stimulate mail to undecided and soft Senators.

7. Chuck Colson is arranging for prominent attorneys from selected states to write key Senators.

8. Harry Dent [director of Nixon's Political Affairs Office] is having influential GOP leaders contact Republican leaners from their home states.

9. National [Republican party] Chairman Rog Morton will personally talk to undecided and soft Republican Senators. Campaign Chairman John Tower [R-Tex.] is being asked to make a pitch to Win Prouty [R-Vt.] and Hiram Fong [R-Hawaii], both up for reelection this year.

10. Justice Department has arranged for Carswell's professional colleagues to write selected Senators.

11. Working through [Rep.] Jerry Ford [R-Mich.] we are applying House pressure on Senators [Marlow] Cook [R-Ky.], [Mark] Hatfield [R-Ore.], [Richard] Schweiker [R-Pa.], [William] Saxbe [R-Ohio], and [James] Pearson [R-Kan.].

12. Congressman Bill Brock [R-Tenn.] will keep up a running attack for [Sen. Albert] Gore [D-Tenn.] to take a public position on Carswell.

13. This office is continuing its day-to-day contacts with Members.[67]

Nixon, like Johnson, was willing to use patronage and politics to secure votes. Examples abound. Nixon's briefing paper for a White House meeting with an undecided senator, Marlow Cook, noted that Cook had a strong interest in having a particular person appointed to the Sixth Circuit Court of Appeals but that the Justice Department had opposed that person because of age and poor qualifications. The briefing paper suggested that "a promise to give [Cook] the judgeship, if he brings it up, might secure his vote for Carswell." This was followed by the reminder: "Cook's support on Wednesday is crucial."[68] Whatever transpired at that meeting, Cook voted against Carswell. In 1986, the Reagan administration reportedly attempted a similar deal with Senator Slade Gorton, a Republican from Washington, to secure Gorton's vote for Daniel Manion, Reagan's nominee to the Seventh Circuit Court of Appeals. Gorton voted for the nominee, but publicity about the alleged deal helped to defeat him in his reelection bid later that year.[69]

Nixon wooed other senators with a simple phone call or through invitations to join him at a Sunday White House church service.[70] Other tactics were more blunt. During the Haynsworth fight, for instance, Political Affairs Director Harry Dent wrote the following about the activities of his office: "We are gathering together the list of favors the target Senators have been asking the Administration for—jobs, projects, grants, etc., and are trying to use this as leverage with the Senators, usually using the State Chairmen as the intermediary parties."[71]

The Congressional Liaison Office routinely provides written material to friendly senators for their use on and off the Senate floor. During 1969 and 1970, Senator Roman Hruska (R-Neb.) was Nixon's point man for Haynsworth and Carswell. Whenever Nixon's chief opponent, Senator Birch Bayh

(D-Ind.), spoke out against the nominees, the White House urged Hruska to come out swinging. The television networks often gave Hruska coverage. The strategy was part of Nixon's "attack" program in Congress. During Nixon's first month in office, H. R. Haldeman wrote that Nixon was "especially anxious . . . [to] set up a system of furnishing attack material on a daily basis to a group of key people on the Hill that Bryce Harlow will be lining up to be our first line of battle for the Administration."[72] The responsibility for writing such material ultimately came to rest with Lyn Nofziger, who joined the congressional liaison staff in July 1969.[73]

Finally, the White House can bully senators through threats, which can take several forms. For instance, the president can threaten to make a "spite" nomination if the current nominee is rejected.[74] Such a nominee may be purposely less qualified or more rigidly ideological than the previous nominee. Reagan threatened a spite nomination if Bork was defeated in 1987 and then nominated Douglas Ginsburg to the Supreme Court. (Ginsburg, younger and less distinguished than Bork, withdrew a few days later, when it was revealed that he had smoked marijuana while teaching at Harvard Law School in the 1970s.) Likewise, Nixon's choice of Carswell may be viewed as a spite nomination in retaliation for Haynsworth's rejection. Carswell was clearly less qualified than Haynsworth and arguably more conservative in his views. After Carswell's defeat, Nixon seriously considered yet another spite nomination. The Senate defeated Carswell in part because of his alleged racism; as a twenty-eight-year old candidate for the Georgia legislature in 1948, Carswell gave a speech in which he said: "I believe the segregation of the races is proper and the only practical and correct way of life. . . . I yield to no man . . . in the firm, vigorous belief in the principles of white supremacy, and I shall always be so governed."[75]

Charles Colson recalls that after Carswell's defeat "Nixon was on the verge of appointing [Senator Robert C.] Byrd to put Congress on the spot."[76] Byrd was a Democrat from West Virginia. In his youth he had been a member of the Ku Klux Klan, advocating a Klan rebirth in every state of the Union as late as 1946. Although Byrd had long repudiated his Klan membership, he had filibustered against the 1964 Civil Rights Act with a fourteen-hour speech, one of the longest in Senate history. Thus, voting for Byrd after voting against Carswell would be awkward for Senate Democrats. At the same time, it would be awkward for the Senate to reject a colleague. As Colson put it, Nixon's plot was *pure* politics. I mean, Bob Byrd wanted it. Bob Byrd was a lawyer. And the idea was, 'We'll put up somebody that the Congress can't afford to say no to.' For the sake of the Court, it's a good thing that vindictive thought didn't come to pass."

Threats can also take the form of direct action against individual senators. During the Haynsworth and Carswell fights, the Nixon administration leaked derogatory stories about Birch Bayh and other Senate opponents to friendly newspapers. This was done at the instigation of the president, who was particularly furious with Bayh. In October 1969, Nixon told Haldeman that they needed "a murderer's row in [the] Senate—need to kick Bayh around."[77]

Another good example of a specific attempt to threaten senators was the Nixon administration's use of corporate campaign contributors during the Haynsworth battle. As we saw in chapter 5, the White House enlisted some fifteen major contributors in Ohio alone to pressure Senator Saxbe to vote for Haynsworth.[78] In like fashion, major contributors from Pennsylvania, Illinois, Tennessee, Oregon, Idaho, Kansas, Missouri, Washington, Iowa, Delaware, and Arkansas were enlisted to pressure particular senators.[79] For the most part, such threats (as well as the more overt tempting of senators with favors) were orchestrated by Nixon's Political Affairs Office rather than the Congressional Liaison Office. In the end, Nixon "froze out" Republican senators who did not support Haynsworth by ignoring them and denying them access to the White House.[80]

In short, the Congressional Liaison Office lobbies senators with threats and reassurances as part of a well-coordinated effort to secure Senate confirmation of court nominees. The office works with other White House staff units to mobilize grassroots pressure on wavering senators. The efforts include building public support for the nominee and orchestrating lobbying efforts by powerful interest groups.

The Office of Public Liaison: Building Interest Group Support

Since 1970, the Office of Public Liaison has existed in the White House Office as an institutionalized mechanism for mobilizing support among interest groups for presidential policy. Presidential use of the office to support judicial nominees is another indication of the politicization of the Supreme Court confirmation process and the extent to which presidents (and special interests) are eager to use the selection process to influence public policy.

The first director of the Office of Public Liaison was Charles Colson. Colson describes his job this way: "I was Special Counsel to the President in charge of relationships with groups outside the White House—any public interest group or any special interest group. My job was to listen to them, represent their points of view at different things that went on in government, and mobilize them to get support for the President."[81]

President Nixon did not create Colson's post until the Haynsworth fight was all but over. Therefore, White House efforts to mobilize interest group support for Haynsworth was done on an ad hoc basis, largely by the Office of Political Affairs headed by Harry Dent. In a memorandum to Attorney General John Mitchell, Dent outlined some of the things his office had done: "The following individuals and organizations were contacted either directly or indirectly by my staff. All of them have been known to favor 'conservative' causes at one time or another in the past and they were asked to use their influence to generate as much pro-Haynsworth mail as possible into the offices of target Senators." This was followed by a nine-page list of contacts, part of which follows:

> G. B. Nalley, a South Carolina lumberman who will contact key leaders of the lumber industry in other states.
>
> Willis Cantey, a South Carolina banker who will contact bankers in other states.
>
> Carter Poe, a South Carolina hardware dealer who will contact hardware associations in other states to get mail coming in.
>
> Phyllis Schlafly, a conservative women's leader is starting a mail campaign. . . .
>
> Captain Robert Orrell of Virginia. Mrs. Orrell is the Procter and Gamble heiress and has a 12,000 person mailing list.
>
> Reed Larson, head of the Right to Work Committee is working on mail. . . .
>
> Harold Stringer of the American Legion is helping on mail.
>
> Roger Fleming of the American Farm Bureau . . . is helping on mail.
>
> Darrell Coover, Vice President for Government Relations of the National Association of Independent Insurers, has begun a mail campaign.
>
> Arch Booth of the National Chamber of Commerce has pledged his support. [Clark] Mollenhoff talked to his people and revved them up.
>
> Paul Harvey, the radio commentator, is going to try to generate mail.[82]

Dent also maintained close ties with Republican organizations and encouraged state Republican organizations and other groups, such as Young Republicans and Young Americans for Freedom, to generate mail.

Colson directed interest group mobilization for the rest of Nixon's Supreme Court appointments. He and the Office of Public Liaison were most active during the Carswell nomination, but they undertook similar efforts for Blackmun, Rehnquist, and Powell. For instance, Colson's handwritten notes indicate the following activity for Rehnquist and Powell: "Calls: 1) Prominent attorneys, 2) Bar Association Leaders, 3) Republican Governors, 4) Party Officials, 5) friendly Editors & Broadcasters, 6) Columnists, 7) Loyalists, 8) Judges, 9) Hill. Group mobilization: 1) Chamber [of Commerce], 2) NAM [National Association of Manufacturers], 3) NAHB [National Association of Home Builders], 4) Police Chiefs, 5) firefighters, 6) VFW [Veterans of Foreign Wars]. [Pat] Buchanan with conservative groups."[83]

The Bork nomination was a watershed in terms of interest group involvement: more than three hundred groups opposed Bork, and these groups "used a wide variety of tactics, including advertising, grass roots events, focus groups, and polling."[84] The White House responded by using its Office of Public Liaison to mobilize group support for Bork. It targeted direct mailings at groups and helped outside groups place favorable editorials in states where there were crucial swing senators.[85] But the White House appeared to have been caught off guard by the groundswell of opposition to Bork, and it never regained the offensive. Presidents since then have learned the lesson and have worked closely with organized interests to mount campaigns on behalf of their nominees. When George Bush nominated Clarence Thomas in 1991, conservative groups waged a campaign, at the behest of the White House, that tended to spend more money and be better organized than Thomas's opponents.[86]

In addition to using interest groups to help secure confirmation, presidents also use judicial appointments as a way of building their own support among particular groups. Republican presidents in the 1980s sought to add several constituencies to the GOP camp, including southern whites. "By concentrating on issues such as abortion, school prayer, and pornography, Republicans . . . sought to politicize the moral concerns of white southerners. . . . Moreover, they . . . used evangelical churches, which are a prominent feature of the southern landscape, to forge institutional links between southern whites and the party." As a result, Republicans secured a strong base in the South "for the first time in the party's 135-year history."[87] The judicial nominations of Reagan and Bush clearly played into this strategy. Reagan defined the Justice Department's "social policy agenda largely in terms of the New Right's opposition to the rulings of the Burger Court (1969–86) on abortion, affirmative action, busing, school prayer, and the like."[88] Reagan and Bush then used their increased control over the judicial selection process to screen candidates to ensure that their judicial philosophy supported such an agenda.

Having built a base in the South, it is not surprising that Bush used a southern strategy to promote Clarence Thomas; in fact, the group that spent the most money on behalf of Thomas during his confirmation battle was the Christian Coalition, a Virginia-based group founded by television evangelist Pat Robertson.[89] Likewise, religious organizations such as the Moral Majority and Focus on the Family played an important role in supporting Bork in 1987.[90]

Conclusion

As we have seen, modern presidents have at their disposal a wide range of resources for screening potential nominees and generating support for them. The development and use of these resources is an important component of the institutional presidency, one in which presidents and their staff play an important role in formulating and implementing policy. In this context, presidents treat the judicial selection process as a way to influence policy and use institutional resources to maximize their influence. However, presidents must compete with other actors, who use their own strategic resources to oppose presidents' nominees. Thus, presidential use of these strategic resources does not guarantee success in securing confirmation of judicial nominees.

In fact, five Supreme Court nominees (Abe Fortas in 1968, Clement Haynsworth in 1969, G. Harrold Carswell in 1970, Robert Bork in 1987, and Douglas Ginsburg in 1987) have failed to win confirmation since 1968.[91] However, other variables have historically put presidents in a weak position to secure confirmation. The nominations of Fortas, Bork, and Ginsburg all took place at the tail end of a presidential term, historically a bad time for presidents to make such nominations. In addition, both Nixon and Reagan faced a Senate majority of the opposition party. As we saw in the introduction to this volume, both of these factors significantly decrease the likelihood that the Senate will confirm nominees.

Compounding the situation were legitimate charges of conflict of interest (in the case of Fortas), legitimate concerns about qualifications (in the case of Carswell and Ginsburg), and unusual political circumstances with both Haynsworth and Bork. With Haynsworth, many liberal senators were retaliating against the nominee for conservative opposition to Fortas. When conflict of interest charges surfaced against Haynsworth, some conservatives felt compelled to vote against him so as to legitimize their opposition to Fortas. With Bork, many liberals were responding to what they perceived as an ongoing attempt by the Reagan administration to pack the courts. In addition, Bork's problems were compounded by his controversial writings, the political climate in the South, the fact that he would replace a moderate swing vote on the Court, and the fact that the White House was not prepared for such intense opposition.

At least three of these failed nominations (Carswell, Ginsburg, and Bork) may be attributed to a breakdown of the initial selection process. Carswell and Ginsburg were chosen for the wrong reason (spite). Moreover, background checks on Ginsburg failed to turn up the damning fact that he had recently smoked marijuana. (One could similarly argue that background checks should have alerted the White House to Fortas's problems; in contrast, Haynsworth's appearance of conflict of interest should, under normal circumstances, have posed no problem.) Finally, Bork was known to be a politically divisive choice from the start. Given Reagan's recent Iran-contra problems and the fact that the opposition party controlled the Senate, the choice of Bork was not politically wise.

The initial selection of nominees is extraordinarily important. Once the president names an ill-considered nominee (one who is clearly mediocre, one who has obvious legal or ethical problems, one who was clearly chosen out of spite, or one who is clearly politically inexpedient), there is little that the White House can do, even with all its strategic resources, to save the nomination. Staff units such as the Office of Communications, the Congressional Liaison Office, and the Office of Public Liaison are most successful at making sure that well-chosen nominations are not derailed by a determined opposition.

The contentiousness of recent nominations, in which so much emphasis was placed on the judicial philosophy of nominees, demonstrates how important the outcome is to so many actors. In this context, the president must be able to compete with other players who wish to influence the selection process. The institutionalization of resources to do this is an important part of modern presidential power and a further example of presidential efforts to lead public policy.

CHAPTER EIGHT

THE CLINTON APPOINTMENTS
AND PROPOSALS FOR REFORM

Despite the rise of the institutional presidency and the additional staff resources it has given modern presidents to use in the Supreme Court selection and confirmation process, presidents do not necessarily dominate the appointment process. In fact, the number of failed nominations has risen dramatically since the late 1960s. Why? There are a number of possible explanations. First, there are limits to the power of staff resources, especially when such staff is opposed by similar resources possessed by other players in the process. Many more players now occupy the field than at any other point in our history. With so many active players, it is more difficult for any one to dominate the process.

Second, most of the presidential staff resources used in the appointment process are a part of the president's personal staff in the White House Office, and this personal staff is inherently political.[1] It is designed to further the interests of the incumbent president, so its members change from administration to administration. It therefore has no institutional memory. At times it is arrogant and woefully inexperienced, making staff more of a curse than a blessing. Moreover, as staff resources multiply and have overlapping jurisdiction, new problems arise. Internal power struggles become more likely, and the chain of command becomes less clear. Public statements from different administration officials may conflict. Moreover, the media, whose penchant for dramatic stories leads to a preoccupation with such conflict, will focus on any apparent dissension within administration ranks.[2] Such stories can increase the tension between those at odds and also make the president look like a poor manager.[3] In the process, the president may lose control of the agenda.

As former White House communications director Thomas Griscom puts it, those who win in politics are those who "have the ability to control and manage the agenda."[4] Former secretary of defense and White House chief of staff Dick Cheney echoes that point. To have an effective presidency, he says, the White House must control the agenda, which means exerting internal discipline among the staff and maintaining an ability to control what the media is reporting about the administration. "You don't let the press set the agenda," Cheney emphasizes. "The press is going to object to that. They like to set the agenda. They like to decide what's important and what isn't important. But if you let them do that, they're going to trash your presidency."[5] In the context of the Supreme Court appointment process, the White House must also prevent opposition players from dominating the agenda and trashing its nominee.

This is more difficult when the presidency and the Senate are controlled by opposite parties. Indeed, the long periods of divided government since 1969 are a third explanation for the high rate of failed Supreme Court nominations in recent years. In addition, controlling the agenda has become more difficult as the appointment process has become more open and as communications technology has advanced. Now, even a peripheral player can dominate the agenda by peddling an attention-grabbing story that can be instantly beamed into American homes via television. The saliency of such stories makes the contemporary process seem more political, more focused on scandal and the personal attributes of nominees.

In fact, scandal and investigations of personal peccadillos have always been a part of the process. Opponents of John Rutledge in 1795 raised questions about his failure to pay his debts and about his reputed insanity. Opponents of George Williams in 1873 charged that he had used public money for private gain when, as U.S. attorney general, he bought an extravagant carriage. Headlines blared with stories of sex and arson in 1887, when opponents charged that Lucius Lamar had had an affair with a woman under indictment for setting fire to a house in Mississippi.[6] Opponents of Louis Brandeis in 1916, Felix Frankfurter in 1939, and William Brennan in 1956 all charged that the nominees were dangerous radicals with socialist or communist ties. And "dry" opponents of Owen Roberts in 1930 questioned his character and ability to enforce the ban on alcohol given his opposition to Prohibition in a 1923 speech. Headlines focused on "dry queries" and the fact that Roberts' law partner was "wet" (appearing, as the *New York Times* put it, as "one of the star witnesses marshaled by the wet association before the House Committee on the Judiciary" during its hearings into the possible repeal of Prohibition).[7]

What *has* changed is that the Senate is neither as isolated from public pressure nor as tightly bound together by norms of elite behavior as it used to be.[8] In part, this is due to the increased visibility of Senate debate and the increased popular accountability brought about by direct election of senators. Now that senators are more responsive to public opinion, they weigh public reaction to such scandals more carefully. Modern-day communication also allows such charges to reach a broader audience much more quickly. Thus, what is different about today's appointment process is not its politicization but the range of players in the process and the techniques of politicization that they use. Today's confirmation battles are no longer government affairs between the president and the Senate; they are public affairs, open to a broad range of players. Thus, overt lobbying, public opinion polls, advertising campaigns, focus groups, and public appeals have all become a routine part of the process.

The highly public nature of modern Supreme Court appointments makes them an important symbolic test of presidential strength. Senate defeat of a nominee can become a potent symbol of presidential weakness or mismanagement (or both), which can in turn reduce a president's prestige in the eyes of the American people and the Washington community. Such a loss is something that no president wants, especially with presidential power now so closely tied to public support. Bill Clinton's early difficulties in gaining Senate confirmation of his attorney general and other nominees damaged his "honeymoon" period with Congress, just as Richard Nixon's problems in filling Abe Fortas's Supreme Court seat early in his first term were both an embarrassment and a symbol of his weakness.

Still, the prime motivation for presidents (and other players in the process) is the desire to influence judicial policymaking. Thus, a nominee's defeat becomes much more than just a symbolic loss to be tallied by media pundits covering the game of politics. Senate refusal to accept a nominee who adheres to a particular approach to constitutional interpretation can significantly alter the outlook of the Court for years to come and have a major effect on policy.[9]

There are, of course, limits to a president's ability to influence policy through judicial appointments. Once on the bench, appointees can disappoint the president who named them by voting against him on important cases or by embracing an ideological approach different from the one he had expected. History books are full of pithy quotes of presidents spurned by their judicial nominees. Betrayed by Justice Tom Clark's votes on important cases, Harry Truman called Clark's appointment his "biggest mistake." Truman had first named Clark as his attorney general and then elevated him to the Supreme Court. "I don't know what got into me," Truman later said. "He was no damn good as Attorney General, and on the Supreme Court . . . it doesn't seem possible, but he's been even worse. He hasn't made one right decision that I can think of. . . . It's just that he's such a dumb son of a bitch."[10] Heightened White House screening of judicial nominees may minimize the likelihood of such "mistakes," but no one can completely predict the behavior of individuals once they sit on the Court. Opposing interest groups can be surprised, too. For instance, the voting behavior of John J. Parker on the U.S. Court of Appeals for the Fourth Circuit belied the predictions of groups who helped bring about the defeat of his earlier Supreme Court nomination.

The Clinton Appointments: Prelude

Confirmation battles over Bill Clinton's nominations of Zoë Baird to be attorney general and Lani Guinier to be assistant attorney general for civil rights in 1993 cast an ominous shadow over the opening months of the Clinton administration. Despite the fact that Democrats controlled both the White House and the Senate, opposition to both nominees became so intense that Clinton withdrew their nominations. The tactics used against Baird and Guinier were similar to those used against earlier Supreme Court nominees such as Robert Bork, and they represent much of what is wrong with contemporary confirmation politics. Legitimate reasons existed to oppose any one of these nominees, but opponents often distorted nominees' records and vilified their characters in order to scare the American people and derail their nominations.

The tactics employed against Baird and Guinier were partly retribution for the tactics Democrats had employed against Republican nominees. Conservatives showed that they could "Bork" as well as their liberal counterparts. Opponents of Guinier used snippets of her academic writing to portray her as a "quota queen," who, if confirmed as assistant attorney general for civil rights, would carry affirmative action programs to an "extreme" by calling for proportional representation of African Americans (that is, a quota of seats in the legislature equal to the proportion of African American voters among the citizenry). Opponents also used her writings to portray her as a dangerous radical who eschewed racial moderation and took the "extreme" stance that black representatives elected from districts with a majority of whites were "inauthentic" since they were neither elected by nor representative of a black constituency. The criticisms played to racial fears, and the out-of-context reading of Guinier's record was what opponents of Robert Bork had done when they used out-of-context snippets of his record to portray him as an advocate of back-alley abortions and forced sterilizations.[11]

The paper trail of any nominee is, of course, a relevant source to examine during confirmation proceedings. There were parts of both Bork's and Guinier's record that critics could legitimately take issue with. But, as Stephen Carter writes, opponents chose the course of "shameless exaggeration" in their portrayal of the two nominees' writings.[12] Carter also argues that Guinier was held to a double standard. African Americans who made "strident" and "ill-conceived" attacks on the black civil rights leadership did not pay the same price as Guinier. Clarence Thomas, for instance, once said that leaders of civil rights organizations "do nothing but bitch, bitch, bitch, moan and moan." "It is hard to imagine that this is the voice of racial moderation that Lani Guinier's conservative critics have demanded. Yet when Thomas apologized, most members of the Senate considered the matter settled." Carter also notes that the Senate unanimously confirmed Webster Hubbell as associate attorney general during the Guinier battle, despite Hubbell's long-time membership in an all-white country club. Hubbell resigned from the club, apologized, and announced his commitment to integration. Carter points out that if this last-minute action was "enough to rescue him from his lifelong habit of relaxing in the company of those who would rather segregate, then surely a public apology from Guinier" for any of her writings that appeared too strident should have been "more than enough" to rescue her nomination.

Opponents of Zoë Baird derailed her nomination by turning a minor offense into a major scandal. Her offense was what came to be known as the "nanny problem." Before Clinton nominated Baird to be attorney general, Baird and her husband had hired a chauffeur and a nanny to help look after their children. The Peruvian couple that they hired for $500 a week were illegal immigrants who lacked work permits. Baird and her husband were aware of this problem and sought advice from their lawyer about hiring the couple. Armed with that advice, they notified the Immigration and Naturalization Service as soon as they hired the couple and then helped them in their efforts to obtain proper documentation. What ultimately sank Baird's nomination was the fact that she failed to pay social security taxes on the couple's salary. This offense (which is not criminal) is committed by a substantial portion of American people who hire babysitters, someone to mow the lawn, or other household help on a regular basis and who fail (usually unwittingly) to pay social security taxes on their salaries. Baird had clearly done wrong. She broke the law, just as those who commit traffic offenses break the law. But, ironically, she had attempted to do right. She and her husband had paid social security taxes on their previous nanny. In fact, they failed to pay the taxes in this case because their lawyer had mistakenly informed them that, until the couple obtained proper documentation (including social security numbers), the government would not accept payment.

When Clinton nominated her, Baird mentioned this indiscretion herself, apologized for it, and paid the back taxes and a fine. Nonetheless, this nanny problem took on sinister proportions. The sound bite was reduced to the fact that Baird broke the law. Moreover, the hiring of a nanny and a chauffeur was used by critics to paint Baird and her husband as part of an uncaring wealthy elite—worse yet, a wealthy elite that evades taxes. President Clinton had promised in his campaign to fight for "the forgotten middle class," those "who work hard and play by the rules." Yet here was a woman who earned half a million dollars a year, a woman who, in the biting words of consumer activist Ralph Nader, could have hired Mary Poppins but instead chose to break the law and hire cheap labor.[13] How, critics asked, could such a person be confirmed as attorney general, a post that oversees law enforcement? The public responded with outrage, and Clinton withdrew Baird's nomination, even though many others (including the current head of the Social Security Administration) were guilty of the same offense.[14]

Since then, many have asked whether this was a legitimate disqualifying factor in Baird's case. In their haste to judge Baird, did her opponents (and the media) portray her case fairly? As Stephen Carter so aptly notes: "There is much to be said for keeping government free from the taint of scandal, but not for creating scandals in order to keep our government free of people we do not like."[15] The tactics used against Baird and Guinier and Bork and Thomas were to Carter, and many others, symptoms of our current "confirmation mess."

Reform Proposals

Proposals to reform the confirmation process and alleviate the "mess" began in earnest shortly after the Bork battle in 1987. The Twentieth Century Fund convened a task force of academics, lawyers, and public servants to assess the Supreme Court selection process and recommend changes.[16] The task force issued its report in 1988. It condemned the politicization and highly public nature of recent Supreme Court confirmation proceedings and concluded that the fundamental problem with the process was that it was "too visible and attract[ed] too much publicity." Indeed, the task force noted that the process had come "dangerously close to looking like the electoral process," with the Senate all but holding a "national referendum" on nominees. Moreover, players in the process, such as White House and Justice Department officials, senators, witnesses before the Judiciary Committee, and even nominees, seemed "tempted to use televised hearings as a forum for other purposes, ranging from self-promotion to mobilizing special interest groups in order to influence public opinion."[17]

Thus, the task force recommended (1) that the confirmation process be "depoliticized by minimizing the potential for participants to posture and distort the basic purpose of the proceedings," (2) that "nominees should no longer be expected to appear as witnesses during the Senate Judiciary Committee's hearings on their confirmation," (3) that if nominees did continue to appear, "senators should not put questions to nominees that call for answers that would indicate how they would deal with specific issues if they were confirmed," and (4) that "the Judiciary Committee and the Senate base confirmation decisions on a nominee's written record and the testimony of legal experts as to his competence."[18] The task force admitted that its recommendations were controversial. Indeed, task force member Joseph A. Califano dissented from all of the conclusions and recommendations of the task force, and Lloyd N. Cutler dissented from the second and fourth recommendations. In addition, task force member Philip B. Kurland strongly dissented from the conclusion that the confirmation process has come dangerously close to looking like the electoral process. These dissents are indicative of ongoing disagreement over how the process should operate.

The dramatic Anita Hill–Clarence Thomas confrontation in 1991 sparked another round of reform proposals. Hill's allegation that Thomas had sexually harassed her led to dramatic televised testimony by both Hill and Thomas. Virtually everyone agreed that the ensuing process was not fair, although many disagreed whether it was Hill or Thomas who was treated worse. The Senate finally confirmed Thomas, but not before he bitterly told the Senate Judiciary Committee that the process had turned into a "high-tech lynching." "I have been harmed worse than I have ever been harmed in my life," he said. "I wasn't harmed by the Klan, I wasn't harmed by the Knights of Camelia, I wasn't harmed by the Aryan race, I wasn't harmed by any racist group, [but] I was harmed by this process."[19]

President Bush called the process a "circus and travesty" that was more akin to "a burlesque show" than a civilized confirmation proceeding.[20] "The present process is simply not fair," he said, "and I think senators on both sides of the aisle are going to want to see changes in several areas."[21] Among those that examined reform proposals was ABC News, which provided an expanded "Town Hall Meeting" edition of *Nightline* on October 16, 1991, as a showcase for debate about how to fix a process that had "run amok." The program included Republican and Democratic senators, interest group representatives, members of the media, and an invited audience made up mostly of people who were involved either directly or indirectly in the Thomas proceedings. It lasted well over its hour-and-a-half time allotment and passions ran high. At times the program itself seemed to run amok. Moderator Ted Koppel attempted to maintain order but often with little success. "You're talking at each other," he finally told his guests in exasperation. "You're not listening to each other. You're not trying to be responsive."

The program underscored the lack of consensus on how to fix the process. Not surprisingly, most reform proposals came to naught. Confirmation hearings since then, starting with Ruth Bader Ginsburg in 1993, have included testimony from the nominee in executive session, to allow for exchanges on sensitive topics, such as sexual harassment, without the glare of publicity. But otherwise, no substantive procedural changes have been made. The 1989 recommendations of the Twentieth Century Fund task force were not implemented.

Should they have been? The major recommendation of the task force was to curtail the public nature of confirmation proceedings in order to minimize "the potential for participants to posture and distort" the basic purpose of the proceedings. The task force argued that public appeals by the White House, interest groups, senators, and others "distract attention from, and sometimes completely distort, the legal qualifications of the nominee." While recognizing that media coverage of the process "may have a salutary effect in informing and educating the public," the task force concluded that the negative effects of such publicity outweigh the positive. In short, the politicization of the process brought about by such publicity "denigrates the Court and serves to undermine its prestige as well as public respect for the rule of law."[22] There certainly is a danger that public appeals will trivialize the confirmation process. The emphasis on the symbolic appeal of nominees may even result in less-distinguished individuals being seated on the Court. This is clearly what the task force feared.

But crass politics has always permeated the Supreme Court appointment process. What is new (indeed, refreshing) in recent years is the degree to which participants now admit that they are engaging in politics. If participants in the confirmation process are going to resort to politics, as history suggests they will, perhaps it is best that such politics be admitted for what it is rather than being hidden behind a cloak of deliberative "objectivity." As Louis Brandeis reminded us, "Sunlight is the best antiseptic."

Public hearings, complete with testimony from the nominee and other types of public appeals, educate the public and make participants in the process more accountable for their actions. It is, after all, the public's only opportunity to influence the process. As reporter Nina Totenberg writes, "senators and their constituencies should not be asked to endorse nominees whose views, if known, would be abhorrent [to them]."[23] We have to hope that misrepresentations and unfounded accusations will be minimized by thorough media coverage of the proceedings and the free exchange of ideas about nominees.

But cannot some procedural change be made to curtail the squalor of so many recent confirmation battles? In the wake of President Clinton's early failures with Baird and Guinier, Stephen Carter assessed various proposals to fix the confirmation mess.[24] He rejects most of them, including suggestions to ban testimony by the nominee and interest groups, to stop televising the confirmation hearings, and to ban public hearings altogether. None of those proposals would make any difference, he argues, "because none of them reduces the stakes that all sides have in each nomination." Carter nonetheless does countenance a reform proposal that would require a constitutional amendment to execute: raising the threshold vote needed to confirm nominees from a simple majority of the Senate to two-thirds. This would arguably force the president to nominate consensus candidates, thereby reducing the political nature of appointments.

Carter also suggests with misgivings, two other possible reforms: (1) the establishment of term limits (without the possibility of reappointment) for Supreme Court justices, and (2) the election of Supreme Court justices. Unlike his proposal to increase the threshold vote for confirmation, these two proposals would likely increase the politicization of the process and reduce judicial independence. Term limits would increase the number and frequency of confirmation battles, and elections would make public appeals even more influential. Carter recognizes these drawbacks but argues that we are so close to confirming nominees by a national referendum anyway that we may as well be honest about it and that term limits would allow everybody a chance to influence the Court at regular intervals.

The flaw in these proposals is the assumption that the confirmation mess is new and the corollary assumption that equilibrium can be restored by fixing what has been broken. In fact, the confirmation mess has less to do with the specifics of the confirmation process (testimony or no testimony, televised hearings or closed hearings, interest group involvement or no interest group involvement) than with the underlying political climate of any given era. The recent confirmation mess was mostly a product of an unusually long period of divided government, coupled with contentious public policy debates—a "cultural civil war," as E. J. Dionne puts it—over some of the most divisive issues imaginable, with race and abortion at the forefront.[25]

Thus, recent nominees have been ensnared in broader political battles, much as nominees in the wake of the Civil War were. The mess comes and goes (witness the uneventful confirmation of Ruth Bader Ginsburg in 1993 and of Stephen Breyer in 1994), and procedural changes will do little to alter that fact. Abuses of the process have certainly occurred. But those abuses are symptoms of other problems, rather than their cause. An examination of President Clinton's Supreme Court appointments may make this clearer. In fact, both of Clinton's appointments are important because they illustrate the importance of the initial selection process in muting confirmation battles.

The Clinton Appointments: Ginsburg and Breyer

During the 1992 presidential campaign, Bill Clinton pledged that, if given the opportunity, he would appoint Supreme Court justices of "far higher quality" than those of his Republican predecessors. "We'd take it out of politics," he said.[26] But Clinton also promised throughout the campaign to appoint justices who believe in the right to privacy. At the first Democratic debate of the primary season, he (along with the rest of the Democratic candidates) even seemed to embrace a "litmus test" to prevent the appointment of justices who would overturn *Roe v. Wade*.[27] These contradictory positions—to take the process out of politics, on the one hand, but to apply a litmus test to ensure that potential justices would vote to uphold abortion rights, on the other—illustrates the contradictory pressures facing contemporary politicians. Yet Clinton came about as close as one could to honoring both promises; he selected highly qualified, moderate nominees who will, in all likelihood, vote to sustain abortion rights but who, nonetheless, provoked no severe confirmation battles.

President Clinton had a number of things going for him when he made the nominations. Both nominations took place during his first two years in office and with a Senate majority of fellow Democrats. Thus, Clinton averted the factors that make bloody confirmation battles more likely: a lame duck presidency and a divided government.[28] Moreover, neither of Clinton's nominations were "critical," which is defined by P. S. Ruckman Jr. as nominations that bring about important shifts in partisan coalitions on the Court (such as a shift from a Democratic to a Republican majority of justices).[29] Nor did either appointment appear to be potentially "transformative," at least with regard to divisive social issues such as abortion. ("Transformative" appointments are those that, regardless of partisan shifts, can lead to important shifts in voting coalitions on the court.)[30] Add to this the fact that Senate confirmation of Supreme Court nominees remains the norm, and it is not surprising that both Ginsburg and Breyer easily won a seat on the Court.[31]

Nonetheless, the Baird and Guinier nominations show that even a newly elected president unhampered by divided government can face bloody confirmation battles. How were Ginsburg and Breyer different? Recent social science research suggests that highly politicized confirmation proceedings occur only under certain circumstances. In a study of Supreme Court nominations since 1954, Charles M. Cameron, Albert D. Cover, and Jeffrey A. Segal show that "when a strong president nominates a highly qualified, ideological moderate candidate, the nominee passes the Senate in a lopsided, consensual vote." On the other hand, "when presidents nominate a less well qualified, ideologically extreme candidate, especially when the president is in a weak political position, then a conflictual vote is likely."[32] By this standard, both Ginsburg and Breyer fit the mold for easy confirmation. The Senate confirmed Ginsburg by a vote of 96 to 3 and Breyer by a vote of 87 to 9.

Neither Ginsburg nor Breyer was Clinton's first choice for the vacancies. In both cases, Clinton wanted to appoint a politician to the Court, a lawyer with "a big heart" and "real-world" experience and the leadership skills necessary to forge a moderate majority among the justices. During the 1992 campaign, Clinton had cited New York governor Mario Cuomo as a potential nominee because "he is a legal scholar who also understands the impact of the law on people's lives."[33] But when Justice Byron White (the last sitting justice named by a Democratic president) announced his retirement in March 1993, Cuomo took himself out of the running. The White House then embarked on a lengthy search for a nominee, during which time Clinton was forced to abandon the nomination of Lani Guinier for assistant attorney general for civil rights.

In its eighty-eight-day search, the White House leaked names, gauged reactions, and ultimately drew criticism for its indecision. It sought a moderate nominee who would not provoke a fight. One finalist, First Circuit Court of Appeals Judge Stephen Breyer, had a variant of the nanny problem—he had failed to pay social security taxes on a housemaid, Breyer had made amends for the indiscretion, but it was less than six months since the Zoë Baird fiasco. Clinton finally chose Ruth Bader Ginsburg, a pioneering litigator on behalf of women's rights who had steered a centrist course as a judge on the U.S. Court of Appeals for the District of Columbia.

The search for a nominee to replace Justice Harry Blackmun in 1994 followed much the same pattern. Again, Clinton wanted to appoint a person with political experience. Blackmun had confided to the president in December 1993 that the current Court term would be his last. Behind the scenes, the White House started its search for a potential nominee. Senate majority leader George Mitchell (D-Maine) became the front-running candidate when he announced that he would not seek reelection to the Senate. Mitchell seemed to have all the qualities the president was looking for. He had served as a U.S. attorney and a federal judge before moving to the U.S. Senate in 1980. The Senate gave him the real-world political experience that appealed to Clinton, and as majority leader Mitchell had honed his skills as a consensus builder. He would be a liberal on the Court, one who could possibly forge a new majority by luring the centrist camp of Sandra Day O'Connor, Anthony Kennedy, and David Souter to vote with the Court's more liberal members: himself, Ginsburg, and John Paul Stevens. And his popularity with members of both parties in the Senate would guarantee easy confirmation.

There were potential problems with Mitchell, but they seemed to be surmountable. For one thing, the "emoluments clause" of the Constitution prohibits lawmakers from being appointed to federal office during a term in which Congress voted to increase that official's pay, and Mitchell had voted in 1990 to increase the salary of associate justices of the Supreme Court from $118,600 to $153,600. But White House Counsel Lloyd Cutler noted that there had been solutions to the emoluments clause problem before and he was certain that one could be found for Mitchell. For instance, Congress could pass special legislation reducing Mitchell's Supreme Court salary to its previous level. Then, without Mitchell in the Senate, the raise could be reinstated in the next term.

A more serious problem involved Mitchell's important role in shepherding the president's health care package through the Senate. Health care reform was a cornerstone of Clinton's domestic policy agenda, and the president did not want to jeopardize its passage. The White House hoped that Blackmun would not announce his retirement until the end of the Supreme Court's term in June 1994, so President Clinton could delay his announcement of a nominee long enough to allow Mitchell to finish his work in the Senate. But Blackmun announced his resignation on April 6. Speculation immediately centered on Mitchell. Four days later, Mitchell said on the CBS news program *Face the Nation* that he would "enjoy being on the Supreme Court." Appearing on the program with Mitchell, Senate minority leader Robert Dole (R-Kan.) said that Mitchell was "a man of integrity and great character and honesty" and that he would "obviously" vote to confirm him if he were nominated. But Dole also made it clear that he did not think Mitchell should continue in the Senate once the nomination was announced. That, he said, would be "a little sticky."[34]

Mitchell had a growing concern that Dole was correct. If he stayed in the Senate through his confirmation hearings and delayed taking his seat on the Court until the end of the Senate term, he could both fuel opposition to his nomination and weaken his leadership position in the Senate. The day after the *Face the Nation* appearance, Mitchell called the White House and asked to speak with the president. At a meeting that evening, Clinton asked Mitchell to serve on the Court, but Mitchell said that he felt he could best serve the president by staying in the Senate and concentrating on health care (an issue he had long championed) and other important issues on the president's agenda. Clinton called Mitchell back the next morning to see if that was still what he wanted to do. Mitchell said yes. Early that afternoon, Clinton and Mitchell appeared before reporters at the White House. "I've asked President Clinton not to consider me for nomination to the vacancy on the Supreme Court to be created by Justice Blackmun's retirement," Mitchell said, explaining his commitment to health care reform and the rest of the president's agenda.[35] The president then thanked Mitchell "for his willingness to forgo a great personal opportunity in anticipation of an enormous struggle with an uncertain result for a goal that is worth the careers of many of us."[36]

The formal search for a nominee had begun only the day before. A group consisting of White House Counsel Lloyd Cutler, White House Chief of Staff Thomas F. McLarty III, Congressional Liaison Director Pat Griffin, Counselor to the President David Gergen, and the Senior Advisers Bruce Lindsey and George Stephanopoulos met at the White House for what was billed as a preliminary "procedural" meeting to chart the selection process, but the group seemed to assume that Mitchell would be the nominee.[37] Now, instead of moving swiftly with a nomination, as they had hoped, they embarked on a full-fledged search. Clinton met with his advisers on April 15 to discuss the search. Lloyd Cutler, who led the search, predicted that the president would have a nominee "within a couple of weeks."[38]

As the search moved forward, the White House felt pressure to appoint a minority justice to the Court. A Hispanic candidate would make good political sense; no Hispanic had ever been appointed to the Supreme Court, and both parties were courting Hispanic votes in important electoral states such as California, Texas, and Florida. But there were few Hispanics with enough judicial experience to merit appointment. Clinton seriously considered José Cabranes, a U.S. district court judge from Connecticut, but passed him over because he was too conservative. (Clinton instead took advantage of an opening on the U.S. Court of Appeals for the Second Circuit to promote him to appellate judge.)

Clinton very much wanted to nominate Richard Arnold, a Court of Appeals judge for the Eighth Circuit. Arnold was brilliant. He had graduated first in his class at both Yale College and Harvard Law School and clerked at the Supreme Court for Justice William Brennan Jr. He had the "big heart" that Clinton said he wanted in a Supreme Court nominee. He also had the potential to forge an important leadership role on the Court as a consensus builder. Arnold had a reputation for "warm, unpretentious humanity and gentle persuasiveness."[39] William Brennan also noted Arnold's "warmth and generosity of spirit," adding that those qualities had "made him enormously popular and beloved." Arnold was "undoubtedly among the most gifted members of the federal judiciary," Brennan said, and he applauded Arnold's "eloquent and passionate" defense of fundamental rights.[40]

Arnold, however, had two problems. First, he came from Arkansas and was a longtime friend of Clinton. Nominating him could smack of cronyism, especially at a time when Clinton's Arkansas dealings—including Whitewater—dominated the news. Second, the fifty-eight-year-old Arnold had a health problem. He had been diagnosed nineteen years earlier with a form of cancer known as non-Hodgkin's lymphoma and had recently been treated with radiation and precautionary chemotherapy for a lymphoma in his mouth. The illness was not life threatening, but Clinton feared that ill health might undermine Arnold's role on the Court and that he might not be able to serve a long term. White House officials reportedly asked independent doctors to review Arnold's medical records in order to give some assurance that he could serve on the court for fifteen years. When the doctors did not give such assurances, Clinton decided not to pick him (prompting some charges of discrimination against those with cancer).[41]

Clinton also seriously considered Interior Secretary Bruce Babbitt (a finalist when Clinton picked Ginsburg the year before). Babbitt had the political experience and leadership skills that Clinton found so appealing, but his liberal reputation would make him a target of conservative Republicans, and several western senators who were angered by his efforts to raise grazing fees on ranchers promised a fight. The president was loathe to waste his limited political capital on a divisive confirmation battle, even though aides assured him that Babbitt would eventually win confirmation. Replacing Babbitt at the Interior Department would also be problematic. The media speculated for several days that Clinton had settled on Babbitt.

Around midnight on May 11 Clinton woke Babbitt up with a telephone call and summoned him to the White House. Babbitt arrived around 12:30 A.M. He and the president watched the end of the Phoenix Suns' basketball game on television, ate apple pie, drank coffee, and talked for three hours. They talked about health care, the Interior Department, and the possibility of naming Babbitt to the Supreme Court. Clinton went over the pros and cons of such a move and, as Babbitt later recalled, "worried out loud about whether or not it made sense to do a sort of double play and have two sets of confirmations," one for Babbitt and one for his replacement at the Interior Department. Clinton "clearly hadn't made a decision," Babbitt added, and he left the White House not knowing what the president would do. Clinton called him the next afternoon and said, "Look, I've thought about this a lot. I want to keep you at the Interior Department."[42]

The president nominated Stephen Breyer the next day. His "nanny problem" was all but forgotten (the IRS had ruled that he was not liable for his failure to pay taxes), and Breyer fit the mold that Clinton was looking for. He was smart (he graduated from Stanford University and Harvard Law School with additional studies at Oxford University), he had clerked for Justice Arthur M. Goldberg, and he had taught at Harvard Law while also serving as an appeals court judge. He was moderate (with a probusiness stance on antitrust and regulatory issues). He had had real-world political experience as an aide to Senator Edward Kennedy (D-Mass.) in 1974–75 and had served as chief counsel of the Senate Judiciary Committee in 1979–80. There he had practiced the art of consensus building and was highly regarded by senators from both ends of the ideological spectrum. Observers called Breyer "gregarious and charming" and "a highly effective small-group politician who inspires genuine affection."[43]

Ironically, some sources said that Clinton had passed over Breyer in 1993 because he was not impressed by him at a luncheon meeting the two had to discuss the possibility of an appointment. A source familiar with the meeting said that the meeting was "pleasant enough but just didn't set sparks flying."[44] According to the media, Clinton found Breyer "uncharming."[45] But many later noted that Breyer had been in pain during the meeting from a recent bicycle accident, in which he had broken a rib. Before joining the president, Breyer was stretched out on the floor of White House Counsel Bernard Nussbaum's office in an attempt to relieve the pain.[46] Thus, if Clinton found Breyer stiff at the meeting, it may have had more to do with his injury than his personality. Others speculated that Clinton chose Ginsburg over Breyer not because of Breyer's demeanor at their meeting but because Ginsburg had a more engaging life story, which would make the selling of the nominee easier and the appointment more dramatic.[47]

The media made much of the fact that Breyer never seemed to be Clinton's first choice. Some, such as National Public Radio's Nina Totenberg, noted that the president seemed unenthusiastic when announcing Breyer's nomination and that he seemed to apply the most enthusiastic praise for those he had not chosen: Arnold and Babbitt.[48] Mishaps in the next couple of days reinforced the image of White House indifference to Breyer. Clinton hastily announced the nomination late on Friday, May 13, without Breyer at his side (an anomaly in recent years, when presidents and nominees have appeared together for such announcements). When Breyer flew to Washington on Sunday, no one from the White House met him. He hailed a cab, but a White House van which had gone to the wrong gate finally showed up for him. Breyer and his family spent the night at the White House. He and the president were scheduled to go jogging together the next morning, but Clinton started the jog without him. Finally, two miles into his three-mile jog, Clinton stopped and waited for Breyer to arrive in a Secret Service vehicle. They then jogged back to the White House together and performed stretching exercises on the White House lawn for the benefit of cameras.[49]

Later in the day, Clinton formally introduced Breyer in a Rose Garden ceremony. The only voices of criticism were from liberal senator Howard Metzenbaum of Ohio and consumer activist Ralph Nader. Both criticized

Breyer's support of big business. (In the end, Metzenbaum voted for Breyer, with all nine negative Senate votes coming from Republicans.)

Throughout the selection process, President Clinton played a major role in the search. He insisted on sitting in on the meetings of his selection team, and in the end the decision was his. "This is not an issue I can defer to aides," he told reporters during the search.[50] The media criticized Clinton for his delay and indecision in naming both Ginsburg and Breyer, yet the two nominations did much to diffuse a politicized confirmation process. In fact, much of the criticism focused on public perceptions created by the White House rather than the selection process itself. For instance, when Mitchell withdrew from consideration, Lloyd Cutler told reporters that the president would have a nominee within a couple of weeks. The search took twice that long. Later, Clinton set a self-imposed deadline for making an announcement and then broke it: he promised an announcement by May 12, but had to come before reporters and say that he needed more time.[51] Some criticized the White House for carrying on such a public search: Stuart Taylor of the *Legal Times,* for example, wrote, "I find it mystifying why [the White House finds] it necessary to leak a new name every day or so. . . . It contributes to this portrait of irresolution."[52]

Despite these criticisms, Clinton did avoid confirmation battles and, as a result, was able to make good on his campaign promise to take politics out of the Supreme Court confirmation process. After the Bork defeat in 1987, President Reagan lamented that "the process of confirming a Supreme Court justice has been reduced to a political, partisan struggle."[53] What he failed to add was that he was largely responsible for that through his politicization of the initial selection process for federal judges. Reagan, who faced little opposition to his judicial nominees during his first six years in office, ultimately provoked opposition by consistently nominating highly ideological candidates.[54]

The point here is not that Clinton was above making ideological appointments. To a large extent, Clinton was forced to nominate centrist candidates because of circumstances beyond his control. (Some suggest that the Ginsburg and Breyer selections were part of a calculated move by Clinton "to reposition and redefine the president within the moderate wing of his party" as part of his reelection strategy.[55] Thus, their selections may have been very politically motivated, even though they did not provoke political fights.) The point to be made is that, when presidents do nominate, for whatever reason, high-quality, moderate candidates, they effectively preclude a highly politicized confirmation fight. If it is true that the initial selection process can alleviate the politicization of the confirmation process, then perhaps reformers should be looking more at the selection (rather than the confirmation) process. Indeed, the selection of highly qualified, ideologically moderate candidates would promote precisely those goals that the Twentieth Century Fund Task Force on Judicial Selection advocated: the depoliticization of the confirmation process and heightened public respect for the "objectivity" of the Court.

David Gergen, counselor to President Clinton, has advocated just such a position. Gergen, who played a direct role in Clinton's search for Supreme Court nominees, had previously served in key positions in the Republican administrations of Ronald Reagan, Gerald Ford, and Richard Nixon. In the *Nightline* "Town Hall Meeting" in the wake of the Clarence Thomas hearings, Gergen suggested genuine consultation between the president and the Senate over the selection of nominees in order to select a nominee who would be acceptable to all sides.[56]

Likewise, Senator Paul Simon (D-Ill.) urged presidents to take seriously the "advice" part of the "advice and consent clause" of the Constitution.[57] "The president should ask senators and others for suggestions and list several names as possibilities in conversations with senators," Simon writes. "It would not take a president long to determine which potential nominees would face difficulty with confirmation if that is done. It is not asking too much to require the president to follow the Constitution." Simon also urges presidents to take their time in selecting nominees. He notes that "generally presidents have served the nation best by taking time to look over the legal landscape carefully" and suggests a search of thirty to sixty days for a nominee. (George Bush chose Clarence Thomas in just five days. Clinton took eighty-eight days to choose Ginsburg and thirty-six to choose Breyer.) Stephen Carter's proposal to require a higher threshold vote for confirmation is yet another reform proposal aimed at the selection process. Again, the goal is to force the president to nominate a consensus candidate. Consensus nominees are even more important since the 1994 midterm elections, which again brought about divided government.

Politics can never be entirely removed from the selection and confirmation of Supreme Court justices, nor should it be. Chief Justice John Marshall, reflecting the view that "law" and "politics" are sharply distinct entities, once wrote: "Judicial power, as contradistinguished from the power of the laws, has no existence. Courts are the mere instruments of the law, and can will nothing."[58]

History has shown us otherwise. Marshall himself was a judicial activist, who read the power of judicial review into the Constitution. Throughout our history, the Supreme Court has willed a great deal. "Judges are human [and] politics is a reflection of human nature."[59] Thus, it is only fitting that

nominees who, if confirmed, will enjoy life tenure and possess broad policymaking powers, be subjected to exacting public and political scrutiny.
But, as Senator Bill Bradley (D-N.J.) so aptly noted: "The system works only
as long as all the players respect the process."[60] Respecting the process starts
in the White House. By setting an example of moderation and a search for
quality, presidents can do much to alleviate the faults in our confirmation
process. Perhaps, then, judges will reflect the better side of human nature.

Little has changed since this book first went to press. Witness, for example, the events of 1997. The Free Congress Foundation's Judicial Selection Monitoring Project—a coalition of more than 250 conservative profamily, small business, victims' rights, and law-enforcement organizations—announced early that year that it was time to stand up to "judicial activism." In a letter sent to President Bill Clinton and all 100 U.S. senators on January 27, the project said that it would "promote judicial restraint and fight judicial activism with whatever tools and resources are legitimately at our disposal."[1]

Less than two months later, House Majority Whip Tom DeLay (R-Tex.) went a step further and said that congressional Republicans would begin efforts to impeach liberal federal judges. "As part of our conservative efforts against judicial activism, we are going after judges," he told the *Washington Times*.[2] By May 1997, even the relatively moderate chairman of the Senate Judiciary Committee, Orrin Hatch (R-Utah), bowed to pressure from his more conservative Republican colleagues and vowed that he would not "stand by to see judicial activists named to the federal bench."[3]

By taking the offense, Republicans sought to limit President Clinton's ability to use his appointment power to influence judicial policymaking through the appointment of liberal judges during his second term. In so doing, Republicans urged strict scrutiny of his lower federal court nominees.[4] Ironically, early studies suggest that Clinton's first-term appointees to both the U.S. Supreme Court and the lower federal courts have had a moderate voting record on the bench.[5] Both of Clinton's Supreme Court appointees—Ruth Bader Ginsburg and Stephen Breyer—were middle-of-the-road, consensus nominees who had enjoyed broad support from both sides of the political aisle, and the same was true of many of the 200 other judges he appointed to the lower federal bench during his first term.

Consensus nominees became an even more important factor in secur-ing confirmation after the 1994 midterm elections, which brought back divided government. In the last two years of his first term, Clinton sought an unusual degree of consultation with the Republican-controlled Senate Judiciary Committee in an effort to win its support for his lower court nominees. Indeed, Clinton seemed more interested in creating a demo-graphically representative judiciary—appointing more women and minorities than any of his predecessors had done—than in creating an ide-ologically rigid one.[6] Even the Judicial Selection Monitoring Project con-ceded that most of Clinton's nominees had enjoyed Republican support, noting that the Senate had confirmed 99 percent of his first-term judicial nominations without a roll call vote. But, the project warned, "grass-roots America . . . demands better."[7] Now conservative interest groups were employing many of the tactics once used by liberals against conservative nominees, including the use of "newsletters, mass mailings, media blitzes, and the World Wide Web" to pressure senators to vote against liberal nom-inees.[8]

During the 1996 presidential election, Republicans tried to make the specter of liberal judicial activism a major campaign theme. During his race for the Republican nomination, Pat Buchanan lashed out at "judicial dictatorship" and accused federal judges of protecting "criminals, atheists, homosexuals, flag burners, illegal aliens (including terrorists), convicts, and pornographers."[9] Republican nominee Bob Dole likewise blasted Clinton's judicial appointees, calling them a "team of liberal leniency," but the issue did not seem to strike a chord with most voters.[10]

After Clinton's reelection, conservative Republicans backed up their rhetoric about blocking activist nominees by orchestrating a major slow-down of the confirmation of lower federal court judges. In the first four months of Clinton's second term, the Senate confirmed only two federal judges, leaving some ninety-nine slots unfilled.[11] Republicans countered that Clinton was slow to nominate judges and that he was responsible for many of the vacancies. For example, during the last session of the 104th Congress, sixty-five slots on the federal judiciary were left vacant. Clinton, however, had nominated replacements for only twenty-one of the slots (of which the Senate confirmed seventeen).[12]

The continued squabbling over judicial appointments is a reminder of the important policymaking role that federal judges play. As I have argued, presidents now use judicial appointments as part of their growing arsenal of resources for influencing public policy. The selling of Supreme Court nominees (as well as the selling of lower federal court nominees) is part of a broader trend toward a White House–centered system of policy-making. In fact, this book is as much about presidential power and its interplay with congressional and interest group power as it is a book about the judiciary.

One change that has taken place since the first publication of this book involves a tug-of-war between congressional and interest group power. In 1947, the Republican-controlled Senate Judiciary Committee invited the American Bar Association to advise it on the qualifications of judicial nominees. As discussed in Chapter 7, the American Bar Association had a distinctly conservative bent in those days. Therefore, it was not surprising that Republicans at both ends of Capitol Hill embraced the ABA's imprimatur of nominees in the 1940s and 1950s. In 1956, Republican President Dwight Eisenhower expanded the ABA's role by formalizing a relationship between the ABA and the Justice Department in order to rate prospective nominees before they were chosen by the president. But by the 1980s, the ideological makeup of the ABA was changing, and Republicans began to distance themselves from their former ally. Republican presidents Ronald Reagan and George Bush both had run-ins with the ABA over its ratings of their nominees, and when Republicans regained control of the Senate in 1994 the new majority on the Judiciary Committee also expressed its displeasure with the ABA. The tension between the ABA and the Republican-controlled Judiciary Committee came to a head in February 1997, when Chairman Hatch severed the ABA's official relationship with the committee. The ABA, he said, was "a political interest group" that should no longer advise the Senate on the qualifications of judicial nominees.[13] Democrat Bill Clinton, on the other hand, continued to seek the advice of the ABA in rating prospective nominees.

Political expediency explains much of how participants in the Supreme Court appointment process act. Just as Republicans once supported ABA ratings and now do not, so Democrats once supported the "Borking" of conservative nominees but now bemoan the "confirmation mess" and urge a kinder, gentler treatment of nominees. The Republican rallying-cry against judicial activism in 1997 was exactly the same rallying-cry used in 1930 by liberal Democrats who decried the judicial activism of conservative judges who read economic rights into the Constitution. Political expediency explains the defeat of Supreme Court nominee John Rutledge in 1789 just as much as it explains the defeat of Robert Bork in 1987. As I stated in Chapter 1, the Supreme Court appointment process is a political process shaped by changing political dynamics and reflecting contemporaneous concerns and balances of power. In tracing those changing dynamics and balances of power, we are reminded that the more things change, the more they stay the same.

NOTES

Preface and Acknowledgments

1. To a certain extent there was de facto "popular" election of U.S. Senators prior to the Seventeenth Amendment through the use of public canvassing. In other words, a "candidate" for the U.S. Senate would campaign in his state for the election of a certain slate of state legislators, who were, in turn, pledged to vote for the Senate candidate if elected. This practice had its origins in the 1830s but reached its zenith in the early 1900s. Popular accountability remained, at best, indirect. William H. Riker, "The Senate and American Federalism," *American Political Science Review* 49 (1955): 463–64.

Introduction

1. *Roe v. Wade*, 410 U.S. 113 (1973); *Bowers v. Hardwick*, 478 U.S. 186 (1986).

2. Linda Greenhouse, "Justice Blackmun's Odyssey: From Moderate to a Liberal," *New York Times*, Apr. 7, 1994.

3. *Planned Parenthood of Southeastern Pennsylvania v. Casey*, 112 S.Ct. 2791 (1992), 2854–55.

4. This number includes Ronald Reagan's nomination of Douglas Ginsburg in 1987. Reagan had publicly announced the nomination, and Ginsburg had already begun meeting with senators on Capitol Hill in anticipation of confirmation hearings, when Ginsburg withdrew. However, Reagan had not formally transmitted Ginsburg's nomination to the Senate before the withdrawal. The number also includes renominations of the same individual for the same post (William Patterson, Edward King, and Stanley Matthews).

5. In addition, John Rutledge, whose nomination was rejected by the Senate, sat briefly on the Court as a temporary "recess appointment," which did not require Senate confirmation.

Four individuals were confirmed twice, first as associate justice and then as chief justice: Edward White, Charles Evans Hughes, Harlan Fiske Stone, and William Rehnquist. Thus, Stephen Breyer became the 108th individual to sit on the Court when the Senate confirmed his nomination in 1994.

6. These were Robert H. Harrison in 1789, William Cushing in 1796, John Jay in

1800, Levi Lincoln in 1811, John Quincy Adams in 1811, William Smith in 1837, and Roscoe Conkling in 1882.

7. George Washington withdrew his nomination of William Paterson in 1783 because of a technicality. Washington resubmitted the Paterson nomination a month later, and the Senate unanimously confirmed him. Lyndon Johnson withdrew his nomination of Homer Thornberry in 1968 because the anticipated vacancy of Abe Fortas's associate justice seat failed to materialize. Neither the Paterson nor the Thornberry withdrawals took place because of Senate opposition to these nominees.

8. P. S. Ruckman Jr., "The Supreme Court, Critical Nominations, and the Senate Confirmation Process," *Journal of Politics* 55 (Aug. 1993): 794. The percentage is based on 120 successful nominations out of the entire 149 Supreme Court nominations that presidents have made. If the Paterson and Thornberry nominations are not included (see n. 7), the success rate rises slightly to 81.6 percent (120 successful nominations out of 147).

9. Tom Charles Huston to President Richard Nixon, Mar. 25, 1969, pp. 1, and 2, in WHCF ExFG 50, the Judicial Branch (1969–1970), Box 1, White House Central Files, FG 50, Nixon Presidential Materials Project, College Park, Md. (hereafter NPMP). My thanks to Professor Sheldon Goldman for locating this memo and sharing a copy with me. Excerpts from the memo were first published in Sheldon Goldman, "The Bush Imprint on the Judiciary: Carrying on a Tradition," *Judicature* 74 (Apr.–May 1991): 295.

Another copy of the memo, apparently with handwritten comments on it by President Nixon, was withdrawn from Nixon's public papers at the National Archives NPMP at the request of the former president. See John Anthony Maltese, "The Selling of Clement Haynsworth: Politics and the Confirmation of Supreme Court Justices," *Judicature* 72 (Apr.–May 1989): 343.

10. Houston to Nixon, Mar. 25, 1969, p. 7, in WHCF ExFG 50, the Judicial Branch (1969–1970), Box 1, White House Central Files, FG 50, NPMP.

11. John D. Ehrlichman to Staff Secretary, Mar. 27, 1969, in News Summaries, Mar. 1969, Box 30, President's Office Files, NPMP.

12. "The Electoral Count," *New York Times*, Jan. 30, 1881.

13. Unelected presidents are those who assumed office after the death or resignation of the previous president. Nominations counted here are only those made during a president's unelected term. For instance, Harry Truman's nominations of Burton and Vinson are counted (since he made them while serving as an unelected president), but his nominations of Clark and Minton (made after he was elected in 1948) are not.

14. These figures include the nominations made by both John Tyler and Andrew Johnson. If Tyler and Johnson are excluded, presidents made twenty-six nominations when the opposition party controlled the Senate, with a success rate of 65.4 percent. (Figures excluding Tyler and Johnson also appear in subsequent notes.)

As a Democrat representing the state of Tennessee in the U.S. Senate, Johnson (alone among southern members of Congress) opposed secession and fought to preserve the Union. He thus became a hero to northern Republicans, who (calling themselves the National Union party) nominated him as Abraham Lincoln's running mate in the 1864 election. He became president after Lincoln's assassination in 1865 but fought bitterly throughout his term with the Republican majority in Congress (who tried, unsuccessfully, to remove him from office through impeachment).

Tyler left the Democratic party to join the Whigs; he served as a Whig senator before being nominated by the Whig party to run as vice president with William Henry Harrison in 1836. As a southerner, he disagreed with many of the policy positions of northern Whigs but, like Johnson, was chosen to balance the ticket. Tyler became president when Harrison died. When Tyler refused to act as a party pawn, all of Harrison's cabinet resigned in protest. Tyler fought bitterly with the Whig-controlled Congress, and it soon became clear that Tyler was a Whig in name only. He ultimately disassociated himself from the party.

15. *Terminal year* signifies the final year that a president served in office. Thus, the last year of a president's term is not considered terminal if he was elected for another term. Presidents made three of these twenty-five nominations just prior to their terminal year (Taney, Barbour, and Pitney), but Senate action took place during their terminal year.

16. Excluding Tyler and Johnson, the following percentages hold: unelected presidents facing divided government made five nominations, with a success rate of 40 percent; terminal-year presidents facing divided government made seven nominations, with a success rate of 28.6 percent; unelected presidents in their terminal year made six nominations without ever achieving success; and presidents made only two nominations when all three of these weak situations occurred—neither was successful.

17. Bruce A. Ackerman, "Transformative Appointments," *Harvard Law Review* 101 (1988): 1164. See also Jeffrey A. Segal, Charles M. Cameron, and Albert D. Cover, "A Spatial Model of Roll Call Voting: Senators, Constituents, Presidents, and Interest Groups in Supreme Court Confirmations," *American Journal of Political Science* 36 (1992): 96.

18. Gregory A. Caldeira and John R. Wright, "Lobbying for Justice: The Rise of Organized Conflict in the Politics of Federal Judgeships," paper prepared for the 1990 annual meeting of the American Political Science Association, 17.

19. "NOW to Fight Thomas's Confirmation," *Washington Post*, July 6, 1991.

20. David M. O'Brien, *Judicial Roulette* (New York: Priority Press, 1988), 9. Two of the ten members of the task force, Joseph A. Califano Jr. and Philip B. Kurland, dissented from the conclusions drawn in the report.

21. Ibid., 11, 10.

22. Henry Paul Monaghan, "The Confirmation Process: Law or Politics?" *Harvard Law Review* 101 (Apr. 1988): 1202.

23. Joel B. Grossman and Stephen L. Wasby, "The Senate and Supreme Court Nominations: Some Reflections," *Duke Law Journal* 1972: 560, n. 9.

24. James E. Gauch, "The Intended Role of the Senate in Supreme Court Appointments," *University of Chicago Law Review* 56 (1989): 337–38.

25. Eugene W. Hickok Jr., "Judicial Selection: The Political Roots of Advice and Consent," in *Judicial Selection: Merit, Ideology, and Politics* (Washington, D.C.: National Legal Center for the Public Interest, 1990), 10.

CHAPTER ONE. The President versus the Senate

1. President Nixon to Senator William B. Saxbe, Mar. 31, 1970, reprinted in the *New York Times*, Apr. 2, 1970. Emphasis added.

2. *Congressional Record* 116 (Apr. 2, 1970): 10180.

3. Robert Griffin, "The Senate's Role of Advice and Consent to Judicial Nomina-

tions: The Broad Role," *Prospectus: A Journal of Law Reform* 2 (Apr. 1969): 285–303; reprinted as "The Historical Context for Advice and Consent," *Congressional Record* 116 (Apr. 2, 1970): 10183.

4. *Congressional Record* 116 (Apr. 2, 1970): 10184.

5. Ibid., 10184–85.

6. Peter G. Fish, "Spite Nominations to the United States Supreme Court," *Kentucky Law Journal* 77 (1988–89): 545; Henry J. Abraham, *Justices and Presidents: A Political History of Appointments to the Supreme Court*, 3d ed. (New York: Oxford University Press, 1992), 15–16.

7. Richard Harris, *Decision* (New York: Dutton, 1971), 11.

8. Charles Colson, interview with author, July 11, 1989, Atlanta, Ga.

9. Jeb Stuart Magruder, *An American Life: One Man's Road to Watergate* (New York: Atheneum, 1974), 110.

10. J. Woodford Howard, "Commentary on the Selection of Federal Judges," *Kentucky Law Journal* 77 (1988–89): 619.

11. Colson interview, July 11, 1989.

12. G. Harrold Carswell, speech before a meeting of the American Legion, Aug. 2, 1949; text reprinted in U.S. Senate, Committee on the Judiciary, *Hearings on the Nomination of George Harrold Carswell*, 91 Cong. 2 sess. (1970), 22–23.

13. See Abraham, *Justices and Presidents*, 16.

14. Daily News Summary (nd), 4, in News Summaries, Feb. 1970, Box 31, President's Office Files, NPMP.

15. Daily News Summary (nd), 3. News Summaries, Mar. 1970, Box 31, President's Office Files, NPMP.

16. Magruder, *An American Life*, 111.

17. Confidential staff memorandum for Senator Charles Mathias, Nov. 5, 1969; quoted in Harris, *Decision*, 32–33.

18. Harris, *Decision*, 33.

19. Magruder, *An American Life*, 110.

20. John Ehrlichman, *Witness to Power* (New York: Simon and Schuster, 1982), 126; see also John Massaro, *Supremely Political* (Albany: SUNY Press, 1990), 116.

21. Ronald Ziegler, interview with author, Nov. 4, 1988, Alexandria, Va.

22. Herbert S. Parmet, *Richard Nixon and His America* (Boston: Little, Brown, 1990), 608. See also Raymond Price, *With Nixon* (New York: Viking, 1977), 199–200.

23. Abraham, *Justices and Presidents*, 16–17.

24. Magruder, *An American Life*, 110.

25. John R. Brown III to Herbert Klein, Apr. 2, 1970, CF FG 51 / A, Supreme Court, 1969–70, Box 22, White House Central Files, NPMP.

26. Ibid.

27. Jeb Stuart Magruder to President Nixon, Apr. 8, 1970, CF FG 51 / A, Supreme Court (1969–70), Box 22, White House Central Files, NPMP.

28. Charles Colson, oral history interview with Frederick J. Graboske, June 15, 1988, at Mr. Colson's office in Reston, Va., p. 46; transcript in NPMP.

29. William Safire, *Before the Fall: An Inside View of the Pre-Watergate White House* (New York: Doubleday, 1975), 486.

30. Colson, oral history interview, June 15, 1988, pp. 17, 20.

31. Magruder, *An American Life*, 111.

32. Stephen E. Ambrose, *Nixon: The Triumph of a Politician (1962–1972)* (New York: Simon and Schuster, 1989), 337.

33. Massaro, *Supremely Political,* 118.

34. Colson interview, July 11, 1989.

35. For a comprehensive discussion of the framers' debate on qualifications, see Michael Nelson, "Qualifications for President," in *Inventing the American Presidency,* ed. Thomas E. Cronin (Lawrence: University Press of Kansas, 1989).

36. Grossman and Wasby, "Senate and Supreme Court Nominations," 559, n. 8.

37. *Congressional Record* 137 (Oct. 15, 1991): 14639.

38. David Broder, "A Way Out of This Mess," *Washington Post,* Oct. 13, 1991; David Gergen, on ABC News, *Nightline,* "A Town Hall Meeting: A Process Run Amok—Can It Be Fixed?" Oct. 16, 1991.

39. Colson interview, July 11, 1989.

40. Alexander Hamilton, "Federalist 76," in *The Federalist Papers,* ed. Clinton Rossiter (New York: Mentor, 1961), 457.

41. Monaghan, "Confirmation Process," 1205. See also Hickok, "Judicial Selection," 9–10.

42. Abraham, *Justices and Presidents,* 18–19; Charles L. Black Jr., "A Note on Senatorial Consideration of Supreme Court Nominees," *Yale Law Journal* 79 (1970): 657; Grossman and Wasby, "Senate and Supreme Court Nominations," 560–61; Albert P. Melone, "The Senate's Confirmation Role in Supreme Court Nominations and the Politics of Ideology versus Impartiality," *Judicature* 75 (Aug.–Sept. 1991): 70.

43. Richard M. Pious, *The American Presidency* (New York: Basic Books, 1979), 22.

44. Hickock, "Judicial Selection," 6.

45. Gauch, "Intended Role of the Senate," 346–50.

46. Joseph P. Harris, *The Advice and Consent of the Senate* (Berkeley: University of California Press, 1953), 20–24; Gauch, "Intended Role of the Senate," 341–42.

47. Gauch, "Intended Role of the Senate," 354.

48. For instance, Tench Coxe, quoted in ibid., 356.

49. W. W. Abbot, ed., *The Papers of George Washington* (Charlottesville: University Press of Virginia, 1989), 401.

50. "The Senate at Its Worst," *New York Herald Tribune,* Feb. 14, 1930.

51. Quoted in "Senate Battles All Day over Hughes Nomination," *New York Times,* Feb. 13, 1930.

52. Quoted in *Congressional Record* 137 (Oct. 15, 1991): 14640.

53. Bruce Fein, "A Circumscribed Senate Confirmation Role," *Harvard Law Review* 102 (1989): 672; William Bradford Reynolds, "The Confirmation Process: Too Much Advice and Too Little Consent," *Judicature* 75 (Aug.–Sept. 1991): 80.

CHAPTER TWO. In the Beginning

1. Article III of the United States Constitution does not set the size of the Supreme Court. This power is left to Congress, which originally set the size of the Court at six in the Judiciary Act of 1789. Congress has passed legislation changing the size of the Court seven times since then: to five in 1801, back to six in 1802, to seven in 1807, to nine in 1837, to ten in 1863, to seven in 1865, and back to nine in 1869. See Elder Witt, ed., *CQ Guide to the Supreme Court* (Washington, D.C.: CQ Press, 1979), 664–65.

2. Richard Barry, *Mr. Rutledge of South Carolina* (New York: Duell, Sloan, and Pearce, 1942), 351.

3. See, for instance, "Letter from an Anonymous Correspondent," *Independent Chronicle*, July 12, 1788, Philadelphia, Pa., and "'Spectator' to John W. Allen," *Massachusetts Gazette*, July 29, 1788, Boston, reprinted in Maeva Marcus and James R. Perry, eds., *The Documentary History of the Supreme Court of the United States, 1789–1800*, vol. 1, *Commentaries on Appointments and Proceedings* (New York: Columbia University Press, 1985), 601–3; hereafter cited as *DH*. These volumes are an extraordinary collection of primary documents relating to the early Supreme Court and are the best single source for information about the first seventeen nominations for the Supreme Court.

4. John Brown Cutting, an aquaintance of both Adams and Thomas Jefferson, wrote Jefferson on Oct. 5, 1788 that Adams had "intimated that the office of Chief-Justice wou'd not be acceptable to him." In *DH*, 604.

5. Copies of many of these letters are found in *DH*.

6. Barry, *Mr. Rutledge*, 351.

7. Abraham, *Justices and Presidents*, 71–72.

8. For brief biographies of these nominees, see *DH*, 3–8, 15–18, 24–27, 31–33, 44–48, 54–56; see also Abraham, *Justices and Presidents*, 72–75.

9. Abraham, *Justices and Presidents*, 73.

10. This and the following parenthetical citations refer to Marcus and Perry, *Documentary History*.

11. At that time, Supreme Court justices also presided over cases in federal appeals courts in the U.S. circuits. Each justice was assigned a circuit and traveled there to hear cases. Before the age of easy transportation, "circuit riding" proved to be an onerous task, one that Iredell feared would be worsened by a vacancy on the Court.

12. These temporary commissions are recorded in *DH*, 74–75, 96.

13. Barry, *Mr. Rutledge*, 355.

14. Charles A. Beard and Mary R. Beard, *The Beards' New Basic History of the United States*, revised and updated by William Beard (Garden City, N.Y.: Doubleday, 1968), 163.

15. News of Rutledge's appointment was first reported in Charleston on July 20. Rutledge did not formally received his commission until Aug. 12, after he had already arrived in Philadelphia to assume his new position. See *DH*, 772, n. 1. Rutledge probably did not yet know of his appointment when he made the speech, although he had clearly placed himself in the running for that office. See *DH*, 812, n. 2.

16. Barry, *Mr. Rutledge*, 355–56.

17. Culver H. Smith, *The Press, Politics, and Patronage* (Athens: University of Georgia Press, 1977), 12.

18. Richard L. Rubin, *Press, Party, and Presidency* (New York: Norton, 1981), 11.

19. Frank Luther Mott, *American Journalism* (New York: Macmillan, 1941), 122.

20. Smith, *Press, Politics, and Patronage*, 13.

21. Mott, *American Journalism*, 124.

22. Martin Mayes, *An Historical-Sociological Inquiry into Certain Phases of the Development of the Press in the United States* (Richmond: Missourian Press, 1935), 48.

23. John Tebbel, *The Compact History of the American Newspaper* (New York: Hawthorn Books, 1963), 64, 65.

24. Willard Grosvenor Bleyer, *Main Currents in the History of American Journalism* (Boston: Houghton Mifflin, 1927), 116.

25. For a copy of Randolph's letter to Rutledge, see *DH*, 95.

26. See, for instance, the letter from William Bradford Jr. to Alexander Hamilton, Aug. 4, 1795, in *DH*, 775.

27. "The Defence No. V by 'Camillus,'" *Argus* (New York), Aug. 5, 1795, in *DH*, 776.

28. "'A Real Republican' to John Rutledge," *Columbia Centinel* (Boston), Aug. 26, 1795, in *DH*, 785.

29. For instance: "John Rutledge, Vindicated: 'A South Carolinean' to Benjamin Rusell," *Columbian Centinel*, Aug. 28, 1795, and "'A Real Republican' to 'The South-Carolinean,'" *Columbian Centinel*, Sept. 5, 1795, in *DH*, 789, 795.

30. Barry, *Mr. Rutledge*, 357.

31. Ibid., 357–58.

32. *DH*, 98–99.

33. Elizabeth Gregory McPherson, "The History of Reporting the Debates and Proceedings of Congress," Ph.D. diss., University of North Carolina at Chapel Hill, 1940, 7, 16.

34. Ibid., 64. See also Gerald L. Grotta, "Philip Freneau's Crusade for Open Sessions of the U.S. Senate," *Journalism Quarterly* 48 (Winter 1971): 667–71.

35. Mott, *American Journalism*, 148.

36. *Marbury v. Madison*, 1 Cr. (5 U.S.) 137 (1803).

37. Thomas Jefferson to Attorney General Caesar Rodney, Sept. 25, 1810, in Daniel S. McHargue, "Appointments to the Supreme Court of the United States," Ph.D. diss., University of California at Los Angeles, 1949, 57.

38. Thomas Jefferson to President James Madison, Oct. 15, 1810, quoted in McHargue, "Appointments to the Supreme Court," 58.

39. McHargue, "Appointments to the Supreme Court," 63.

40. Quoted in ibid., 68.

41. Abraham, *Justices and Presidents*, 89.

42. In theory, Whigs controlled both the presidency and the Senate, but President Tyler was a Whig in name only. The result was de facto divided government.

43. Abraham, *Justices and Presidents*, 115–16.

44. McHargue, "Appointments to the Supreme Court," 129; Laurence H. Tribe, *God Save This Honorable Court: How the Choice of Supreme Court Justices Shapes Our History* (New York: Random House, 1985), 87.

45. See n. 1. If Congress reduces the size of the Court, justices are not expelled. Rather, no replacements for departing justices are appointed until the membership has been reduced to the new size.

46. See, for example, Richard D. Friedman, "The Transformation in Senate Response to Supreme Court Nominations: From Reconstruction to the Taft Administration and Beyond," *Cardozo Law Review* 5 (1983): 4.

47. John P. Frank, "The Appointment of Supreme Court Justices: Prestige, Principles and Politics," *Wisconsin Law Review 1941* (May 1941), 343.

CHAPTER THREE. The Rise of Organized Interests

1. Gregory A. Caldeira and John R. Wright embarked on a thorough study of interest group involvement in twentieth-century judicial nominations. They developed impressive data regarding all nominations since 1980 and the controversial nominations beginning with Louis Brandeis's 1916 nomination. See Caldeira and Wright, "Lobbying for Justice: The Rise of Organized Conflict"; and Caldeira and

Wright, "Lobbying for Justice: Organized Interests before the Senate, 1916–90," *Vox Pop Newsletter* 10 (1991): 4–6.

2. Scott Ainsworth and John Anthony Maltese, "National Grange Influence on the Supreme Court Confirmation of Stanley Matthews," *Social Science History* 20 (Spring 1996): 41–62.

3. Frank, "Appointment of Supreme Court Justices," 343.

4. Paul A. Freund, "Appointment of Justices: Some Historical Perspectives," *Harvard Law Review* 101 (Apr. 1988): 1157–58.

5. McHargue, "Appointments to the Supreme Court," 263.

6. Abraham, *Justices and Presidents*, 136.

7. For discussions of the Hayes-Tilden election and Matthews' role in it, see Paul L. Haworth, *The Hayes-Tilden Election* (Indianapolis: Bobbs-Merrill, 1906); Ari Hoogenboom, *The Presidency of Rutherford B. Hayes* (Lawrence: University of Kansas, 1988); C. Vann Woodward, *Reunion and Reaction: The Compromise of 1877 and the End of Reconstruction* (Boston: Little, Brown, 1951).

8. Julius Grodinsky, *Transcontinental Railway Strategy, 1869–1893* (Philadelphia: University of Pennsylvania Press, 1962), 68, n. 28.

9. "Another Corporation Judge," *Louisville Post*, Feb. 3, 1881, in National Archives, Record Group 46, Judiciary Committee, 47 Cong. NA 47B-A5 (hereafter National Archives).

10. For a discussion of the Granger cases, see Charles Warren, *The Supreme Court in United States History*, vol. 2, *1836–1918* (Boston: Little, Brown, 1926), 574–96.

11. National Grange, *Journal of Proceedings: 1881*, 23. These *Proceedings* (of which few copies survive) are housed in the U.S. Dept. of Agriculture in Beltsville, Md.

12. Editorial, *Cincinnati Grange Bulletin*, Mar. 17, 1881, in National Archives.

13. For a discussion of Matthews' opposition to the Thurman Act, see "The Supreme Court Vacancy," *New York Times*, Feb. 2, 1881. For a discussion of the Thurman Act and the events surrounding it, see Lewis H. Haney, *A Congressional History of Railways in the United States*, vol. 2, *1850 to 1887* (New York: Augustus M. Kelley, 1968), chap. 8.

14. "The Pacific Railroads to Pay Up," *New York Times*, Apr. 10, 1878.

15. *Sinking Fund Cases*, 99 U.S. 700 (1879).

16. McHargue, "Appointments to the Supreme Court," 273.

17. Ibid., 270.

18. "The Supreme Court Vacancy."

19. "Pacific Railroads to Pay Up."

20. National Grange, *Journal of Proceedings: 1881*, 22–23.

21. Editorial, *Louisville Post*, Feb. 3, 1881, in National Archives.

22. "Stanley Matthews as a Judge," *New York Times*, Jan. 27, 1881.

23. Editorial, *New York Times*, Feb. 2, 1881.

24. Editorial, *New York Times*, Feb. 9, 1881.

25. Stanley Matthews to President Rutherford Hayes, Jan. 31, 1881, in Ronald B. Jager, "Stanley Matthews for the Supreme Court," *Cincinnati Historical Society Bulletin* 38 (Fall 1980): 195.

26. President Rutherford B. Hayes to W. M. Rogers, Feb. 5, 1881, in McHargue, "Appointments to the Supreme Court," 264.

27. "Making National Laws," *New York Times*, Feb. 9, 1881.

28. "The Obnoxious Nominations," *New York Times*, Feb. 10, 1881.

29. McHargue, "Appointments to the Supreme Court," 265.

30. "The Next Administration," *New York Times*, Feb. 15, 1881.

31. "Stanley Matthews Renominated," *New York Times*, Mar. 15, 1881.

32. Abraham, *Justices and Presidents*, 137.

33. McHargue, "Appointments to the Supreme Court," 614.

34. C. Peter Magrath, *Morrison R. Waite: The Triumph of Character* (New York: Macmillan), 246 (esp. n. 42).

35. Under Hayes, Democrats controlled the Senate by a margin of forty-two to thirty-three. Under Garfield, both Democrats and Republicans had thirty-seven members. In both cases, there was one senator from neither party.

36. Leonard Rhone, master of the Pennsylvania State Grange, to the Senate Judiciary Committee, Mar. 11, 1881, in National Archives.

37. Senate Judiciary Committee File, in National Archives.

38. C. F. Huhlein to Senator Allen Thurman, Feb. 3, 1881, in National Archives.

39. Jager, "Stanley Matthews," 203.

40. "Confirmed by One Vote," *New York Times*, May 13, 1881.

41. John W. Stevenson to Senator Allan Thurman, Jan. 30, 1881, in National Archives.

42. See the probit models in Ainsworth and Maltese, "National Grange Influence on the Supreme Court Confirmation of Stanley Matthews."

43. See, for example, Robert H. Salisbury, "Parties and Pluralism," in *American Political Parties*, ed. Eric M. Uslaner (Itasca, Ill.: F. E. Peacock, 1993); Scott H. Ainsworth, "The Evolution of Interest Representation and the Emergence of Lobbyists," Ph.D. diss., Washington University, 1989.

44. Stanley Matthews to Rutherford Hayes, May 22, 1881, in Jager, "Stanley Matthews," 205.

45. *New York Sun*, quoted in Jager, "Stanley Matthews," 205.

46. "Justice Matthews' First Decision," *New York Times*, May 27, 1881.

47. Abraham, *Justices and Presidents*, 137.

48. McHargue, "Appointments to the Supreme Court," 280, 282.

49. Edward Mayes, *Lucius Q. C. Lamar: His Life, Times, and Speeches*, 2d ed. (New York: AMS Press, 1974), 534, 537. Originally published in 1896 by the Publishing House of the Methodist Episcopal Church.

50. Abraham, *Justices and Presidents*, 141.

51. Mayes, *Lucius Q. C. Lamar*, 525.

52. McHargue, "Appointments to the Supreme Court," 284.

53. Ibid., 289.

54. Abraham, *Justices and Presidents*, 149.

55. McHargue, "Appointments to the Supreme Court," 309; Abraham, *Justices and Presidents*, 150.

56. Frank, "Appointment of Supreme Court Justices," 369.

57. Abraham, *Justices and Presidents*, 151–52.

58. See, for example, Robert H. Bork, *The Tempting of America: The Political Seduction of the Law* (New York: Free Press, 1990), 51–52.

59. *Lochner v. New York*, 198 U.S. 45 (1905), 53.

60. Ibid., 75.

61. President Theodore Roosevelt to Senator Henry Cabot Lodge, July 10, 1902, in McHargue, "Appointments to the Supreme Court," 346. For a full account of the

Holmes appointment, see Liva Baker, *The Justice from Beacon Hill: The Life and Times of Oliver Wendell Holmes* (New York: Harper Collins, 1991), chap. 16.

62. David M. O'Brien, *Storm Center: The Supreme Court in American Politics*, 3d ed. (New York: Norton, 1993), 123.

63. Abraham, *Justices and Presidents*, 163.

64. Frank, "Appointment of Supreme Court Justices," 373.

65. Abraham, *Justices and Presidents*, 167.

66. McHargue, "Appointments to the Supreme Court," 364–66.

67. Ibid., 367.

68. Ibid., 366; Frank, "Appointment of Supreme Court Justices," 374–75.

69. H. B. Peckham to President William Howard Taft, Dec. 17, 1909, in Frank, "Appointment of Supreme Court Justices," 374.

70. A. B. Garretson to President William Howard Taft, Dec. 9, 1909, in Frank, "Appointments of Supreme Court Justices," 374.

71. President William Howard Taft to A. B. Garretson, Dec. 11, 1909, in McHargue, "Appointments to the Supreme Court," 366.

72. Horace H. Lurton to Secretary of War John M. Dickenson, Nov. 25, 1909, in McHargue, "Appointments to the Supreme Court," 364–66.

73. *New York Evening Post*, Feb. 19, 1912, in McHargue, "Appointments to the Supreme Court," 403–4.

74. "Taft Names Pitney for Supreme Court," *New York Times*, Feb. 20, 1912.

75. "Oppose Pitney, as Justice," *New York Times*, Feb. 22, 1912; "Pitney Opposition Wanes," *New York Times*, Mar. 1, 1912.

76. "Halt Pitney's Confirmation," *New York Times*, Mar. 9, 1912; "Fight Pitney Confirmation," *New York Times*, Mar. 12, 1912; "Many Oppose Pitney," *New York Times*, Mar. 13, 1912; "Confirm Justice Pitney," *New York Times*, Mar. 14, 1912.

77. Abraham, *Justices and Presidents*, 178–80.

78. Philippa Strum, *Louis D. Brandeis: Justice for the People* (Cambridge: Harvard University Press, 1984), 291.

79. *Muller v. Oregon*, 208 U.S. 412 (1908). See also Louis Fisher, *Constitutional Structures: Separated Powers and Federalism* (New York: McGraw-Hill, 1990), 475.

80. For an account of the Brandeis brief, see Strum, *Louis D. Brandeis*, chap. 8.

81. A. L. Todd, *Justice on Trial: The Case of Louis D. Brandeis* (Chicago: University of Chicago Press, 1964), 64–65.

82. Melvin I. Urofsky, *Louis D. Brandeis and the Progressive Tradition* (Boston: Little, Brown, 1981), 112.

83. Strum, *Louis D. Brandeis*, 291; Todd, *Justice on Trial*, 120, 37.

84. Strum, *Louis D. Brandeis*, 293.

85. Todd, *Justice on Trial*, 78, 79.

86. Ibid., 75–77.

87. Urofsky, *Louis D. Brandeis*, 106.

88. Todd, *Justice on Trial*, 71–72.

89. Ibid., 86; Urofsky, *Louis D. Brandeis*, 107.

90. Todd, *Justice on Trial*, 136.

CHAPTER FOUR. The Defeat of John J. Parker

A generous Herbert Hoover Presidential Research Grant funded my research for this chapter at the Herbert Hoover Presidential Library in West Branch, Iowa.

1. Donald J. Lisio, *Hoover, Blacks, and Lily-Whites: A Study of Southern Strategies* (Chapel Hill: University of North Carolina Press, 1985), 212.

2. Judiciary, Supreme Court of the United States, Correspondence, 1930–31, White House Central Files Box 191, HHPL.

3. Eager to make use of the new medium of radio, the Hoover campaign telegraphed Hughes to return from Paris to make a series of campaign speeches across the United States in support of Hoover, each with a nationwide radio hookup, and each delivered at night to secure the widest possible radio audience. Hughes agreed to make five such speeches. Hoover later informed Hughes that the effect of the speeches was "the most profound of any campaign in our history," adding that he heard of them "from every town and village across the continent." See Hubert Work to Charles Evans Hughes, Aug. 29, 1928; John Q. Tilson to Herbert Hoover, Sept. 25, 1928; and Herbert Hoover to Charles Evans Hughes, Nov. 1928, General Correspondence: Hughes, C&T Box 37, HHPL.

4. Merlo J. Pusey, "The Nomination of Charles Evans Hughes as Chief Justice," *Yearbook 1982* (Washington, D.C.: Supreme Court Historical Society, 1982), 98.

5. Hoover rejected this story. See Herbert Hoover to Charles Evans Hughes, Feb. 19, 1939; Hughes to Hoover, Feb. 20, 1937; Hoover to Hughes, Feb. 25, 1937; Hughes to Hoover, Mar. 8, 1937; in Hughes: Correspondence, 1934–1948, PPI Box 95, HHPL. Henry J. Abraham argues that, while Hoover and Stone were intimate friends, Hoover felt comfortable with Hughes's "jurisprudential politics" and that Hughes really was Hoover's first choice. See Abraham, *Justices and Presidents*, 201. For an overview of the differing accounts of the Hughes nomination, see Frederick Bernays Wiener, "Justice Hughes' Appointment—The Cotton Story Re-Examined"; and James M. Buchanan, "A Note on the 'Joe Cotton Story,'" both in *Yearbook: 1981* (Washington, D.C.: Supreme Court Historical Society, 1981); see also Pusey, "Nomination of Charles Evans Hughes."

6. "Fight to Bar Hughes from Bench Opened by Senator Norris," *New York Times*, Feb. 11, 1930. Senator Norris himself had predicted prompt and favorable action by the full Senate just a week earlier; see "Action on Hughes Set for Next Week," *New York Times*, Feb. 5, 1930.

7. "Fight to Bar Hughes from Bench."

8. "Senate Battles All Day over Hughes Nomination," *New York Times*, Feb. 13, 1930.

9. William G. Ross, "Participation by the Public in the Federal Judicial Selection Process," *Vanderbilt Law Review* 43 (Jan. 1990): 10.

10. "Hughes Confirmed by Senate," *New York Times*, Feb. 14, 1930.

11. Ibid.

12. "Senators Attack the Supreme Court for 'Seizing Power,'" *New York Times*, Feb. 15, 1930; "'Lawmaking' Curb on Supreme Court Is Urged in Senate," *New York World*, Feb. 15, 1930.

13. *International Organization, United Mine Workers of America v. Red Jacket Consolidated Coal and Coke Company*, 18 F.2d 839 (1927).

14. "Labor Opposes Parker on Supreme Bench," *New York Times*, Mar. 26, 1930.

15. Richard L. Watson Jr., "The Defeat of Judge Parker: A Study in Pressure Groups and Politics," *Mississippi Valley Historical Review* 50 (Sept. 1963): 216. Details about the circumstances leading up to the case can be found in 18 F.2d 840–42.

16. Watson, "Defeat of Judge Parker," 213.

17. Kenneth W. Goings, *The NAACP Comes of Age: The Defeat of Judge John J. Parker* (Bloomington: Indiana University Press, 1990), 23.

18. *Hitchman Coal & Coke Company v. Mitchell*, 245 U.S. 229 (1917).

19. Lisio, *Hoover, Blacks, and Lily-Whites*, 212.

20. Department of Justice memorandum, in Judiciary, Supreme Court of U.S., Endorsements: Parker, 3/29–4/10/30, WHCF Box 192, HHPL.

21. William Green to President Hoover, Apr. 16, 1930, in Endorsements: Parker, 4/11–4/15/30, WHCF Box 192, HHPL. *Scott v. Sandford*, 60 U.S. (19 How.) 393 (1857), commonly known as the Dred Scott case, held that the Constitution did not accord blacks the rights of citizenship.

22. William Green to George W. Norris, Apr. 4, 1930, in Endorsements: Parker, 3/29–4/10/30, WHCF Box 192, HHPL.

23. President Hoover to William Green, Apr. 14, 1930, in Endorsements: Parker, 4/11–4/15/30, WHCF Box 192, HHPL.

24. Green to Hoover, Apr. 16, 1930, in Endorsements: Parker, 4/11–4/15/30, WHCF Box 192, HHPL.

25. "Opposes Parker on Supreme Bench," *New York Times*, Mar. 26, 1930.

26. "Labor Federation Will Fight Parker," *New York Times*, Mar. 29, 1930.

27. Watson, "Defeat of Judge Parker," 217, n. 34.

28. H. W. Gross to Senator Henry Allen, Apr. 4, 1930, in Endorsements: Parker, 3/29–4/10/30, WHCF Box 192, HHPL.

29. Watson, "Defeat of Judge Parker," 217.

30. W. T. Bost, "Republicans Happy in Progress of Negroes to Democratic Party," *Greensboro Daily News*, Apr. 19, 1920; see Goings, *NAACP Comes of Age*, 24.

31. Lisio, *Hoover, Blacks, and Lily-Whites*, 209.

32. Ibid.

33. Bost, "Republicans Happy in Progress of Negroes."

34. Goings, *NAACP Comes of Age*, 24; Lisio, *Hoover, Blacks, and Lily-Whites*, 210.

35. Watson, "Defeat of Judge Parker," 220.

36. Goings, *NAACP Comes of Age*, 24–25.

37. Lisio, *Hoover, Blacks, and Lily-Whites*, 213.

38. Goings, *NAACP Comes of Age*, 48; Lisio, *Hoover, Blacks, and Lily-Whites*, 221–22; Watson, "Defeat of Judge Parker," 220–21.

39. Lisio, *Hoover, Blacks, and Lily-Whites*, 219–21.

40. Goings, *NAACP Comes of Age*, 31.

41. Ibid., 25.

42. Lisio, *Hoover, Blacks, and Lily-Whites*, 211.

43. U.S. Senate, Subcommittee of the Committee on the Judiciary, *Hearing on the Confirmation of Hon. John J. Parker to be an Associate Justice of the Supreme Court of the United States*, Apr. 5, 1930, 71 Cong. 2 sess.; reprinted in Roy M. Mersky and J. Myron Jacobstein, eds., *The Supreme Court of the United States: Hearings and Reports on Successful and Unsuccessful Nominations of Supreme Court Justices by the Senate Judiciary Committee, 1916–1975*, vol. 9 (Buffalo: William S. Hein, 1977). Green's testimony, 23–60; White's testimony, 74–79. Page numbers in text refer to either source, whose pagination is the same.

44. *Hearing on the Confirmation of Parker*, 75.

45. Ibid., 76.

46. Ibid., 77.

47. "Senators Favor Withdrawal of Parker's Name," *New York Herald Tribune,* Apr. 12, 1930, copy in Parker Clippings, WHCF Box 193, HHPL.

48. "President Is Told of Protest Made on Judge Parker," *U.S. Daily News,* Apr. 12, 1930, copy in Parker Clippings, WHCF Box 193, HHPL.

49. "Parker Clash Fails to Sway Mr. Hoover," *New York Herald Tribune,* Apr. 13, 1930, copy in Parker Clippings, WHCF Box 193, HHPL.

50. Ibid.; see also "President Is Firm in Backing Parker in Face of Attacks," *New York Times,* Apr. 13, 1930.

51. "Answer to charge that Judge Parker advocated denial of rights to colored people," in Endorsements: Parker, 3 / 29–4 / 10 / 30, WHCF Box 192, HHPL. The document is also discussed and quoted in "Fight over Parker Laid before Hoover," *New York Times,* Apr. 12, 1930.

52. *City of Richmond v. Deans,* 37 F.2d 712 (1930).

53. These cases were *Buchanan v. Warley,* 245 U.S. 60 (1917), and *Harmon v. Taylor,* 273 U.S. 668 (1926).

54. "Fight over Parker Laid before Hoover."

55. Lisio, *Hoover, Blacks, and Lily-Whites,* 222; Watson, "Defeat of Judge Parker," 222–23.

56. Robert R. Moton to Walter H. Newton, Apr. 18, 1930, in Endorsements: Parker, 4 / 16–4 / 20 / 1930, WHCF Box 192, HHPL.

57. Lisio, *Hoover, Blacks, and Lily-Whites,* 214.

58. John J. Parker to Senator Henry D. Hatfield, Apr. 19, 1930, in Endorsements: Parker, 4 / 16–4 / 20 / 1930, WHCF Box 192, HHPL.

59. Lisio, *Hoover, Blacks, and Lily-Whites,* 214–15.

60. Memo from "H," n.d., in Endorsements: Parker, 4 / 16–4 / 20 / 30, WHCF Box 192, HHPL.

61. Memo from "MHH," Apr. 18, 1930, 5:55 P.M., in Endorsements: Parker, 4 / 16–4 / 20 / 30, WHCF Box 192, HHPL.

62. For instance, "Hoover Approves Parker Quiz Plan," *New York Evening Post,* Apr. 18, 1930, copy in Parker Clippings, WHCF Box 193, HHPL.

63. "Parker Is Willing to Testify, He Says," *New York Times,* Apr. 20, 1930.

64. Watson, "Defeat of Judge Parker," 222.

65. Lisio, *Hoover, Blacks, and Lily-Whites,* 223.

66. John J. Parker to Senator Lee S. Overman, Apr. 24, 1930, in Endorsements: Parker, 4 / 21–4 / 25 / 30, WHCF Box 192, HHPL.

67. *Coppage v. Kansas,* 236 U.S. 1.

68. Donald Lisio makes much of this decision (*Hoover, Blacks, and Lily-Whites,* 223–24), although it is doubtful that the inclusion of the three omitted sentences would have made much difference. The omitted sentences read: "I have heard it charged that in accepting the nomination for Governor I said that I would resign if my election were due to a single Negro vote. That is not true, and the press accounts of my speech show no such statement. Likewise, the charge that I supported the adoption of the Suffrage Amendment to the North Carolina Constitution is absurd when it is remembered that I was only fourteen years old when it was adopted." Draft letter transmitted to the White House from New York at 1:09 P.M., Apr. 24, 1930, in Endorsements: Parker, 4 / 21–4 / 25 / 30, WHCF Box 192, HHPL.

69. Lisio, *Hoover, Blacks, and Lily-Whites,* 224.

70. "Mr. Ashurst Says Offers Were Made for Parker Votes," *U.S. Daily News,*

May 6, 1930; "Senate Votes Today on Parker; Ashurst Charge Is Withdrawn," *New York Herald Tribune,* May 7, 1930, copies in Parker Clippings, WHCF Box 193, HHPL.

71. Diary, Campbell B. Hodges, May 9, 1930, p. 157, in Hodges Papers, HHPL. See also Lisio, *Hoover, Blacks, and Lily-Whites,* 225.

72. Lisio, *Hoover, Blacks, and Lily-Whites,* 228.

73. The full text of the letter was published in "Urged Judge Parker as Political Move," *New York Times,* May 1, 1930.

74. Goings, *NAACP Comes of Age,* 48; Watson, "Defeat of Judge Parker," 221.

75. "Senate Rejects Judge Parker, 41 to 39," *New York Times,* May 8, 1930.

76. Draft statement by Herbert Hoover, May 7, 1930, in Endorsements: Parker, 5/6–5/10/30, WHCF Box 193, HHPL. In addition, the Hoover papers include an undated draft of a presidential statement to be issued in the event that Parker withdrew his nomination before a Senate vote.

77. Draft statement by Herbert Hoover, undated, in Endorsements: Parker, 5/1–5/5/30, WHCF Box 192, HHPL.

78. "Hoover Is Silent on Parker Repulse," *New York Times,* May 9, 1930; "Hoover Names O. J. Roberts for the Supreme Court," *New York Times,* May 10, 1930. Donald Lisio incorrectly asserts that Hoover made a public statement about the Parker defeat (*Hoover, Blacks, and Lily-Whites,* 228).

In a letter to the editor of the Grand Rapids, Iowa, *Gazette-Republican,* Hoover wrote: "As to my making a statement on the action of the Senate over Judge Parker, this matter has given me a great deal of concern. I had prepared such a statement, but subsequently concluded that the stronger answer would be to present a new man at once." Herbert Hoover to Verne Marshall, May 9, 1930, in Hoover, 1929–1933, Box 1, Verne Marshall Papers, HHPL.

79. Final draft of statement by Herbert Hoover, May 8, 1930, in Endorsements: Parker, 5/6–5/10/30, WHCF Box 193, HHPL.

80. Herbert Hoover, *The Memoirs of Herbert Hoover: The Cabinet and the Presidency (1920–1933)* (New York: Macmillan, 1952), 269.

81. Lisio, *Hoover, Blacks, and Lily-Whites,* 229.

82. Watson, "Defeat of Judge Parker," 234.

CHAPTER FIVE. The Defeat of Clement Haynsworth

1. Carl M. Brauer, *Presidential Transitions: Eisenhower through Reagan* (New York: Oxford University Press, 1986), 126.

2. Interview with Richard Nixon by David Frost, 1977.

3. Bruce Allen Murphy, *Fortas: The Rise and Ruin of a Supreme Court Justice* (New York: Morrow, 1988), 552.

4. For an account of the relationship between Fortas and Wolfson, see Murphy, *Fortas,* chaps. 8 and 24. For further accounts of the Fortas incident, see Abraham, *Justices and Presidents,* 290–92; Robert Shogun, *A Question of Judgment: The Fortas Case and the Struggle for the Supreme Court* (Indianapolis: Bobbs-Merrill, 1972); "The Fortas Case in Perspective," *CQ Weekly Report,* May 16, 1969, 705ff. See also Massaro, *Supremely Political,* chap. 2, for a discussion of the ill-fated Fortas nomination to be chief justice.

5. Nigel Bowles, *The White House and Capitol Hill: The Politics of Presidential Persuasion* (New York: Clarendon, 1987), 156. Murphy counts 254 contacts between Johnson and Fortas from October 1966 to December 1969; see Murphy, *Fortas,* 235, and chap. 10 generally.

6. Murphy, *Fortas*, 553–56.

7. Ibid., 559.

8. Richard Nixon, *RN: The Memoirs of Richard Nixon* (New York: Grosset and Dunlap, 1978), 418.

9. Haynsworth wrote two of the prominority opinions: *Hawkins v. North Carolina Dental Society*, 355 F.2d 718 (1966), and *Coppedge v. Franklin County Board of Education*, 404 F.2d 1177 (1968). For a complete list of the prominority cases, see U.S. Senate, Executive Report 91–12, *Nomination of Clement F. Haynsworth, Jr.*, 91 Cong. 1 sess. 17–18; reprinted in Mersky and Jacobstein, *Supreme Court*, vol. 10. The three desegregation opinions are *Griffin v. Board of Supervisors of Prince Edward County*, 322 F.2d 332 (1963), reversed, 377 U.S. 218 (1964): *Bradley v. School Board of City of Richmond, Va.*, 345 F.2d 319 (1965), reversed, 382 U.S. 103 (1965); *Bowman v. County School Board*, 382 F.2d 326 (1967), reversed, 391 U.S. 430 (1968). His dissents were to opinions on *Dillard v. School Board of the City of Charlottesville*, 308 F.2d 920 (1962); *Simkins v. Moses Cone Memorial Hospital*, 323 F.2d 959 (1963); and *Griffin v. County School Board*, 363 F.2d 206 (1966).

10. See, for instance, "Statement by Floyd B. McKissick, National Conference on Black Lawyers," and "Statement by Victor Rabinowitz, President, National Lawyers Guild," both in U.S. Senate, Committee on the Judiciary, *Hearings on the Nomination of Clement F. Haynsworth, Jr., To Be Associate Justice of the Supreme Court of the United States*, Sept. 1969, 91 Cong. 1 sess., 612–18; reprinted in Mersky and Jacobstein, *Supreme Court*, vol. 10.

11. John P. Frank, *Clement Haynsworth, the Senate, and the Supreme Court* (Charlottesville: University Press of Virginia, 1991), 19, 31.

12. "Haynsworth Statements," *CQ Weekly Report*, Sept. 19, 1969, 1718.

13. *Darlington Manufacturing Company v. National Labor Relations Board*, 325 F.2d 682 (1963).

14. Frank, *Clement Haynsworth*, 69.

15. Abraham, *Justices and Presidents*, 15.

16. Ehrlichman, *Witness to Power*, 120; see also Harry Dent, *The Prodigal South Returns to Power* (New York: Wiley, 1978), 208–9.

17. Abraham, *Justices and Presidents*, 15.

18. H. R. Haldeman, *The Haldeman Diaries: Inside the Nixon White House* (New York: Putnam's, 1994), 95.

19. Excerpts of the statement are in *CQ Weekly Report*, Sept. 12, 1969, 1687.

20. Clark Mollenhoff, *Game Plan for Disaster* (New York: Norton, 1976), 50–53.

21. Frank, *Clement Haynsworth*, 43–44, 37.

22. Haldeman, *Haldeman Diaries*, 93.

23. Ehrlichman, *Witness to Power*, 120.

24. A copy of the report is in EX FG 51 / A, 10 / 1 / 69–10 / 31 / 69, (1 of 2), in WHCF Box 1, FG 51, NPMP.

25. Mollenhoff, *Game Plan for Disaster*, 57–60.

26. Herb Klein to Ken Cole, 8 Oct. 1969, in CF FG 51 / A, Supreme Court, 1969–70, WHCF Box 22, FG 51, NPMP.

27. *Public Papers of the Presidents of the United States: Richard Nixon, 1969*, 815, 818.

28. Robert C. Odle Jr. to Jeb Stuart Magruder, Oct. 28, 1969, p. 1, in Haynsworth (2 of 3), Harry Dent Files Box 6, NPMP.

29. Ibid., 2–3.

30. "Papers Favorable to Judge Parker," Apr. 26, 1930, in Endorsements: Parker,

4/26–4/30/30, WHCF Box 192, HHPL. An example of the Hoover administration's contacts with friendly newspapers during the Parker fight can be seen in its correspondence with Verne Marshall, editor of the *Cedar Rapids Gazette* in Iowa; see, for instance, "Parker Appointment by Hoover," Verne Marshall Papers Box 14, HHPL.

31. Pat Buchanan to John Brown, Nov. 4, 1969, in EX FG 51/A, 11/1/69–12/31/69, WHCF Box 3, FG 51, NPMP.

32. Tom Huston to H. R. Haldeman, Mar. 25, 1969, in News Summaries, Mar. 1969, President's Office Files Box 30, NPMP.

33. John D. Ehrlichman to Staff Secretary, Mar. 27, 1969, in News Summaries, Mar. 1969, President's Office Files Box 30, NPMP.

34. Haldeman, *Haldeman Diaries*, 110; see also Mollenhoff, *Game Plan for Disaster*, 59.

35. Gordon S. Brownell to Harry Dent, Oct. 8, 1969, in Haynsworth (3 of 3), Harry Dent Files Box 6, NPMP.

36. Harry Dent to Ken Belieu, Oct. 17, 1969, in Haynsworth (2 of 3), Harry Dent Files Box 6, NPMP.

37. James E. Holshouser Jr. to all county and district chairmen, Oct. 25, 1960, in EX FG 51/A, 10/1/69–10/31/69 (2 of 2), WHCF Box 3, FG 51, NPMP.

38. Ronald C. Romans to All Members—Young Republican Federation of Pennsylvania, Oct. 29, 1969, in Haynsworth (2 of 3), Harry Dent Files Box 6, NPMP.

39. Dent to Belieu, Oct. 17, 1969, in Haynsworth (2 of 3), Harry Dent Files Box 6, NPMP.

40. President Nixon to Harry Dent, Oct. 21, 1969, in Haynsworth (2 of 3), Harry Dent Files Box 6, NPMP.

41. Harry Dent to John Mitchell and Bryce Harlow, Oct. 27, 1969, in Haynsworth (2 of 2), John Ehrlichman Files Box 34, NPMP.

42. Gordon S. Brownell to Harry Dent, Oct. 14, 1969, in Haynsworth (3 of 3), Harry Dent Files Box 6, NPMP. See also Dent to Belieu, Oct. 17, 1969, p. 2, in Haynsworth (2 of 3), Harry Dent Files Box 6, NPMP.

43. Jack A. Gleason to Kevin Phillips, Oct. 15, 1969, in Haynsworth (3 of 3), Harry Dent Files Box 6, NPMP.

44. Jack A. Gleason to Harry Dent, Oct. 24, 1969, p. 1, in Haynsworth (Brownell), Harry Dent Files Box 6, NPMP.

45. Louis M. Kohlmeier, *God Save This Honorable Court* (New York: Scribner's, 1972), 138.

46. Gleason to Dent, Oct. 24, 1969, in Haynsworth (Brownell), Harry Dent Files Box 6, NPMP.

47. Dent to Belieu, Oct. 17, 1969, p. 1, in Haynsworth (2 of 3), Harry Dent Files Box 6, NPMP.

48. Mollenhoff, *Game Plan for Disaster*, 59.

49. Ibid., 63.

50. H. R. Haldeman notes, meeting between President Nixon and H. R. Haldeman, Oct. 21, 1969, in Haldeman Notes: July–Dec. 1969 (Oct.–Dec. 1969, pt. 2), H. R. Haldeman Files Box 40, NPMP.

51. Harry Dent to President Nixon, Oct. 15, 1969, in Haynsworth (3 of 3), Harry Dent Files Box 6, NPMP.

52. Dent to Belieu, Oct. 17, 1969, p. 3, in Haynsworth (2 of 3), Harry Dent Files Box 6, NPMP.

53. Ibid., p. 2.

54. John C. Whitaker to Members of the Cabinet and Under-Secretaries, Oct. 28, 1969, with copy of the Mollenhoff summary attached, in EX FG 51/A, 10/1/69–10/31/69 (2 of 2), WHCF Box 3, FG 51, NPMP.

55. Ken Cole to Jeb Stuart Magruder, Oct. 22, 1969, in EX FG 51/A, 10/1/69–10/31/69 (2 of 2), WHCF Box 3, FG 51, NPMP. See also Odle to Magruder, Oct. 28, 1969, p. 3, in Haynsworth (3 of 3), Harry Dent Files Box 6, NPMP.

56. Daily News Summary, n.d., p. 5, in News Summaries, Oct. 1969, President's Office Files Box 31, NPMP. For a similar response by the president, see Alexander Butterfield to the President, Oct. 10, 1969, reprinted in Bruce Oudes, ed., *From: The President—Richard Nixon's Secret Files* (New York: Harper and Row, 1989), 60.

57. Daily News Summary, Oct. 2, 1969, p. 3, with President Nixon's handwritten margin note, in News Summaries, Oct. 1969, President's Office Files Box 31, NPMP.

58. R. W. Apple, "Nixon's Soft Voice: Herbert George Klein," *New York Times*, Nov. 26, 1968.

59. Herbert Klein, *Making It Perfectly Clear* (Garden City, N.Y.: Doubleday, 1980), chap. 6.

60. Klein to Cole, Oct. 8, 1969, in CF FG 51/A, Supreme Court, 1969–70, WHCF Box 22, FG 51, NPMP.

61. Herbert Klein to Benjamin Bradlee, Oct. 27, 1969, in EX FG 51/A, 10/1/69–10/31/69 (2 of 2), WHCF Box 3, FG 51, NPMP.

62. Benjamin Bradlee to Herbert Klein, Oct. 30, 1969, in EX FG 51/A, 10/1/69–10/31/69 (2 of 2), WHCF Box 3, FG 51, NPMP.

63. Herbert Klein to H. R. Haldeman, Nov. 11, 1969, in H. R. Haldeman I (2 of 3), Herbert Klein Files Box 1, NPMP.

64. Odle to Stuart Magruder, Oct. 28, 1969, p. 3, in Haynsworth (2 of 3), Harry Dent Files Box 6, NPMP; see also Oudes, *From: The President*, 59–60.

65. Daily News Summary, n.d., p. 2, in News Summaries, Oct. 1969, President's Office Files Box 31, NPMP.

66. President Nixon to Bryce Harlow, Nov. 12, 1969, in Political Memos, Harlow 1969, Staff Secretary Box 85, NPMP.

67. Jeb Stuart Magruder to Bryce Harlow, Nov. 18, 1969, in Haynsworth (1 of 2), John Ehrlichman Files Box 34, NPMP.

68. Jeb Stuart Magruder to Bryce Harlow, Nov. 21, 1969, in Memos/Jeb Magruder, November 1969, H. R. Haldeman Files Box 54, NPMP.

69. Nixon and Mitchell are quoted in Kohlmeier, *God Save This Honorable Court*, 140, 142.

70. President Nixon to H. R. Haldeman, John Ehrlichman, Bryce Harlow and Henry Kissinger, Nov. 24, 1969, in Oudes, *From: The President*, 69–70.

71. The following is based on a memo from John Ehrlichman to the president's file, "Meeting between the President of the United States and Judge Clement Haynsworth," Dec. 4, 1969, in Haynsworth (1 of 2), John Ehrlichman Files Box 34, NPMP.

CHAPTER SIX. Speaking Out

My thanks to Karen J. Maschke for her help in collecting data for this chapter. See Karen J. Maschke and John Anthony Maltese, "Lobbying in the Supreme Court Confirmation Process," paper prepared for the 1991 meetings of the American Political Science Association.

1. For a thorough account of the Butler hearings, see David J. Danelski, *A Supreme Court Justice Is Appointed* (New York: Random House, 1964).

2. Steven S. Smith and Christopher J. Deering, *Committees in Congress* (Washington, D.C.: CQ Press, 1984), 13; Frank, "Appointment of Supreme Court Justices," 173.

3. Frank, "Appointment of Supreme Court Justices," 173.

4. An excellent source for information about Supreme Court nominations and confirmation proceedings prior to Williams is Warren, *Supreme Court in United States History.*

5. Michael Pertschuk and Wendy Schaetzel, *The People Rising* (New York: Thunder's Mouth Press, 1989), 152–53.

6. Ethan Bronner, *Battle for Justice: How the Bork Nomination Shook America* (New York: Norton, 1989), 146.

7. Pertschuk and Schaetzel, *People Rising,* 173.

8. Bronner, *Battle for Justice,* 155.

9. Pertschuk and Schaetzel, *People Rising,* 155.

10. Bronner, *Battle for Justice,* 146.

11. Neil A. Lewis, "Law Professor Accuses Thomas of Sexual Harassment in 1980's," *New York Times,* Oct. 7, 1991.

12. Preliminary figures showed that ABC coverage of Thomas's testimony from 9:00 to 10:30 P.M. received an average 13.9 national Nielson rating (with each rating point representing 431,028 homes with television sets) and a 23 percent audience share. NBC coverage of the testimony for the same time period received a 12.6 rating and a 21 percent share. In contrast, CBS coverage of the Toronto-Minneapolis baseball game received a 9.2 rating and a 15 percent share. Ratings for the last half-hour of the baseball game, after the hearings ended, went up to 11.6, with a 19 percent share. See John Carmody, "The TV Column," *Washington Post,* Oct. 14, 1991.

13. John Carmody, "The TV Column," *Washington Post,* Oct. 15, 1991.

14. President Bush, "Remarks in a Teleconference with the Associated Press Managing Editors," Oct. 17, 1991, *Weekly Compilation of Presidential Documents, 1991,* 1458; President Bush, "News Conference," Oct. 25, 1991, *Weekly Compilation of Presidential Documents, 1991,* 1508–9.

15. Abraham, *Justices and Presidents,* 45–26, 130; Frank, "Appointment of Supreme Court Justices," 195, n. 66; Warren, *Supreme Court,* 2:555.

16. *Springfield Republican,* Jan. 2, 1874; see Warren, *Supreme Court,* 2:555.

17. Frank, "Appointment of Supreme Court Justices," 193–94.

18. Ibid., 198–202.

19. "The Chief-Justiceship," *New York Herald Tribune,* Jan. 6, 1874.

20. "The Chief-Justiceship," *New York Herald Tribune,* Jan. 9, 1874.

21. George H. Williams to President Grant, Jan. 7, 1874, in "Attorney-General Williams's Letter Requesting the Withdrawal of His Nomination," *New York Herald Tribune,* Jan. 9, 1874.

22. Frank, "Appointment of Supreme Court Justices," 201–2.

23. "The Chief-Justiceship," *New York Herald Tribune,* Jan. 17, 1874.

24. Frank, "Appointment of Supreme Court Justices," 207.

25. John Marshall Harlan to Senator James B. Beck, Oct. 31, 1877, John Marshall Harlan Papers, the Filson Club, Louisville, Kentucky. My thanks to my colleague Loren P. Beth, for alerting me to the existence of this letter, and to the Filson Club,

for granting me permission to quote from it. For a more thorough discussion, see Loren P. Beth, "President Hayes Appoints a Justice," *Yearbook: 1989* (Washington, D.C.: Supreme Court Historical Society, 1989), 68–77; see also Frank, "Appointment of Supreme Court Justices," 207–9.

26. Frank, "Appointments of Supreme Court Justices," 209.

27. Harlan to Beck, Oct. 31, 1877, in John Marshall Harlan Papers, Filson Club, Louisville, Kentucky.

28. James Speed to Senator George F. Edmunds, Nov. 10, 1877, in Frank, "The Appointment of Supreme Court Justices," 208.

29. *Civil Rights Cases*, 109 U.S. 3 (1883); *Plessy v. Ferguson*, 163 U.S. 537 (1896). "If the [Civil War] amendments be enforced, according to the intent with which, as I conceive, they were adopted, there cannot be, in this republic, any class of human beings in practical subjection to another class, with power in the latter to dole out to the former just such privileges as they may choose to grant," Harlan wrote in the *Civil Rights Cases*, in Louis Fisher, *Constitutional Rights: Civil Rights and Civil Liberties* (New York: McGraw-Hill, 1990), 984. In *Plessy*, Harlan wrote that the "separation of citizens, on the basis of race, while they are on a public highway, is a badge of servitude wholly inconsistent with the civil freedom and the equality before the law established by the Constitution. It cannot be justified upon any legal grounds," in ibid., 989.

30. Frank, "Appointment of Supreme Court Justices," 210.

31. Beth, "President Hayes Appoints a Justice," 73–74.

32. John Marshall Harlan to President Rutherford B. Hayes, Oct. 31, 1877, in ibid., 74.

33. Melville W. Fuller to Senator George Edmunds, June 13, 1888, in McHargue, "Appointments to the Supreme Court," 295; see also Frank, "Appointment of Supreme Court Justices," 356.

34. George Shiras III and Winfield Shiras, *Justice George Shiras, Jr., of Pittsburgh* (Pittsburgh: University of Pittsburgh Press, 1953), 90–91.

35. Alpheus Thomas Mason, *Brandeis: A Free Man's Life* (New York: Viking, 1946), 465, 467.

36. Shiras and Shiras, *Justice George Shiras, Jr.,* 96.

37. Todd, *Justice on Trial*, 113; see also Mason, *Brandeis*, 473.

38. Mason, *Brandeis*, 469.

39. Todd, *Justice on Trial*, 113, 114–15.

40. Mason, *Brandeis*, 473.

41. U.S. Senate, Subcommittee of the Committee on the Judiciary, *Nomination of Louis D. Brandeis: Hearings Before the Subcommittee of the Committee on the Judiciary of the United States Senate*, 64 Cong. 1 sess. Doc. 409, 682–705, 713–47, 773–807, 815–45, 847–57, 986–1004, 1246–66.

42. Mason, *Brandeis*, 478.

43. Louis Brandeis to Edward McClennen, Mar. 9, 1916; Edward McClennen to Louis Brandeis, Mar. 10, 1916, in Mason, *Brandeis*, 486–87.

44. Mason, *Brandeis*, 503–4; Todd, *Justice on Trial*, 221–26.

45. Frank, "Appointment of Supreme Court Justices," 492.

46. Alpheus Thomas Mason, *Harlan Fiske Stone: Pillar of the Law* (New York: Viking, 1956), 181.

47. Frank, "Appointment of Supreme Court Justices," 489.

48. Ibid., 491; Mason, *Harlan Fiske Stone*, 188.

49. Mason, *Harlan Fiske Stone*, 141. The following passages also draw from this work; see ibid., 188–89, 191.

50. Ibid., 192–94; Frank, "Appointment of Supreme Court Justices," 491–92.

51. Mason, *Harlan Fiske Stone*, 197.

52. James A. Thorpe erroneously reports that Reed did answer questions; see "The Appearance of Supreme Court Nominees before the Senate Judiciary Committee," *Journal of Public Law* 18 (1969): 375. The transcript of the hearing shows that one witness suggested that the subcommittee ask Reed certain questions. The chairman, Senator M. M. Logan, then asked: "Does any member of the committee desire to ask Mr. Reed any questions?" After a pause, he said: "Apparently not." Thereupon the subcommittee went into executive session and within two minutes unanimously endorsed Reed. U.S. Senate, Subcommittee of the Committee on the Judiciary, *Hearings on the Nomination of Stanley F. Reed*, Jan. 20, 1938, 75 Cong. 3 sess., 25–26; reprinted in Mersky and Jacobstein, *Supreme Court of the United States*, vol. 4.

53. Joseph Alsop Jr., "Black Confirmed," *New York Herald Tribune*, Aug. 18, 1937.

54. For a transcript of the six stories, see Justice Hugo Black (KKK Membership), PPS Box 36, HHPL.

55. Russell B. Porter, "Alabama Aware of Black's Ties," *New York Times*, Sept. 13, 1937.

56. "New Dealers Want Black to Disprove Klan Link or Resign"; and Mark Sullivan, "Black, If Now a Klansman, Held Subject to Impeachment," *New York Herald Tribune*, Sept. 16, 1937.

57. David Lawrence, "Freedom of the Radio," *San Francisco Chronicle*, Oct. 4, 1937, in Justice Hugo Black (KKK Membership), PPS Box 36, HHPL.

58. Transcript of Hugo Black's radio address, Oct. 1, 1937, 9:30 P.M. ET, in Justice Hugo Black (KKK Membership), PPS Box 36, HHPL.

59. Institute of Public Opinion, "Public Opinion Shifts as Justice Takes Seat Following Radio Speech," Oct. 1937, in Justice Hugo Black (KKK Membership), PPS Box 36, HHPL. It is not clear what the sample size of this poll was nor how generalizable its results are.

60. Thorpe, "Appearance of Supreme Court Nominees," 376.

61. W. Dressler (attorney, Omaha, Neb.) to Senate Judiciary Committee, Jan. 9, 1939, in Frank, "Appointment of Supreme Court Justices," 506.

62. Testimony of Elizabeth Dilling, U.S. Senate, Subcommittee of the Committee on the Judiciary, *Nomination of Felix Frankfurter: Hearings*, 11–12 Jan. 1939, 76 Cong. 1 sess., 45–47; see also: "Frankfurter Goes to Hearing Today," *New York Times*, Jan. 12, 1939; and Frank "Appointment of Supreme Court Justices," 507–8.

63. Thorpe, "Appearance of Supreme Court Nominees," 376.

64. Dean Acheson, *Morning and Noon: A Memoir* (Boston: Houghton Mifflin, 1965), 202.

65. "Frankfurter Goes to Hearing Today."

66. Frank, "Appointment of Supreme Court Justices," 508.

67. Acheson, *Morning and Noon*, 201.

68. Ibid., 203.

69. U.S. Senate, *Nomination of Felix Frankfurter*, 107–8.

70. Ibid., 126.

71. "Frankfurter Wins Senate Group Vote," *New York Times*, Jan. 13, 1939.

72. Acheson, *Morning and Noon*, 207.

73. U.S. Senate, *Nomination of Felix Frankfurter*, 128.

74. Acheson, *Morning and Noon*, 208.

75. U.S. Senate, Subcommittee of the Committee on the Judiciary, "Executive Session (Confidential) on Confirmation of Nomination of Earl Warren of California to be Chief Justice of the United States," Feb. 20, 1954, pp. 22 and 23; copy in CIS microfiche of unpublished Senate Committee Hearings.

76. U.S. Senate, Committee on the Judiciary, *Nomination of William Joseph Brennan, Jr., Hearings before the Committee on the Judiciary*, Feb. 26–27, 1957, 85 Cong. 1 sess., pp. 17, 23, 28, 34, 36–40.

77. Nat Hentoff, "Profiles: The Constitutionalist," *New Yorker*, Mar. 12, 1990, p. 52.

78. U.S. Senate, *Nomination of William Brennan*, 28, 34.

79. U.S. Senate, Committee on the Judiciary, *Hearings on the Nomination of Potter Stewart to be an Associate Justice of the Supreme Court of the United States*, Apr. 9, 1959, in Mersky and Jacobstein, *Supreme Court*, 6:26–28, 34–36, 41.

80. Stuart Taylor Jr., "Bork's Evolving Views: Far from the New Deal," *New York Times*, July 8, 1987.

81. Louis Romano, "Leading the Charge on Bork," *Washington Post*, Sept. 15, 1987.

82. Timothy M. Phelps and Helen Winternitz, *Capitol Games: Clarence Thomas, Anita Hill, and the Story of a Supreme Court Nomination* (New York: Hyperion, 1992), 179.

83. U.S. Senate, Committee on the Judiciary, *Hearings on the Nomination of Judge Clarence Thomas to be Associate Justice of the Supreme Court of the United States*, Sept. 1991, 102 Cong. 1 sess., pt. 1, 222–23; see also Phelps and Winternitz, *Capitol Games*, 192–93.

84. U.S. Senate, Committee on the Judiciary, *Hearings on the Nomination of David H. Souter to be Associate Justice of the Supreme Court of the United States*, Sept. 1990, 101 Cong. 2 sess., 114–15.

85. Daniel H. Pollitt, "David Souter, the Dark Side," in U.S. Senate, *Hearings on Souter*, 1008–9.

86. U.S. Senate, *Hearings on Souter*, 54.

87. "My view is that there is a right to privacy in the 14th amendment," Thomas said, in U.S. Senate, *Hearings on Thomas*, pt. 1, 127.

88. *Planned Parenthood of Southeastern Pennsylvania v. Casey*.

89. Jeffrey K. Tulis, *The Rhetorical Presidency* (Princeton: Princeton University Press, 1987), 95.

90. Samuel Kernell, *Going Public: New Strategies of Presidential Leadership* (Washington, D.C.: CQ Press, 1986), 23. See also George C. Edwards, *The Public Presidency: The Pursuit of Popular Support* (New York: St. Martin's, 1983); and John Anthony Maltese, *Spin Control: The White House Office of Communications and the Management of Presidential News*, 2d ed., rev. (Chapel Hill: University of North Carolina Press, 1994).

91. Kernell, *Going Public*, 35.

92. Richard Rose, *The Postmodern President: The White House Meets the World* (Chatham, N.J.: Chatham House, 1988), chap. 7.

93. John Benjamin Ashby, "Supreme Court Appointments Since 1937," Ph.D. diss., University of Notre Dame, 1972, 158.

94. News Conference, Sept. 18, 1945, in *Public Papers of the Presidents of the United States: Harry S. Truman, 1945*, 326.

95. Vanderbilt University, *Television News Index and Abstracts,* Nashville, Tenn.

96. The data on the list is from *Weekly Compilation of Presidential Documents.* Initial statements of nomination or statements issued upon confirmation, rejection, or withdrawal are not included.

CHAPTER SEVEN. The Institutional Presidency

1. Clinton Rossiter, *The American Presidency* (Baltimore: Johns Hopkins University Press, 1987).

2. See, for instance, John P. Burke, "The Institutional Presidency," in *The Presidency and the Political System,* ed. Michael Nelson, 3d ed. (Washington, D.C.: CQ Press, 1990).

3. James L. Sundquist, *The Decline and Resurgence of Congress* (Washington, D.C.: Brookings, 1981), 39.

4. Lester M. Salamon, "The Presidency and Domestic Policy Formulation," in *The Illusion of Presidential Government,* ed. Hugh Heclo and Lester M. Salamon (Boulder, Colo.: Westview, 1981), 179.

5. Sundquist, *Decline and Resurgence of Congress,* 33.

6. Erwin C. Hargrove and Michael Nelson, *Presidents, Politics, and Policy* (Baltimore: Johns Hopkins University Press, 1984), 175.

7. Matthew A. Crenson and Francis E. Rourke, "By Way of Conclusion: American Bureaucracy since World War II," in *The New American State,* ed. Louis Galambos (Baltimore: Johns Hopkins University Press, 1987), 93.

8. Ibid., 94.

9. James P. Pfiffner, *The Modern Presidency* (New York: St. Martin's, 1994), 57–58.

10. Harold Seidman, *Politics, Position, and Power,* 3d ed. (New York: Oxford University Press, 1980), 111.

11. Gary King and Lynn Ragsdale, eds., *The Elusive Executive* (Washington, D.C.: CQ Press, 1988), 205, 208.

12. Tom Charles Huston to President Richard Nixon, Mar. 25, 1969 (emphasis in the original). My thanks to Professor Sheldon Goldman for giving me this copy of the memo, which he located in the White House Central Files of the Nixon Presidential Materials Project. Another copy, which apparently included Nixon's handwritten comments on it, was withdrawn from Nixon's public papers at the request of the former president.

13. Ehrlichman to Staff Secretary, Mar. 27, 1969. in News Summaries, March 1969, President's Office Files Box 30, NPMP.

14. For a more thorough discussion of senatorial courtesy, see Harold W. Chase, *Federal Judges: The Appointing Process* (Minneapolis: University of Minnesota Press, 1972), 6–13.

15. Attorney General William D. Mitchell, radio speech, Apr. 26, 1929, in Justice, Press Releases, Attorney General, 1929–30, WHCF Box 25, HHPL.

16. David M. O'Brien, *Judicial Roulette: Report of the Twentieth Century Fund Task Force on Judicial Selection* (New York: Priority Press, 1988), 33.

17. Larry C. Berkson and Susan B. Carbon, *The United States Circuit Judge Nominating Commission: Its Members, Procedures, and Candidates* (Chicago: American Judicature Society, 1980).

18. Alan Neff, *The United States District Judge Nominating Commissions: Their Members, Procedures, and Candidates* (Chicago: American Judicature Society, 1981).

19. O'Brien, *Judicial Roulette*, 61.

20. Mitchell, radio speech.

21. Sheldon Goldman, "Reagan's Judicial Legacy: Completing the Puzzle and Summing Up," *Judicature* 72 (Apr.–May 1989): 319–20.

22. Stephen J. Markman, "Judicial Selection: The Reagan Years," in *Judicial Selection: Merit, Ideology, and Politics* (Washington, D.C.: National Legal Center for the Public Interest, 1990), 38.

23. For overviews of the debate concerning original intent, see Lief H. Carter, *Contemporary Constitutional Lawmaking* (New York: Pergamon, 1985); and Jack N. Rakove, ed., *Interpreting the Constitution: The Debate over Original Intent* (Boston: Northeastern University Press, 1990). For alternative perspectives on original intent, compare Bork, *Tempting of America;* and Leonard W. Levy, *Original Intent and the Framers' Constitution* (New York: Macmillan, 1988).

24. David M. O'Brien, "The Reagan Judges: His Most Enduring Legacy?" in *The Reagan Legacy,* ed. Charles O. Jones (Chatham, N.J.: Chatham House, 1988), 68; see also Herman Schwartz, *Packing the Courts: The Conservative Campaign to Rewrite the Constitution* (New York: Scribner's, 1988).

25. O'Brien, *Judicial Roulette,* 61–62, 23–24.

26. Huston to Nixon, Mar. 25, 1969, 1.

27. Sheldon Goldman, "Bush's Judicial Legacy: The Final Imprint," *Judicature* 76 (Apr.–May 1993): 295.

28. Figures obtained by the author from the Senate Judiciary Committee, Mar. 1994.

29. Goldman, "Bush's Judicial Legacy," 285.

30. White House and Justice Department officials, interviews with author, Mar. 1994.

31. McHargue, "Appointments to the Supreme Court."

32. See, for example, Bronner, *Battle For Justice,* 29–36; and Mark Gitenstein, *Matters of Principle: An Insider's Account of America's Rejection of Robert Bork's Nomination to the Supreme Court* (New York: Simon and Schuster, 1992), 28–37.

33. McHargue, "Appointments to the Supreme Court," 505–6.

34. Ashby, "Supreme Court Appointments Since 1937," 16.

35. For a discussion of representational considerations, see Barbara Perry, *A Representative Supreme Court? The Impact of Race, Religion, and Gender on Appointments* (New York: Greenwood, 1991).

36. Paul Simon, *Advice and Consent* (Washington, D.C.: National Press Books, 1992), 32; O'Brien, *Judicial Roulette,* 40–41.

37. O'Brien, *Storm Center,* 88–89.

38. Rena B. Smith to the White House, Mar. 17, 1930, with enclosed clipping, "A Woman on the Supreme Bench?" from the *Christian Science Monitor* (Mar. 11, 1930), in Judiciary—Supreme Court of U.S., Correspondence, 1930–31, WHCF Box 191, HHPL.

39. Beverly B. Cook, "The First Woman Candidate for the Supreme Court—Florence E. Allen," *Yearbook: 1981* (Washington, D.C.: Supreme Court Historical Society, 1981), 19.

40. Schwartz, *Packing the Courts,* 61.

41. Harry P. Stumpf, *American Judicial Politics* (New York: Harcourt Brace Jovanovich, 1988), 256.

42. O'Brien, *Judicial Roulette*, 84–85.

43. Schwartz, *Packing the Courts*, 99.

44. *Public Citizen v. U.S. Department of Justice*, 491 U.S. 440 (1989). Justice Scalia did not participate in the case. See also Schwartz, *Packing the Courts*, 99; O'Brien, *Storm Center*, 80.

45. O'Brien, *Storm Center*, 80.

46. Richard Neustadt, *Presidential Power: The Politics of Leadership* (New York: Wiley, 1960).

47. Mason, *Brandeis*, chaps. 30 and 31.

48. For a complete history of the office, see Maltese, *Spin Control*.

49. Cole to Magruder, Oct. 22, 1969; and Whittaker to Members of the Cabinet and Under-Secretaries, Oct. 28, 1969; in EX FEG 51/A, 10/1/69–10/31/69, (2 of 2), WHCF Box 3, NPMP.

50. Magruder, *An American Life*, 94.

51. Odle to Magruder, Oct. 28, 1969, in Haynsworth (2 of 3), Harry Dent Files Box 6, NPMP.

52. Magruder, *An American Life*, 95.

53. Ron Baukol to Charles Colson, Apr. 26, 1971, in Senate Select Committee on Presidential Campaign Activities, *Final Report*, 93 Cong. 2 sess., 1974, S. Rept. 93–981, 151.

54. Thomas Griscom, interview with author, Dec. 5, 1988, Chattanooga, Tenn.

55. Martha Joynt Kumar, "Free Lancers and Fogmeisters: Party Control and White House Communications Activities," paper prepared for the annual meeting of the American Political Science Association, Sept. 1993. Quotation on 19.

56. Taylor, "Bork's Evolving Views."

57. Griscom interview, Dec. 5, 1988.

58. Exchange with reporters, Oct. 13, 1991, in *Weekly Compilation of Presidential Documents (1991)*, 1438.

59. Remarks at a Kickoff Ceremony for the Eighth Annual National Night Out Against Crime, Aug. 6, 1991, in ibid., 1119.

60. Bowles, *White House and Capitol Hill*, 159–60, 166–68; Johnson is quoted on 166.

61. Magruder, *An American Life*, 110.

62. Egil "Bud" Krogh to John Ehrlichman, Sept. 24, 1971, in Supreme Court Nominations, David R. Young Files Box 17, NPMP.

63. Colson interview, July 11, 1989.

64. For example, Patrick B. McGuigan and Dawn M. Weyrich, *Ninth Justice: The Fight for Bork* (Washington, D.C.: Free Congress, 1990), 219.

65. Bronner, *Battle for Justice*, 200.

66. Griscom interview, Dec. 5, 1988.

67. William E. Timmons to the President, Mar. 25, 1970, in CF FG 51/A, Supreme Court (1969–70), WHCF Box 22, NPMP.

68. Bryce Harlow to the President, Apr. 6, 1970, in CF FG 51/A, Supreme Court (1969–70), WHCF Box 22, NPMP.

69. Schwartz, *Packing the Courts*, 107–8.

70. Action Items—Carswell Nomination, Apr. 2, 1969, in CF FG 51/A, Supreme Court (1969–70), WHCF Box 22, NPMP.

71. Dent to Belieu, Oct. 17, 1969, in Haynsworth (2 of 3), Harry Dent Files Box 6, NPMP.

72. H. R. Haldeman to Herbert Klein, Feb. 9, 1969, in H. R. Haldeman I (1 of 3), Herbert Klein Files Box 1, NPMP.

73. Klein, *Making It Perfectly Clear*, 120.

74. For a discussion of spite nominations, see Fish, "Spite Nominations," 545.

75. Carswell, speech before a meeting of the American Legion, Aug. 2, 1948.

76. Colson interview, July 11, 1989. H. R. Haldeman's private diary confirms this; see Haldeman, *Haldeman Diaries*, 147.

77. H. R. Haldeman notes, meeting between the President and H. R. Haldeman, Oct. 21, 1969, in Haldeman Notes: July–Dec. 1969 (Oct.–Dec. 1969, pt. 2), H. R. Haldeman Files Box 40, NPMP.

78. Gleason to Dent, Oct. 24, 1969, in Haynsworth (Brownell), Harry Dent Files Box 6, NPMP; see also Gleason to Phillips, Oct. 15, 1969, in Haynsworth (3 of 3), Harry Dent Files Box 6, NPMP.

79. Gleason to Dent, Oct. 24, 1969, in Haynsworth (Brownell), Harry Dent Files Box 6, NPMP.

80. Oudes, *From: The President*, 69–70.

81. Colson interview, July 11, 1989.

82. Harry S. Dent to the Attorney General and Bryce Harlow, Oct. 27, 1969, in Haynsworth (2 of 2), John Ehrlichman Files Box 34, NPMP.

83. Handwritten notes, Charles Colson, n.d., in Supreme Court, Charles Colson Files Box 115, NPMP.

84. Caldeira and Wright, "Lobbying for Justice," 2, 17.

85. Kumar, "Free Lancers and Fogmeisters," 19; McGuigan and Weyrich, *Ninth Justice*, 125.

86. Phelps and Winternitz, *Capitol Games*, 133–36.

87. Benjamin Ginsberg and Martin Shefter, "The Presidency, Interest Groups, and Social Forces: Creating a Republican Coalition," in Nelson, ed., *Presidency and the Political System*, 346–47.

88. O'Brien, "Reagan Judges," 64.

89. Phelps and Winternitz, *Capitol Games*, 24, 133.

90. McGuigan and Weyrich, *Ninth Justice*, 124.

91. Even though his name had not been formally submitted to the Senate when he withdrew under fire, it is clear that Douglas Ginsburg withdrew because Senate defeat was inevitable.

CHAPTER EIGHT. Clinton Appointments and Proposals

1. Even the institutional staff contained in the Executive Office of the President is not the nonpartisan, independent staff that the Brownlow Committee envisaged. Instead, the EOP has been politicized and is largely directed by the White House. See John Hart, *The Presidential Branch* (New York: Pergamon, 1987), 128–29.

2. David L. Paletz and Robert M. Entman, *Media Power Politics* (New York: Free Press, 1981), 16.

3. Robert M. Entman, "The Imperial Media," in *Politics and the Oval Office*, ed. Arnold J. Meltsner (San Francisco: Institute for Contemporary Studies, 1981), 89.

4. Griscom interview, Dec. 5, 1988.

5. Dick Cheney, interview with author, Mar. 10, 1989, Washington, D.C.

6. John P. Frank, "Supreme Court Appointments: II," *Wisconsin Law Review 1941* (May 1941): 348–49.

7. "New Dry Queries Raised on Roberts; His Partner 'Wet,'" *New York Times,* May 11, 1930; see also "Hoover Names O. J. Roberts for the Supreme Court; Drys Bring Up Old Speech."

8. Kernell, *Going Public,* 23.

9. Empirical analysis of civil liberties decisions during the 1946–85 terms of the Supreme Court confirms that membership change was the primary source of collective voting change on the Court. See Lawrence Baum, "Membership Change and Collective Voting Change in the United States Supreme Court," *Journal of Politics* 54 (Feb. 1992): 3–24.

10. O'Brien, *Storm Center,* 121–22.

11. For a discussion of Lani Guinier's writings and how they were taken out of context, see Stephen L. Carter, *The Confirmation Mess: Cleaning up the Federal Appointments Process* (New York: Basic Books, 1994), 37–53; and Lani Guinier, *The Tyranny of the Majority: Fundamental Fairness and Representative Democracy* (New York: Free Press, 1994). See Bork, *Tempting of America,* for Bork's discussion of how his writings were taken out of context.

12. Carter, *Confirmation Mess,* 51. The following is also based on this source; see 43–44, 25–26, 28.

13. Howard Fineman with Mark Miller, Ann McDaniel, and Bob Cohn, "Off the Books, Out of the Chair," *Newsweek,* Feb. 1, 1993, 32.

14. Carter, *Confirmation Mess,* 174.

15. Ibid., 30–31.

16. The members of the task force were Hugh L. Carey (chairman), Walter Berns, Joseph A. Califano Jr., Lloyd N. Cutler, Philip B. Kurland, David M. O'Brien, Jack W. Peltason, Nicholas J. Spaeth, Michael M. Uhlmann, and Robert F. Wagner.

17. O'Brien, *Judicial Roulette,* 8–9.

18. Ibid., 9–11.

19. Testimony of Clarence Thomas, U.S. Senate, *Hearings on the Nomination of Judge Clarence Thomas,* 205.

20. Phelps and Winternitz, *Capitol Games,* 425.

21. ABC News, *Nightline,* "A Town Hall Meeting."

22. O'Brien, *Judicial Roulette,* 9.

23. Nina Totenberg, "The Confirmation Process and the Public: To Know or Not to Know," *Harvard Law Review* 101 (1988): 1228.

24. Carter, *Confirmation Mess.* The following is from pp. 195, 196–98, 199–203.

25. E. J. Dionne, on ABC News, *Nightline,* "A Town Hall Meeting."

26. "Excerpts from the Democratic Candidates' Debate in Maryland," *Washington Post,* Mar. 2, 1992.

27. "Dem Debate: Raucous National Outing for 6 Dems," *Abortion Report,* Dec. 16, 1991. The debate, moderated by Tom Brokaw, took place on NBC television on the evening of Dec. 15, 1991.

28. Jeffrey Segal, "Senate Confirmation of Supreme Court Justices: Partisan and Institutional Politics," *Journal of Politics* 49 (Nov. 1987): 998–1015.

29. Ruckman, "Supreme Court, Critical Nominations, and the Senate Confirmation Process."

30. Bruce Ackerman coined the term *transformative appointments,* but no one has performed a rigorous empirical analysis to test whether they are less likely to be confirmed; see Ackerman, "Transformative Appointments."

31. Even in the last twenty-five years, when contentious confirmations have been more prevalent, nominees are confirmed 71 percent of the time; overall, the Senate has confirmed Supreme Court nominees over 80 percent of the time.

32. Charles M. Cameron, Albert D. Cover, and Jeffrey A. Segal, "Senate Voting on Supreme Court Nominees: A Neoinstitutional Model," *American Political Science Review* 84 (June 1990): 532.

33. Dan Freedman and Vic Ostrowidski, "Speculation Whirls around Cuomo," *Albany Times Union,* Mar. 20, 1993.

34. "Mitchell Signals He'd Like Court Post, Dole Vows Support for Old Senate Foe," *Atlanta Constitution,* Apr. 11, 1994.

35. *CNN News,* Apr. 12, 1994, 2:04 P.M. ET. Transcript 668-1.

36. Ibid., 6:04 P.M. ET. Transcript 632-2.

37. Gwen Ifill, "Work Begins on Court Selection," *New York Times,* Apr. 12, 1992.

38. Ruth Marcus, "Clinton 'at the Beginning' in Hunt for Court Nominee," *Washington Post,* Apr. 16, 1994.

39. Stuart Taylor Jr., "In High Court Race, Arnold Is Class of the Field," *Fulton County Daily Report,* May 4, 1994.

40. Ibid.

41. Former presidential candidate Paul Tsongas, a cancer survivor, criticized Clinton for rejecting a potential nominee because of cancer. "If he had been rejected because of race or color, there would have been outrage, but this kind of discrimination is accepted," he said. The Americans with Disabilities Act (which does not apply to judicial appointments) makes such considerations illegal in most types of hiring situations. Tony Mauro, "From Cancer Survivors, a Cry of Discrimination," *USA Today,* May 19, 1994.

42. Bruce Babbitt, on CNN, *Larry King Live,* May 23, 1994. Transcript 1127.

43. David Lauter, "Breyer's Public Life Offers Few Clues to Private Beliefs," *Los Angeles Times,* May 31, 1994.

44. Ruth Marcus, "Court Runners-Up Drew President's Warmest Praise," *Washington Post,* May 15, 1994.

45. Froma Harrop, "Charm Holds the Key," *Atlanta Constitution,* May 26, 1994.

46. Lauter, "Breyer's Public Life."

47. Marcus, "Court Runners-Up."

48. Nina Totenberg, on NPR, *All Things Considered,* May 16, 1994. Transcript 1346-8.

49. John M. Broder, "Clinton Formally Introduces Breyer as a Reformer," *Los Angeles Times,* May 17, 1994.

50. Paul Richter, "Clinton Takes More Time on Court Choice," *Los Angeles Times,* May 13, 1994.

51. Ibid.

52. Stuart Taylor, on CNN, *Inside Politics,* May 10, 1994, 4:37 P.M. ET. Transcript 578-2.

53. PBS, *The MacNeil/Lehrer NewsHour,* Oct. 1, 1987.

54. Schwartz makes this argument in *Packing the Courts.*

55. Donald Lambro, "Political Plotting . . . and Raiding," *Washington Times,* May 23, 1994.

56. ABC News, *Nightline,* "A Town Hall Meeting."

57. Simon, *Advice and Consent*,309–10.

58. *Osborne v. Bank of the United States*, 9 Wheat. 738 (1824).

59. Howard Ball, *Courts and Politics*, 2d ed. (Englewood Cliffs, N.J.: Prentice-Hall, 1987), 297.

60. ABC News, *Nightline*, "A Town Hall Meeting."

Afterword, 1998

1. Press Release, Judicial Selection Monitoring Project, Jan. 23, 1997 (available on the World Wide Web at <http://www.fcref.org/jsmp/oppose.htm>).

2. Quoted in Michael Kelly, "Judge Dread," *New Republic*, Mar. 31, 1997, 6.

3. Orrin Hatch, "Speech to Federal Judges," Federal Judges Association, May 14, 1997.

4. Roger E. Hartley and Lisa M. Holmes, "Increasing Senate Scrutiny of Lower Federal Court Nominees," *Judicature* 80 (May–June 1997): 274–78.

5. Ronald Stidham, Robert A. Carp, and Donald Songer, "The Voting Behavior of President Clinton's Judicial Appointees," *Judicature* 80 (July–Aug. 1996): 16–20.

6. Sheldon Goldman and Matthew D. Saronson, "Clinton's Nontraditional Judges: Creating a More Representative Bench," *Judicature* 78 (Sept.–Oct. 1994): 68–73.

7. Press Release, Judicial Selection Monitoring Project, Jan. 23, 1997.

8. Terry Carter, "A Conservative Juggernaut: Judicial Attacks Push Debate to Right, Put Hatch in Middle," *ABA Journal* 83 (June 1997): 32.

9. James Bennet, " 'Judicial Dictatorship' Spurns People's Will, Buchanan Says," *New York Times*, Jan. 30, 1996, sec. A, p. 9.

10. Sheldon Goldman and Elliot Slotnick, "Clinton's First Term Judiciary: Many Bridges to Cross," *Judicature* 80 (May–June 1997): 254–73.

11. Viveca Novak, "Empty-Bench Syndrome: Congressional Republicans are Determined to Put Clinton's Judicial Nominees on Hold," *Time*, May 26, 1997, 37.

12. Hatch, "Speech to Federal Judges," May 14, 1997.

13. Congressional Press Release, "Hatch on the Role of ABA in Judicial Nomination Process," Feb. 18, 1997.

INDEX

Acheson, Dean, Frankfurter and, 105–7
Adams, John: as potential chief justice, 23–24; on Rutledge defeat, 31; appointments of, 31–32
Adams, John Quincy, 34
Advice and consent. *See* Senate, advice and consent function
Allen, Florence E., 126
American Bar Association, 82; on Parker, 69; on Haynsworth, 81; exclusion of African-Americans, 125, 127; rating of nominees, 127–28
American Federation of Labor, 85; opposition to Lurton, 47–48; support of Brandeis, 50; Taft resignation and, 53–54; opposition to Parker, 57–59, 61; opposition to Haynsworth, 72
Anderson, George, 98
Arnold, Richard, 153–54
Ashurst, Henry F., 67; Frankfurter and, 107

Babbitt, Bruce, 154
Baird, Zoe, 144–46, 150, 151
Baker, Howard: role in Carswell nomination, 15, 132; role in Bork nomination, 124, 133
Baukol, Ron, 130
Bayh, Birch: on Nixon's interpretation of advice and consent, 13; Nixon's attempts to discredit, 15, 16, 79, 136; opposition to Haynsworth, 73, 81

Beck, James B., 96
Biden, Joseph, 18
Black, Hugo: 1937 nomination of, 101; response to Klan membership stories, 101–4
Black, Jeremiah S., 35
Blackmun, Harry A., resignation of, 1, 151, 152
Bork, Robert: 1987 nomination of, 7, 110, 124, 130, 133, 139; and interest groups, 36, 137–38, 144; hearings on, 87–88; ABA rating of, 128
Bradlee, Benjamin, 81
Bradley, Bill, 158
Brandeis, Louis D., 148; 1916 nomination of, 49–51, 75, 142; hearings regarding, 51, 86–87, 88, 89, 98–99; public silence of, 97; use of surrogate lobbyists, 98; and Jewish seat, 125
Brennan, William J., Jr.: 1957 nomination of, 108–9, 142; on Arnold, 153
Breyer, Stephen, 1994 nomination of, 149, 150, 151–56
Broder, David, 18
Brownlow Committee, 117–19, 183 n.1
Brown v. Board of Education, questioning of Stewart about, 109–10
Bryce, Lord, 11
Buchanan, James, 35
Buchanan, Patrick: role in Haynsworth nomination, 76, 80, 81; letter-writing campaign, 130

Library of Congress Cataloging-in-Publication Data

Maltese, John Anthony.
  The selling of Supreme Court nominees / John Anthony Maltese.
      p.   cm. — (Interpreting American politics)
  Includes index.
  ISBN 0-8018-5102-5 (acid-free paper).
    1. United States. Supreme Court—History.   2. United States. Supreme Court—
Officials and employees—Selection and appointment.   3. Judges—Selection and
appointment—United States.   4. Political questions and judicial power—United
States.   I. Title.   II. Series.
KF8742.M36   1995
347.73'26'34—dc20
[347.3073534]   95-3536

ISBN 0-8018-5883-6 (pbk)